Entrepreneurship and Social Entrepreneurship in the MENA Region

Nehme Azoury • Taïeb Hafsi
Editors

Entrepreneurship and Social Entrepreneurship in the MENA Region

Advances in Research

palgrave
macmillan

Editors
Nehme Azoury
Faculty of Business
Holy Spirit University of Kaslik
Jounieh, Lebanon

Taïeb Hafsi
HEC Montréal
Montreal, QC, Canada

ISBN 978-3-030-88446-8 ISBN 978-3-030-88447-5 (eBook)
https://doi.org/10.1007/978-3-030-88447-5

This Palgrave Macmillan imprint is published by the registered company Springer Nature Switzerland AG.
The registered company address is: Gewerbestrasse 11, 6330 Cham, Switzerland

Contents

Notes on Contributors

Marwan Azouri, Ph.D. Specialist in Marketing and Social Media studies.Currently holds the position of Assistant Professor at the Notre Dame University, Lebanon. Part of the Department of Marketing and Management. Active in research and holds a PhD from the University of Burgundy, Dijon France in 2016. His course load evolve around: Fundamentals of Marketing, Digital Business, Business Research, Consumer Behavior, and Salesmanship. He has also taught in a multitude of universities in Lebanon and France.

Nehme Azoury is a Professor and Deputy President for Corporate and Employment Affairs at the Holy Spirit University of Kaslik—USEK. Former Deputy President for Research and former Dean of the Faculty of Business, he lectures in the fields of marketing, strategy, and corporate governance in several universities and teaches strategic management and corporate governance. He is one of the eight members of the scientific committee of Eduniversal, as a representative of the Eurasian region. He has been Professor and Distinguished Professor at various universities, including Panthéon-Assas (Paris II), Euromed-Marseille, La Rochelle, Lyon 3, and the George Washington University, which presented him with an appreciation award for Active Contribution to the Education of MSF Students. He is the author of several publications and the editor-in-chief of the Arab Economic & Business Journal and the

Lebanese Journal of Economics and Management. He is also a Managing Partner at Widein, a consultancy firm based in Lebanon. Prof. Azoury has published several books with Palgrave Macmillan, *Business and Education in the Middle East, Business and Society in the Middle East* and *Business and Social Media in the Middle East.*

Sofiane Baba is an assistant professor of strategic management at the University of Sherbrooke in Québec, Canada. His research focuses on the organization–society nexus from a variety of theoretical perspectives and research interests, mainly related to institutional change, sustainability, and strategic management. He holds a Master of Science in strategy and a PhD in organizational theory and strategy from HEC Montreal.

Meriem Benslama is director of The Algerian Center for Social Entrepreneurship, an organization whose mission is to promote social entrepreneurship among young Algerians. She holds a bachelor's degree in language and business engineering and a master's degree in Culture and Communication Engineering from the University of Versailles, France. Her thesis focused on the enablers and barriers to social entrepreneurship in Algeria. Along with her professional experiences in communication and cultural journalism, she has several years of experience in Algerian and French associations.

Lindos Daou Assistant Professor at the Management and Marketing Department at the Faculty of Business Administration and Economics—Notre Dame University—Louaize.Holder of a PhD in Marketing from USEK, Lindos Daou is an Assistant Professor lecturing in Marketing at the Faculty of Business Administration and Economics at NDU. Dr Daou used to teach at USEK Business School at the University of Holy Spirit University of Kaslik. He also occupied the position of Chairperson of Management, in addition to Transport and Logistics Departments. Besides teaching, Dr. Daou was also a researcher and member of the CIRAME research center at the school and part of the scientific committee of Research and Business Link Review (RBL). In the scope of conducting research and studies for BEPS, he has initiated several studies involving the Arab Business Schools. His areas of research in Marketing include university branding, student satisfaction, social media, and advertising. He was also selected by the Institute of International Education (IIE) and US State Department to participate in the Fulbright Scholarship program for Junior Faculty Development program for Lebanon at the University of Illinois, USA. He was also a visiting Professor at Varna University of Management-Bulgaria in lecturing in "Global Marketing in the Digital Era." Furthermore, he also occupies the position of a senior consultant at Professional Financial Consultancy—Beirut focusing on marketing strategy and market research projects.

Dora Jurd De Girancourt is a brand strategist and a researcher in the field of marketing and communication of family businesses.In 2002, she wrote her first book on the topic, Leur nom est une marque, published by Éditions d'Organisation, France. The book deals with the marketing specificities of family businesses that bear patronymic names. In 2017, she co-authored *Embracing Paradoxes in South African Family Businesses*, which unveils the special features of South African family businesses. She co-authored Femmes au cœur des entreprises familiales—La Croisée des Chemins, 2021, with Prof. Thami Ghorfi, Dean of ESCA École de Management, Casablanca, Morocco. The book explores the place of women in Moroccan family businesses and brings to light their prominent roles and new forms of leadership.She holds a Master in Marketing from ESCP Business School, Paris, and a Master in Semiotics from La Sorbonne. Besides her researches, she has been working in the marketing field for almost 20 years, in leading companies both in France and in the USA (Clarins Group, Saint Gobain) and then in global communication agencies (TBWA Group, Kantar Consulting) as a senior brand strategist, advising leading international FMCG brands. Most recently, she was a guest lecturer in marketing strategy at ESCA École de Management.

Vladimir Dzenopoljac He teaches Strategic Management and is Director of MBA program at the College of Business Administration, American University of the Middle East, Kuwait. He received his PhD Degree from the University of Kragujevac, Serbia, in the field of impact of intellectual capital on value creation in contemporary enterprises. Alongside his academic career, Vladimir was providing consultancy services in the fields of strategy development and execution, business planning, and financial planning and analysis. He has published a significant number of research papers in his field of professional expertise and has been involved in the implementation of several projects for small, medium, and big companies. His areas of professional interest are strategic financial management and intellectual capital management.

Ayman El Tarabishy is the deputy chair and a teaching professor in the Department of Management at The George Washington University School of Business. His expertise involves entrepreneurship and the creative, innovative, and humane-focused practices existing within the field. Dr. El Tarabishy now sits as the President & CEO of the International Council for Small Business (ICSB), the oldest and largest non-profit organization across the globe devoted to advancing small business research and practices. The Council stands as a coalition of over a dozen national organizations, being represented in over 180 countries.Dr. El Tarabishy is an award-winning author and teacher. In 2019, the George Washington University New Venture Competition awarded Dr. El Tarabishy the kind honor of being named the "Most Influential Faculty." Having developed the first Social Entrepreneurship, Innovation, and Creativity courses offered to MBA and undergraduate students, El Tarabishy is constantly striving to find the perfect balance between tradition and modernization in his teaching pedagogy. Currently, Dr. El Tarabishy is the sole faculty member in the GW School of Business to teach in two nationally ranked programs.Remembered as one of his greatest achievements, Dr. El Tarabishy played a central role in the creation and promotion of the United Nations Micro, Small and Medium-Sized Enterprises (MSMEs) Day. Recognized by the United Nations and the Permanent Mission of Argentina to the United Nations, this Name Day is designated on specific dates to mark particular events or topics, in order to consciously and actively promote the objectives of the organization. With his novel idea, Dr. El Tarabishy managed to work closely with the Permanent Mission of Argentina to propose a resolution to dedicate a United Nations International Name Day to MSMEs. Approved by the United Nations General Assembly, the proposal was presented by the Permanent Mission of Argentina and 54 countries; thus, 5.5 billion people acted as co-signers of this resolution. From that day forward, June 27 has been recognized as the official UN MSME Day.

Thami Ghorfi is Dean of ESCA École de Management, an African leading Business School based in Casablanca, Morocco.He published "Entreprises familiales—Des paradoxes aux opportunités"—La croisée des Chemins May 2016. Thami Ghorfi coauthored "Preparing Executives for 2030 (ESCA publication © December 2015). He authored "Indispensables entrepreneurs africains" in Constructif N° 47 June 2017. Thami Ghorfi coauthored "The Impact of Businesses in the MENA Region" a chapter in "Business and Society in the Middle East, Exploring Responsible Business Practice"—Palgrave Macmillan Feb 2017. Thami authored "L'enseignement du management, au service de l'influence en Méditerranée in "La Méditerranée, terrain de la géopolitique mondiale ?" L'Harmattan 2019. He also coauthored "Impact of Social media usage on MENA countries economy" a chapter in "Business and Social Media in the Middle East"—Palgrave Macmillan Jul 2020. Thami coauthored "Femmes au cœur des entreprises familiales"—La Croisée des Chemins 2021.He contributes to the development of Management Education in the region. Thami chairs the AACSB MENA Advisory Council. He is an International Academic Member of the EDAF Committee of the EFMD (European Foundation for Management Development). Thami Ghorfi is also a member of the Academic Leadership Council of GBSN (Global Business School Network).Thami Ghorfi had been appointed in 2011 as an expert member of the Economic, Social, and Environmental Council (CESE), a constitutional institution of the Kingdom of Morocco.Thami is a graduate of ISG-Paris and ESSEC Business School.

Taïeb Hafsi is the Strategy and Society Professor of management at HEC Montréal. He has written numerous articles and books dealing with strategic management and change in organizations. His work has been published in most major journals including *Administrative Science Quarterly*, the *Academy of Management Review*, the *British Journal of Management*, and *Journal of Management Studies*. He holds a Master's of science degree in management from the Sloan School of Management, at the Massachusetts Institute of Technology, Boston, and a Doctorate in business administration, from the Harvard Business School.

Yara Harb is a PhD graduate in Management and International Affairs from the Holy Spirit University of Kaslik (USEK), and an experienced business development executive in cards and innovative e-payment solutions. Her research works concern strategic management and entrepreneurship, notably in regard to financial performance in SMEs. Her doctoral thesis was dedicated to identify the antecedents and implications of Entrepreneurial Orientation on firm performance while tackling the case of SMEs in an emerging economy.

Imad-eddine Hatimi holds a PhD in Business Administration (Strategy & Innovation) and a master in Management from HEC Montréal (1st Triple Crown Institution in North America) as well as a Master in Civil Engineering from Sherbrooke University (Canada). Dr Hatimi has focused his consulting and research activities on Strategic Management, Organizational Development and Innovation Management. In 2004, jointly with Taïeb Hafsi, he was awarded the Best Article Prize by the *Canadian Journal of Administrative Sciences*. In Canada, he was researcher and lecturer at HEC Montreal and a management consultant for various firms. Since his return to Morocco, he has been a Professor and a Dean of the Facultyof Management at Mundiapolis University (2008–2011). Dr. Hatimi has been also the Director General of ESCA École de Management, a business school he joined in 2012 as an Associate Dean Accreditations of ESCA EM and succeeded in achieving its AACSB Accreditation as the first institution in Morocco and French-speaking Africa. He has developed a consulting and training expertise in various fields like Strategic Planning, Organizational design, HR Recruitment and Development, Innovation and Entrepreneurship, and Education Management.

Omar Hemissi is a professor at the École Supérieure de Commerce d'Alger. He graduated from the National School of Administration (Algeria), holds a Master's in finance and a Doctorate in Management Sciences. His research focuses mainly on issues related to change management, governance and growth strategies. His publications focus on both the public sector and family businesses, largely in developing countries. He also acts as an expert and consultant to various organizations.

Sherif Kamel is a professor of management, dean of the school of business at The American University in Cairo, and president of the board of governors of the American Chamber of Commerce in Egypt. He is an

Eisenhower Fellow. He is the co-chair of the board of stewards of the African Women Entrepreneurship Cooperative (USA) and a founding member of the Internet Society (Egypt). He was a member of the World Bank Knowledge Advisory Commission (USA) and chairman of the Chevening Association (Egypt). His research and teaching interests include digital transformation, information technology transfer to developing nations, decision support systems, and entrepreneurship. His work is broadly published in over 250 academic and business articles, chapters, and cases in information systems, business and management journals, books, and magazines. He is the author of the NileView article series https://sherifkamel.substack.com. Kamel holds a PhD in information systems from the London School of Economics and Political Science, an MBA, a BA in business administration, and an MA in Islamic Art and Architecture from the American University in Cairo.

Diala Kozaily holds a Master of Sciences degree in Business administration with an emphasis on Finance. She previously contributed to the editing and writing of a book about higher education governance in the Arab world. She is a PhD candidate at USEK Business School. In fact, she is studying social entrepreneurship. Adding to that, she takes part in editing different book projects. Moreover, she is assisting in giving different courses for the bachelor and master levels. Furthermore, she is a professor at GBSB Global. She is also a manager at Maison Kozaily SARL, a company based in Lebanon that produces and distributes a variety of natural foods and beverages to the local and international market.

Sung Joo Park is an emeritus professor at the KAIST Business School in Seoul, Korea. He was the former Dean and Vice President of KAIST, and served as the founding President of AAPBS (Association of Asia-Pacific Business Schools). He also served as a member of global business education boards including AACSB and GFME (Global Foundation for Management Education), an Asian Advisory Board member of EFMD, and scientific committee member of Eduniversal.For more than 10 years, he was the mentor or reviewer of business school accreditation for AACSB and EFMD for schools such as Tsinghua SEM in China (Mentor), Chinese U. Business School of Hong Kong, Keio Business School in Japan, Chengchi Business School and Soochow Business School in

Taiwan, Sogang Business School in Korea, and University of Malaya in Malaysia. He is also an advisor for Sasin Graduate Institute of Business Administration of Chulalongkorn University in Thailand, FPT University in Vietnam, and a board member of the Higher School of Business Kazan Federal University in Russia.He received a PhD at the Michigan State University in 1978 and worked for the KAIST since 1980. He was a visiting professor at UCLA Anderson Graduate School of Management in the US, Tsinghua SEM in China, and Keio Business School in Japan.He was an advisory consulting professor for Samsung Group for 10 years, including the companies like Samsung Corning, Samsung SDS, Samsung Advanced Institute of Technology among others.He sits on the editorial boards of international academic journals such as *Decision Support Systems, J. of Operational Research, International J. of Modeling, Simulation and Scientific Computing.*He also was committee member and advisor for Korean government, such as Ministry of Education, Ministry of Science & Technology, Ministry of Agriculture & Fisheries, and was a member of advisory committee of National Assembly Budget Office, an advisor for Supreme Prosecutor's Office. Additionally, he was a member of Korean Presidential Advisory Council on Science & Technology and currently is a lifetime member of the Korean Academy of Science & Technology.

Georges Yahchouchy is the President of the American University of the Middle East (AUM), Kuwait. He is known for his commitment to excellence in Higher Education and expertise in academic leadership given his vast educational background and exposure to multicultural environments during his educational and professional paths. He is professor in business administration and he received his PhD in Business Administration from Montesquieu Bordeaux University, France, in 2004 and earned a Postgraduate Certificate in Learning and Teaching in Higher Education from the University of Chester, UK in 2013. He completed the Professional Education Certificate in Institute for Educational Management (IEM Class of 2019) offered by the Harvard Graduate School of Education. He is the author of several research papers in business, leadership, and educational management.

List of Figures

List of Tables

Introduction

Where others see risks and trouble, some see profit and opportunities. Despite constrained resources, they start new businesses. Many have agreed to name this concept "entrepreneurship." Add to it launching a company that also seeks to serve a social cause, and you have "social entrepreneurship" also known as "altruistic entrepreneurship."

As this concept has become a major economic force that proved, in many cases, to be related to a company's growth, we have sought to gather eminent academics and professionals from around the world to help shed light on various aspects of this phenomenon, particularly in the Arab world.

Reputed experts from Washington, Korea, Kuwait, Lebanon, Morocco, Canada, Egypt, and Algeria discuss in this book how and whether social entrepreneurship, which has emerged over the past decade in the region, can improve the lives of people and make an actual change and difference in a specific field.

This book is divided into three parts. The first part focuses on the importance of establishing a culture of humane entrepreneurship in the Arab world to enhance sustainability. It also studies closely the correlation between innovation and entrepreneurship to ensure business survival. Moreover, it reflects critically on the advantages and setbacks of social entrepreneurship and addresses the determinants of entrepreneurial orientation as an influential factor of business performance and growth.

The second part examines the intrinsic link between education and entrepreneurship as the latter has become a popular college major with a focus on new venture creation. The part also emphasizes the prominent role assumed by women in social entrepreneurship in the Arab world. It ends with a qualitative analysis that shares the experience of four Algerian entrepreneurs who strive to overcome the institutional challenges they face in a dynamic and turbulent context.

The third and last part look at practical case studies of entrepreneurship which examine the impact of this concept on job creation in Lebanon and the influence of entrepreneurship on the culture and economy in Egypt. It ends with the emergence of social entrepreneurship as a new field, which is confronted with several hurdles, in Algeria.

With the wide variety of the aspects that are tackled, this book offers a unique insight to better understand how social entrepreneurship operates in the Arab world now that it is gaining more attention and instigating regulations' amendments to accommodate to its needs. In struggling economies like Lebanon, which suffer from devaluation and the effects of the COVID-19 pandemic, it could be leveraged as an inspiration that could address society's problems and empower the youth to drive social growth.

I wish you a pleasant reading and hope you will enjoy, as much as I did, uncovering many interesting aspects of the social entrepreneurship phenomenon as you delve into the chapters of the insightful "Entrepreneurship and Social Entrepreneurship in the MENA Region".

Part I

Entrepreneurship: Trends and Concepts

1

The Intersection of Social Entrepreneurship, Sustainability, and the UN SDGs in the Arab World: A Humane Entrepreneurship Perspective

Ayman El Tarabishy

The Arab Ecosystem

At the turn of the twentieth century, there was an explosion of research on the Arab World, including the next steps needed for the countries categorized in this region to enter the next phase of their evolution—financially, socially, and ecologically. The Arab World includes 22 countries spread throughout the Middle East and North Africa (MENA), more specifically, Algeria, Bahrain, the Comoros Islands, Djibouti, Egypt, Iraq, Jordan, Kuwait, Lebanon, Libya, Morocco, Mauritania, Oman, Palestine, Qatar, Saudi Arabia, Somalia, Syria, Tunisia, the United Arab Emirates, and Yemen. Given their vast geographic and cultural landscapes, these nations have a very important and rare opportunity to

A. El Tarabishy (✉)
Department of Management, The George Washington University School of Business, Washington, DC, USA
e-mail: ayman@gwu.edu

N. Azoury, T. Hafsi (eds.), *Entrepreneurship and Social Entrepreneurship in the MENA Region*, https://doi.org/10.1007/978-3-030-88447-5_1

engage the Arab region in transforming the way in which they function in and throughout the society. By centering themselves in a certain type of entrepreneurship—one which seeks to center the way wealth is created, rather than one that analyzes solely the way in which money is made—the Arab world will lead us all into the next phase of growth.

Generally, individuals in Arab countries typically feel positively about entrepreneurship, and specifically about 3/4th of the region's population recognizes entrepreneurship as a successful and generally "good" choice in career (GEM, 2017). Upon surveying, it was concluded that the way that people perceive entrepreneurship depends [on] how people feel about or respond to risk-taking in entrepreneurial activities (Aminova, 2019). It is important to note that even in each nation's individual analysis, many of the Arab countries had improved in their individual standings around fear of failure, as well as the indicator of female entrepreneurial activity, indicating that their culture was moving closer to or including more aspects of entrepreneurship (GEM, 2017).

Over the past 10 years, many of these Arab nations have looked to multinational organizations, as well as to the Western example, for guidance in their transitions towards entrepreneurship, including how to engage their populations in becoming more entrepreneurial, but also in a way that helps civil society.

A great example of this multi-purpose enterprise is the case of Sekem, a social enterprise founded by Ibrahim Abdou. Abdou established Sekem in his home nation of Egypt after spending much time abroad. This enterprise began with the intention of creating and managing an organic farm, but gradually took on many other projects, all of which had the intent of profit and/or people, building Sekem's portfolio into what it is today (El Tarabishy & Sashkin, 2008). Within the realm of social entrepreneurship, the social entrepreneur is "innovative, resourceful, and results oriented as they draw on the best thinking in both the business and nonprofit worlds to develop strategies that maximize their social impact" (Abdou et al., 2010). This case study provides us many insights regarding who social entrepreneurs are and what they do; however, it also provides an example of what a thoroughly successful social enterprise might resemble in MENA and specifically in Egypt.

Despite standalone examples and the large visibility around the need for some type of expansive entrepreneurship in the MENA, this region has been a historically "underrepresented region in the growing literature of social entrepreneurship" (Abdou et al., 2010). Therefore, in a collaborative effort to better understand the current nature of social entrepreneurship, specifically in the Middle East, Abdou et al. created a comprehensive study of the region's current ecosystem in 2010 in order to better plan for sustainable decisions in the future, especially noting the growing population of young people across the region. In observing the specific challenges that ultimately led to the limiting nature of both the access to becoming a social entrepreneur and the reach of these individual's social enterprises, obstacles to success included "policy making and governance related challenges; the need for greater institutional, operational, and financial support; and a lack of social and cultural awareness and recognition of their work" (Abdou et al., 2010). This report pointed out that social entrepreneurship [had] flourished globally where key institutions and economic actors were actively engaged in creating a conducive environment that supports and cultivates new, indigenous ideas and innovative practices; the study provided this examination as a way to hopefully propel the organization of social entrepreneurship into the future (Abdou et al., 2010).

As previous articles and reports have argued that "the seeds for social entrepreneurship can be sowed in any context" (Abdou et al., 2010), our argument brings light to the cultural differences at play and offers possible solutions for addressing sustainability through the lens of entrepreneurship in the Arab World.

Entrepreneurship and Sustainability: What Can Be Done?

From this place, it seems important, if not essential, to note the ways in which sustainability may perform or appear in a society. In analyzing the three specific pillars of sustainability, we identified key social, financial, and ecological variables at play. Social sustainability can appear as inclusive and equitable access to opportunity. Financial sustainability involves a cyclical economy, through which money and resources are constantly exchanged and reused. Lastly, ecological sustainability can be taken from many perspectives. It can and does, of course, consider the natural environment and a community's care for that environment; however, it additionally includes the community (i.e. people) and their lifestyles, as well as the status of the ecological system of entrepreneurship for that particular environment. When we speak of ecological matters, we are more specifically referring to the symbiosis of that specific environment's stakeholders.

It is necessary that we have and use these expansive definitions for sustainability. If we narrow the definition of sustainability, we may indirectly limit our ability to work on sustainable projects and to create a healthier and more prosperous economic and ecological environment in Arab countries. The dynamics of "population change, ecological degradation, and resource scarcity with development policies and practice, all occurring in complex and highly unstable geopolitical and economic environments," have and will continue to create nearly impossible barriers from which the nations in these regions can respond (El-Zein et al., 2014). That will place incredible pressures on the government and public sector as they constantly react to the needs of their populations. Entrepreneurship, and specifically a type of entrepreneurship that aims to do well for the greater society, can relieve some of the stress and, in so doing, help the government so that they can focus on caring for the needs of their people, which includes fostering a strong and ample entrepreneurial ecosystem.

The Ancestors of Social Entrepreneurship

Looking specifically at social entrepreneurship in the Arab world, and potentially more generally at social giving, it is clear that Arab countries have extremely different patterns and institutionalized habits for giving as compared with Western nations, from which the term of social entrepreneurship emerged (*What is Social Entrepreneurship?*, 2017). Therefore, through the examination of social entrepreneurship, it is necessary to take into account the major differences in culture that accumulate to produce the many different results of social entrepreneurship throughout the world.

In looking at the many aspects that play into social entrepreneurship, we tracked its evolution in order to plan for the future of social consideration and giving in the sector of entrepreneurship.

Looking at Fig. 1.1, traditional philanthropy includes a contribution of financial or in-kind resources to development projects. The MENA region has many institutionalized pathways of philanthropy, originating in business and typical culture. The experience of poverty and relations between those who are impoverished and those who are not differs majorly between MENA and the Western world.

As the first institution to shepherd in the principles of corporate social responsibility (CSR) in the Arab region, the Egyptian Corporate Responsibility Center (ECRC) was a leader in transforming Egypt's fresh, yet growing Corporate Social Responsibility movement. Founded in

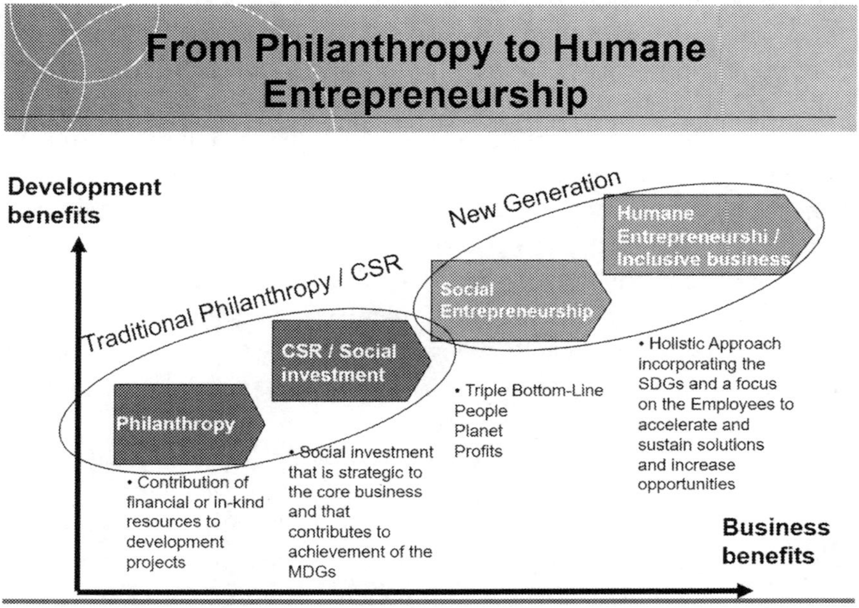

Fig. 1.1 From philanthropy to humane entrepreneurship (Source: Copyright Dr. Ayman El Tarabishy)

2005 with an intention to propel the conversation about CSR beyond philanthropy, the ECRC proposed a "perspective that the well-being of businesses and society are fundamentally interdependent, rather than mutually exclusive. By operating in harmony with all its stakeholders and managing its social and environmental impacts, [the ECRC advocated that] a business [could safeguard] its long-term success" (El Tarabishy, 2008). Learning from the global recession of 2008, countries saw the ways in which funds that were initially set aside for philanthropic contributions had been the first to be repurposed towards more "necessary" ventures, and therefore, decided that investments in society needed to be "be fully integrated with their core operations for the business to be truly sustainable" (El Tarabishy, 2008). In the wake of the recession, CSR, seen as holding the "potential to link business, government, and civil society around poverty reduction and sustainable development" (El Tarabishy, 2008), had the power to determine less how businesses spent their money and more about how they made their money, which set the stage for modern-day interactions between business and society.

Despite the ideological importance of CSR, its implementation in the Arab world faced many challenges, including lack of effective government interaction and cultural obstacles. This cultural piece is essential to explore as it leaves its imprint on the social giving practices of today. Given Egypt's strong culture of philanthropy, which "offers a powerful foundation for a more strategic, coordinated approach to [social giving], the government [had] the opportunity to build on this foundation, embracing CSR activities for the sustainable development of the country" (El Tarabishy, 2008). The failed widespread implementation of CSR must not be considered a failure, however, as it gave way to an imperative conversation about the private sector's role and responsibility in providing for their communities.

CSR in Egypt and much of the rest of the Arab World struggled to take hold as it did not take an expansive enough approach in defining the roles of stakeholders. Firms often separated CSR into only two stakeholder categories—the employees and the people, or the community. This is an indicator of these firms' inability to appropriately establish CSR in their enterprise as it does "not recogniz[e] suppliers, competitors, or government regulators as [additional] CSR stakeholder groups" (El

Tarabishy, 2008). This limited involvement of stakeholders created a limit on "resources for CSR, [so that] most firms [narrowed] their focus to two or three topics," which was ultimately a disservice to the firms and their surrounding community (El Tarabishy, 2008). We will return to the conversation around stakeholders later in this review.

Understanding that Culture Matters

In looking towards solutions, many companies have been able to fabricate models that demonstrate value creation for both public and private spheres by specifically enlisting community members. These models provide much short-term success; however, these companies will need to find innovative solutions to create long-term success and reach their goal of ensured sustainability for the community and environment. These solutions will most likely come from the entrepreneur, who is "just as important to the success of an entrepreneurial effort as the innovation itself" (El Tarabishy & Sashkin, 2008). As Schumpeter (1934) described it, the entrepreneur "is merely the carrier of the innovation into society" (El Tarabishy & Sashkin, 2008). Within the realm of social entrepreneurship, El Tarabishy and Sashkin (2008) pointed to three major and essential elements of social entrepreneurship. The first is the innovation itself, as it is the curator of entrepreneurial activity. The second is the entrepreneur who, as mentioned above, is someone able to "(a) develop (or identify) an innovation, (b) take a highly active role in creating an organizational venture based on that innovation, and (c) take high (but realistic) risks to successfully establish that venture" (El Tarabishy & Sashkin, 2008). The last element is the social context of entrepreneurship, which plays into the first two parts. If the innovation and the entrepreneur are not socially conscious of the community within which they are operating (or planning to operate), then their venture will decrease in its importance as well as its likelihood for success (El Tarabishy & Sashkin, 2008).

Because of this importance of social context, the practice of frugal innovation has taken hold in many places in the world. Frugal innovation is the creation of a new idea, product, or service which uses limited resources to serve a community need in a widespread manner. It works from the greater understanding that humans are creative and innovative in nature; therefore, no matter the limits placed on our resources, if one is given the time and space, they will be able to create a product or service that fits the needs of a population. A key concept within this practice, though, is that the best frugal innovators or frugal entrepreneurs are those who have an extremely thorough understanding of the community that they are serving. This means that most frugal entrepreneurs will work in a community that fits their (or a similar) identity.

In Egypt and many other MENA nations, as mentioned earlier, the culture varies incredibly as compared to the Western nations from which many concepts of social entrepreneurship have evolved. Three essential features that appear in the MENA region, which are seen as vital characteristics to implementation and success, include trust, communication, and awareness (El Tarabishy, 2008). Before understanding the notion of social intervention or giving, we must recognize that "even the translation of the term 'social' in Arabic is related to hand-to-mouth charity, raising the question of whether new terminology is needed for the CSR concept to truly take root" (El Tarabishy, 2008). We are called to "look beyond philanthropy" as we seek a more sustainability-oriented approach to social giving in the regional context which requires business, government, and civil society to integrate in a way that views each other as one and the same as opposed to other and different from one another.

Social Entrepreneurship as the Next Rung on the Giving Ladder

The Arab World is experiencing a rare and opportune moment in history due to their growing youth population. With approximately 110 million youth between the ages of 15 and 29 years living in the Middle East, this population makes up more than 30% of the region's population (*MENA: Youth Facts*, 2020). Additionally, the youth unemployment rate in the Middle East is nearly double that of the world's total. Countries in the region are experiencing increased pressure on public systems, such as health and education, as well as a great need for employment opportunities as young people enter the job market. These challenges, coupled with a need to transition away from nonrenewable energy sources, indicate that future "development [in the Arab World] will depend on active collaboration across institutions on the national level as well as greater cooperation between countries at the regional level" (Abdou et al., 2010).

This is a moment for partnerships, and social entrepreneurship is a platform upon which these partnerships might take form and flourish. Social entrepreneurship necessitates that "key institutional actors work together to create a supportive environment for innovation and growth in the area of sustainable development" (Abdou et al., 2010). An analysis on the opportunity for social entrepreneurship in Middle East reported: "As this increasingly educated generation comes of age, expectations are high—both among the youth themselves, who seek meaningful opportunities for economic and social advancement, and among the region's reform advocates, who expect that this increasingly globalized and educated generation will pave the way for sustainable growth and stability in the region" (Abdou et al., 2010). As governments become increasingly restricted and unable to assure the safety nets that they provided older populations, there is a great "need for the public and private sector to work together to create new jobs and meaningful opportunities for work, in addition to managing the broader set of services needed by this young population" (Abdou et al., 2010). The compilation of past and present pressures on these traditional spaces of government support have greatly decreased the government's ability to both "creatively and effectively deal with emerging challenges such as water shortages and other environmental concerns" (Abdou et al., 2010). For this reason, many MENA governments have attempted to advance the private sector in taking on more responsibility in "economic production and the provision of services, and, thus, in spurring economic diversification and sustainable growth" (Abdou et al., 2010).

Despite these efforts, MENA governments need an innovative development framework to empower the private sector to step into their role as leading partners, "ensuring an inclusive environment and sound governance for private initiatives that are promoting macroeconomic growth, job creation, and social impact" (Abdou et al., 2010). Although the Arab World has witnessed much economic growth in recent years, research demonstrates that this growth is not necessarily coupled with equitable development nor accessible opportunities for the most vulnerable groups within these communities.

Individual firms have been taking it upon themselves to "move beyond charity" (Abdou et al., 2010), given the reality that "traditional sources of philanthropy have been somewhat dormant or restricted due to historical developments related to the balance of power between such institutions and the state, or have been crowded out by the historically dominant role of the state in social service delivery" (Abdou et al., 2010). Some enterprises are aiming to resuscitate the region's tradition for philanthropic action; however, all private philanthropic action is limited in its scope due to confined religious interpretations and practice (Abdou et al., 2010).

This environment gives a great opportunity for the next evolution of social interaction and giving—the social enterprise. This enterprise is most generally defined as "an organization with a clear social mission and a strategy that combines resourcefulness and innovation, which allow it to be financially sustainable" (Abdou et al., 2010). Separated into four specific categories, social enterprises can be leveraged nonprofits, enterprising nonprofits, hybrid enterprises, or social businesses. A leveraged nonprofit is defined by its ability to "capitalize on the interest of a variety of stakeholders to operate and to secure ongoing support based on a diversified portfolio of funding," whereas enterprising nonprofits typically "have a self-financing component contributing to the organization's sustainability" (Abdou et al., 2010). Hybrid enterprises are a compilation of the qualities detailed in "for-profit and nonprofit legal models, either through an innovative legal structure or by using a for-profit subsidiary to support the social activities of the non-profit" (Abdou et al., 2010). Lastly, social businesses are enterprises "that can demonstrate market-level financial performance and competitiveness while expressing an equal or greater commitment to a social aim" (Abdou et al., 2010). Within these social enterprises exist teams, and specifically leaders, who operate in specific ways that promote (or restrict) the firm as a socially operating enterprise. Social enterprises necessitate buy-in from a variety of stakeholders in order to truly be successful.

A study examining the ecosystem of entrepreneurship in the Middle East took a look at many aspects of social entrepreneurship, including the specific qualities of a social entrepreneur, noting that all those studied come from a "highly educated group, with the majority of them having attained university degree and post-graduate degrees" (Abdou et al., 2010). Additionally, as "children and youth, most of these individuals were engaged in extracurricular activities, including sports, the arts and youth organizations," and "a third of this group has studied, lived, or worked abroad and cite their experience abroad as a factor that has shaped their professional aspirations" (Abdou et al., 2010). Almost all of these social entrepreneurs had "an intimate understanding of, or personal experience with, the problems they are trying to solve," and therefore a "majority of them are pursuing systemic change" (Abdou et al., 2010). Lastly and quite interestingly, "due to issues of organizational and funding priorities, 73 out of the 78 internationally recognized social entrepreneurs are drawn from only 5 counties in the region: Egypt, the West Bank and Gaza, Jordan, Lebanon, and Morocco" (Abdou et al., 2010). Research shows that unfortunately, SE has been created into something that is only for the well-educated and well-trained. The necessity of high connections and stature in the Arab World makes SE an "invitation only" type of entrepreneurship (El Tarabishy & Sashkin, 2008).

It is unfortunate that social entrepreneurship has not taken widespread hold in the Arab World. In hypothesizing the potential reason for this, one might be directed towards their different (as compared to the West) way and method of giving. In a culture where "giving back" to the community is part and practice of nearly all communities, we might postulate if social entrepreneurship has a place. In order to understand why social entrepreneurship has not integrated into Arab countries, we might want to transition our attention from ways in which we can create more receptive operating environments for social entrepreneurs, and move to an enhanced understanding that recognizes the limitations of social entrepreneurship, especially in addressing the pillars of sustainability in a global manner.

In other words, let us note that social entrepreneurship is a Western term, created out of a Western ideology in response to the demands of Western societies. This is not to say that social entrepreneurship cannot exist in the Arab World, but more so that it already does exist (in some capacity). Therefore, to engage with sustainability thoroughly and productively, we must engage with a furthered concept within the realm of Entrepreneurship—that being, Humane Entrepreneurship.

Beyond Social Entrepreneurship: Possible Solutions for Sustainable Change in the Arab World

In analyzing the shortfalls of SE in the Arab World, we can develop a workable concept by expanding upon and taking into account the shortfalls of social entrepreneurship. In thinking about the role of the social entrepreneur(s) with a mission of systemic change, where is the gap between intention and impact? How might we conceptualize a model or construct that does not look to create "long-term charity," but rather seeks sustainable and equitable justice? In what ways has the current integration of social entrepreneurship promoted systemic injustices in its ability to determine who can act as a social entrepreneur? How might we engage with the people—employees, community, customers, and so on—to bring about both widespread and sustainable impact? What might this look like in the Arab World, and can we categorize this new concept for the Arab World at-large, or might we need to look at individual countries and communities to assess their specific needs?

It is here that we would like to propose the concept of Humane Entrepreneurship, or inclusive business, as a more appropriate solution for the inclusion of societal good in businesses in the MENA region. As indicated in the Appendix, Human Entrepreneurship (HumEnt) is the next evolution of "giving," which in fact works to do away with the concept of giving in order to recenter the space of operation around individual perspective. HumEnt, at large, offers us another variation to the solution. Instead of pushing policies that could improve the standing of social entrepreneurship in the Arab World, we can examine the ways in which we can find and optimize the strengths that are already present in the Arab countries and their communities to create innovative and sustainable cycles of growth (i.e. cyclical economy).

HumEnt is a holistic approach, which incorporates the United Nations Sustainable Development Goals (SDGs) and focuses on all stakeholders (especially employees) to accelerate and sustain solutions and increase opportunities. The main objective of HumEnt is to create healthy business models which, with appropriate leadership and human resource management (HRM), are able to create wealth and further employment opportunities.

The Theory of Humane Entrepreneurship

HumEnt is a new theory in entrepreneurship research best described as "virtuous and sustainable integration of Entrepreneurship Leadership, and HRM, in which successful implementation leads to a beneficial increase in wealth and quality job creation, perpetuated in a continuous cycle" (Kim et al., 2018). A satisfactory application of HumEnt opens the opportunity to create more of a desired result, which would then generate additional desired results or successes in a continuously moving chain of action (Kim et al., 2018). Within any specific population or firm, we can easily measure their specific state of HumEnt. Broken into four specific categories, these states include:

- IDEAL: Virtuous and Sustainable Integration, Beneficial with Continuous Cycle.
- MODERATE: Non-Virtuous and Sustainable Integration, Beneficial in Broken Cycle.
- NEGATIVE: Vicious and Disconnected, Disadvantageous in Broken Cycle.
- HARMFUL: Vicious and Disconnected Disadvantageous with Continuous Cycle.

In order to understand these categories to their fullest capacities, it is essential to highlight the key nature of humanistic management, which provides the main basis from which Humane EO and EO diverge (Kim et al., 2018).

Humanistic management describes a style of management which "emphasizes the human condition and is oriented to the development of human virtue, in all its forms, to its fullest extent" (Melé, 2003). Within this theory, top managers must enter into human needs to properly and fully motivate employees, or citizens. These actions, then, create a culture that "considers the ethical impact of actions, and motivates people around them to acquire virtues in order to build a strong community" (Melé, 2003). Throughout all society, including business, "respect for human dignity demands respect for human freedom" (Kim et al., 2018). When looking at the multidimensional nature of HRM, we can see how there are management practices that "increase profitability through people, including participation and empowerment, employee ownership, training and skills development, cross-utilization and cross-training, employment security, selective recruiting, high wages, and information sharing" (Pfeffer, 1998). Understanding that high-performance HRM can also mean high-commitment HRM, humanistic management is at the centerfold of Humane Entrepreneurship, in its focus on mutual gains for the employee and employer.

An organization of any size or stature has the opportunity to enhance their structure and strategy with empathy, equity, enablement, and empowerment. By harnessing these four domains, organizations can create very powerful synergies for their internal and external relations and activities (Kim et al., 2018). An empathetic orientation acts as the key driving factor for employee engagement and a communicative business culture, which will result in better relations between both organizational members and stakeholders (Choi, 2006). As empathy can be greatly utilized to gain insights into other people's understandings and beliefs, it can also be "considered the starting point of design thinking and is essential to understanding the needs of customers" (Ickes & Simpson, 1997; Brown, 2008).

Empathy leads to the next element of equity, or the extent to which a company treats individuals in a fair and equal manner (Kim et al., 2018). Equity-based justice, an important part of society, is founded in a sense of proportion, meaning that the "outcomes [that an] individual receives should be awarded in proportion to their inputs and outputs" (Kim et al.,

2018). The creation of a justice-based ecosystem will allow organizations to reach the next dimension of entrepreneurial humanism.

Enablement is the extent to which a company provides the environment in which each individual employee is able to develop their skills and knowledge (Kim et al., 2018). However, to reach a place of enablement, there must already be a company culture that has equitable following of performance rewards.

The last element within this analysis of humanistic management is empowerment. A necessity for long-term, sustainable growth, empowerment is "the delegation of power and responsibility from higher levels of the organizational hierarchy to lower levels, especially in regard to an employee's ability to make their own decisions" (Kim et al., 2018). It reminds us to breed a culture of collective autonomy. This leads us to the greatest outcome of HRM, which is "to improve organizational performance by facilitating organizational members' spontaneous motivation and inducing employees' active participation in organizational decision-making, leading to enhanced organizational efficiency" (Kim et al., 2018). In sum, employees are seen and heard as human beings who are "self-motivated to enhance organizational efficiency, empowered to achieve better quality of work by developing their individual capabilities, and trusted as partners in the development and growth of the organization" (Kim et al., 2018).

In creating this theory, we hope that organizations incorporate these elements into their management strategies, while aiming to build upon them to develop population-specific education and training programs to better understand, prepare, and improve their unique workforce. Therefore, humane enterprises transform from a singular enterprise into a community-supporting enterprise that seeks to uplift humanity throughout their entire business model. HumEnt offers us a key insight into possible solutions for populations that have been historically left out, looking specifically at the Arab World in this case.

When understanding the ways in which HumEnt can embed itself into an organization, firm, or nation, it is essential to recognize the important role of culture in value and movement. Leadership and management create a culture of entrepreneurial orientation (EO) and humane entrepreneurial orientation (H-EO) through their own actions, thus enhancing performance at large. Culture contains the "attitudes, values, beliefs, and behaviors shared by a particular group of people, therefore [defining the] structures and systems, [guiding] management processes, [impacting] work-unit climate, and, ultimately, [affecting] organizational performance" (Kim et al., 2018). A humanely entrepreneurial culture is thus created and originally shaped by the intention and impact of the entrepreneur and leadership team.

Qualification of HumEnt

The main driving forces working amongst the three main pillars of HumEnt include: leadership and firm performance; leadership to EO; leadership to H-EO; H-EO to EO (and EO to H-EO); EO to firm performance; and H-EO to firm performance. Therefore, having defined these interactions, it is essential to return to the four categories or states of H-EO (as mentioned in previous section *The Theory of Humane Entrepreneurship*), being IDEAL, MODERATE, NEGATIVE and HARMFUL. In understanding these four components, we can dive into the ways that umEnt can be practiced and utilized.

Those organizations qualifying for an IDEAL Humane Entrepreneurial state, or status, include those adhering to a people-centered entrepreneurial orientation, resulting in cyclical growth that benefits all stakeholders. MODERATE HumEnt includes a social and financial capital clash amongst their EO and H-EO practices, which ultimately leads to mixed results that inhibit continuous cyclical growth. NEGATIVE HumEnt is founded in the absence of a people-centered model from entrepreneurial orientation, then causing disadvantageous trends and broken growth cycles. Lastly, HARMFUL HumEnt portrays an organization that directly or indirectly causes active harm to some of their stakeholders, commonly their employees and their surrounding communities, which certainly results in a destructive cycle of growth.

It is important to note that in a changing world, such as that of today, the collective business conscience is shifting more towards the leveraging of social capital in and for organizational success. This shift demonstrates that although those currently placed within the HARMFUL HumEnt state are capable of growing wealth, their lack of greater understanding of humane wealth will ultimately break their cycles of growth (Kim et al., 2018) (see Appendix).

Once clear markers are created to determine the state of an organization or firm, either through self-nomination or an external auditing system, there must be incentive for companies and nations to break away from their destructive cycles of growth. Through this, we will be able to more greatly specify the culture which we collectively desire to uphold. It is only those placed within the IDEAL and MODERATE categories that have the potential to increase the wealth of all national populations while simultaneously creating quality jobs for the well-educated and trained youth in the Arab World who are prepared to take on the demands of the workforce. To more greatly cement the power of these top states, the theory of HumEnt proposes a way of connecting both GDP and national growth, which will ultimately "address the growing public concern over inequality, in terms of both income and wealth" (Kim et al., 2018).

In thinking specifically about a population or nation, HumEnt can be practiced to bring about serious change amongst the groups affected and their greater reach in their communities. We can use the same criteria to determine the wealth of a nation, using the four states or criteria and observing the ways in which a country's leaders manage EO and H-EO in their culture. Striving for an IDEAL association, by tapping into one's potential for HumEnt, nations can create just, green economies that seek to uplift their citizens and, in doing so, generate wealth and improve quality job opportunities, environmental standards, as well as nutrition, health, and education systems.

The above section "Qualification of HumEnt" was taken from El Tarabishy, Healing a Hurt Generation with Humane Entrepreneurship, 2020.

Looking Further: Who Is Considered When Sustainable Patterns Are Created?

Reflecting on the elements necessary for establishing a concept of entrepreneurship that is equally focused on innovation for humanity and the pursuit of business opportunities for profit, society's well-being, sustainability, and the integration of all people, we need to examine our understanding of the role and relationship between stakeholders, shareholders, and enterprises (which can be extrapolated to larger entities such as regions or nations).

Humane Entrepreneurship can be thought of as the harmony of applied innovation, the pursuit of business opportunities for profit, and the sustainable well-being of society, which is for the people and by the people. It is, in essence, a humane way of treating entrepreneurship, where the well-being of each individual is paramount. A better picture of the concept is gained by examining the historical roots of its operational environment. Returning to 1970, Nobel Prize winner Milton Friedman announced that any business pursuing a goal other than making money was "an unwitting puppet of the intellectual forces that have been undermining the basis of a free society these past decades" (Friedman, 1970). His declaration was taken as religion, and for the next 40 some years, we, collectively, viewed shareholders as the only group to indeed have a moral claim on the corporation, which existed, in essence, to maximize their value—specifically, the bottom line. However, corporations, just as individuals and communities, do not exist in silos, nor do their company practices. In recent years, the evil and unprecedented harm done to communities worldwide for the sake of the bottom line has become more visible, thanks to innovations in technology, allowing people to see both the social successes and havoc globally caused by enterprises.

Next, we might look to Edward Freeman, an American philosopher. He, around the same time as Friedman, stated, conversely, that many groups can make moral claims on the corporation because the corporation has the potential to harm or benefit these groups. Freeman's theory encompasses a variable that Friedman forgot, which would be the stakeholders. Stakeholders—including the owners, corporate managers, the local community, customers, employees, and suppliers—are essential to the survival and success of the corporation as their relationship with the corporation affects them.

Movement towards stakeholder inclusion, promoted by the lens of Humane Entrepreneurship, is not intended to enable philanthropic or socially responsible acts, nor are we promoting the re-establishment of social entrepreneurship. We are specifically and directly asking for a holistic approach that incorporates social achievements (the UN Sustainable

Development Goals) and focuses on the employees as vehicles to accelerate and sustain solutions and increase opportunities on a local and global level.

How are foundational organizations providing an equitable policy that allows parents to successfully do their work? How can we ensure that we keep up with ecological policies that care for our local communities and are necessary ways to continue our combat against climate change? How are organizations advocating for fair and inclusive policies for micro, small, and medium-sized enterprises, and appropriate measures that ensure that these MSMEs have access to such aid?

The five paragraphs above were taken from El Tarabishy, The Stakeholder Share, 2020.

For businesses, organizations, and governments who are looking to take a more human-centric view of their operations, it is essential to bring all these concepts together and recognize that humane includes not only those people who are typically considered in business transactions, but additionally the groups that have been significantly disenfranchised. Within the Arab World, and most of the rest of the world as well, these groups include women, young people, and those living in poverty. It is necessary to note that these groups are not mutually exclusive, and many individuals exist at the intersections of these identities.

These concepts work from the fact that a "local communities' growing economic health boosts profits and prosperity for everyone along the value chain," meaning that the 116 million people at the "base of the pyramid" in MENA are not a "monolith" (Khouri, 2019). Throughout the world, the outputs of the base of the pyramid create one-third of the world's economy. As "business models that call for creating private and public value while aiming for scale become more prevalent," it is essential that "companies commit to learning what constitutes value for the various components of this population" (Rangan et al., 2011). In doing so, enterprises, organizations, and governments must gain a greater understanding of the people at the "base of the pyramid," so as to best create a relationship with them that generates value and fits their needs. We might divide this group at the bottom of the pyramid into three sections: consumers, coproducers, and clients.

Enterprises and organizations can ensure "value to consumers by directly addressing their needs for services such as clean water, better sanitation, education, and credit" (Rangan et al., 2011). This section gives significant visibility to the innovative creation of high-quality products and services with goals to "lower overall usage costs and [provide] greater convenience than those of present alternatives [to consumers]. The result: a profound effect on productivity" (Rangan et al., 2011). Next, coproducers are those for whom companies might provide work (and, therefore, income). Lastly, clients are those at the extreme base of the pyramid, indicating that they encompass the "extreme-poverty segment." These individuals are seen to need "agents" in order to "garner resources on their behalf" in our current system (Rangan et al., 2011). Agents can be companies, organizations, and government or regional entities. It is important to note that it is necessary that these agents understand the specific needs of the community with which they are working. Bottom-up communication is essential and may oftentimes include programs that work less to provide resources for individuals, and more to deconstruct the barriers that keep these people in harmful cycles of poverty, or from existing within an environment which could be categorized as having a harmful status of HumEnt.

Companies in the past have failed time and time again because they forgot or overlooked the key component of "bolstering the success of the base-of-the-pyramid communities where they do business" (Rangan et al., 2011). Essentially, the companies "had failed to recognize how people in the region defined success for themselves and, therefore, failed to contribute to that success" (Rangan et al., 2011).

A key example of this misstep in the Middle East is the experience of microfinance. Many microfinanciers have "appeared to be profiting on the backs of the poor, less because of their interest rates than because of the policies that ignore social value" (Rangan et al., 2011). These firms' inability to see and understand that although individuals received loans, many of them were "unable to achieve a higher standard of living, [and] as a result, the companies [became] scapegoats when customers faced tough economic times" (Rangan et al., 2011).

In captivating the youth in the Arab World, we can establish a culture of HumEnt which will allow us to specify our usage of entrepreneurial ecosystems and frugal innovation to include all stakeholders in a greater conversation around entrepreneurship. To capture the economically forgotten groups in the region, while also recognizing that populations have endured great feats already, we must recognize that these groups come ready to innovate in alternative ways. Born out of and into systemic oppression, MENA youth, for example, are proactive in searching for solutions that have yet been discovered. They are powerful and innovative. It is time that we let their gifts find a place and take hold in our broken world so as to bring about positive and lasting change for young people themselves and the world at large. Humane entrepreneurship offers the nation a strong, human-centered foundation from which every individual member of the population may find prosperity in a sustainable, circular economy.

An Arab Ecosystem

Given the issues in the MENA region's educational systems, as well as the demands of the emerging private sector's human resources, "youth increasingly find themselves excluded from the employment opportunities provided within the formal private sector" (Abdou et al., 2010). For this reason, the concept of humane entrepreneurship will fit more seamlessly and advance the society more efficiently than that of social entrepreneurship. The private sector necessitates a fresh development framework that has the capacity to play a "greater role in transferring skills to young people and in fostering their creativity, innovation and entrepreneurial ambition" (Abdou et al., 2010). The goal for both theories of social and humane entrepreneurship is for "private businesses and corporations [to] forge stronger connections with the social sector, moving beyond ad hoc partnerships and traditional charitable activities," in addition to creating sustainable cycles of change that would lessen the region's reliance on foreign direct investment, which is unstable and inconsistent (Abdou et al., 2010).

The Arab ecosystem may not necessarily exist at large. Each nation in the region has an entire history and culture which, although grouped together, remains independent of its overarching geographic region. In the process of becoming in this new status quo, we hear references to creating, (re)building, and maintaining entrepreneurial ecosystems. Ecosystem, originally a biological term, describes a community or environment in which organisms (or entities) interact with each other and their physical environment. Alternatively, it is the structure that creates the confounds and limits on that particular system. We can find ecosystems practically everywhere. Nature consists of many ecosystems, there are ecosystems within our institutions, and we can even find ecosystems within and throughout the inner workings of the human body. There seems to be, however, one specific commonality that holds for all of these ecosystems, and that is that they operate and function better and more efficiently when left alone.

We are spending time and money looking to create an artificial ecosystem that can occur naturally in our societies. Is the problem truly that we do not have enough or enough well-built ecosystems, or is it instead that our institutions are not ready to recognize their problematic nature? Throughout the discussion on ecosystems, Humane Entrepreneurship, and more, we hear time and time again, the need to center the entrepreneur, or "place the entrepreneur in the driver seat." We want to intensely and deeply return the natural balance to our communities, so we speak of focusing on the human as if it is a hard thing to do. Humans focus on humans. Seemingly a simple equation, but for some reason, a much more complex formulation.

As we take so much effort to center the entrepreneur and their needs in to our constructed artificial system, we must question, what is an entrepreneurial ecosystem more than the act of removing our institutions and organizations to get them out of the way of the entrepreneurs? We have spent centuries building the society that we now inhabit; however, one must postulate that the need for entrepreneurial ecosystems has advanced as a need to "return to our roots" and find a more natural and organic balance within the ecosystem.

Similar to the havoc being wreaked on the Amazon River by human development, the ecosystem will survive when we stop pretending that there is nothing we can do to enable entrepreneurship and empower entrepreneurs, other than give them the space to do just that. Humane

Entrepreneurship provides a solution to help institutions, regions, and governments better understand how humanity must be at the forefront of decisions regarding entrepreneurship. If we change our thinking and refocus our attention from the entity in which people exist to the people themselves, then we will be simultaneously creating solutions in two frameworks of understanding: one of HumEnt and that of entrepreneurial ecosystems.

In both theories and practices, two essential concepts hold true in both our natural and artificial systems, those being bottom-up and intangible. In nature, ecosystems are created by the symbiosis of microscopic living organisms working synergistically together. The masses (bottom-up) are responsible for creating and maintaining the system, while it is inexplicable energy (the intangible) that provides the conduction of an ecosystem's seamless flow.

We can think of the intangible in an entrepreneurial ecosystem, or frankly any human ecosystem, as the culture. Culture works as a significant driving force that, although very difficult to describe, guides an ecosystem. Culture—created, accepted, and perpetuated by the people that belong to a shared group—decides the parameters of success, failure, and an ecosystem's ability to flow seamlessly. I want to posit that this might be a missing piece in the discussion of ecosystem building. There is essentially no framework that we can construct that can truly describe a "framework" for ecosystems because an ecosystem's success is typically based on its ability to capture the least common denominators of a community, or the groups typically left out of the discussion. The ability of an ecosystem to adequately engage with women, young people, and the disenfranchised will change depending on each culture. Yet, it is a guiding and determining factor for prosperity in every entrepreneurial ecosystem. We can easily find contradictions in all theories and most practices, and therefore, it is our responsibility to find our seat in the uncertainty of the gray area. It is from this uncertainty that we advance and also in which entrepreneurship lies.

The above section "An Arab Ecosystem" was taken from El Tabarabishy, Evoking Ecosystems, 2020.

Conclusion

Bringing It All Together

The Arab World constitutes 22 nations with long and beautiful traditions. It is time that these nations, and the region at large, reflect inward. Instead of looking to copy Western practices, these countries can contemplate how they might truly capture their strengths and recognize that these strengths include the individuals who are ready and able to begin working.

A wonderful example for Arab countries of a movement that highlights opportunity for and within a nation is BUBU, or Buy Uganda Build Uganda. BUBU is a "policy geared towards promoting use of locally manufactured goods and use of local skills/personnel" (BUBU, 2014). This policy brings visibility to the notion that by turning attention and money towards one's own nation, and especially toward populations in need, citizens are actively able to take part in rebuilding a post-conflict and hurt nation. In advertisements for BUBU, the creators and proponents clearly state, "the success of the BUBU concept will require us as Ugandans to position ourselves in order to play our respective roles in building the Ugandan economy and reaping from it" (BUBU, 2014).

To change culture, it takes simultaneous desire and motivation from both the government and its constituents. Humane entrepreneurship thrives when the top-down meets the bottom-up movement halfway.

Final Thoughts

From connecting social entrepreneurship and the pursuit of humane entrepreneurship, we are able to establish a collective goal with measurable outcomes for which we, and our enterprises, organizations, and governments, ultimately get to choose the behaviors to achieve said outcomes.

Being aware of the important and necessary role of the Sustainable Development Goals—global goals to reduce poverty and promote prosperity throughout the world—in ensuring wealth and job creation, while working from a humanistic approach, the Arab World has an incredible opportunity to restructure its economic policy so as to embody HumEnt for the achievement of the SDGs. With such a large and stagnant population of young people, the Arab World has much untapped potential. If its citizens are given the innovative ecosystem that they deserve, they will be able to create important products and provide purposeful services, even in a frugal manner. With even the smallest increase in access to financial markets, the entrepreneurs of MENA will build something truly incredible and, most likely, currently unimaginable.

It is important to recognize the changes that can be made from a simple shift in mindset. This change to awareness can transform an individual, an enterprise, and even a nation. From awareness comes embodiment, and through this undertaking of clear and virtuous principles, organizations can begin to build up communities within our nations and the world, at large. Looking forward, the inclusion of an "agreed-upon macroeconomic indicator of sustainability that measures a country's change in entrepreneurship and wealth per capita over time can potentially help fill [the] void" within the current measuring system of HumEnt (Kim et al., 2018). Regarding the importance of an H-EO, it is essential to note that "the function of organizations, globally, goes far beyond purely bottom-line incentives. Investing in human capital can be a springboard for diversification of national wealth and the economy, reducing many countries' dependence on unnatural capital and the commodity-driven boom-and-bust cycles common to many low- and middle-income countries" (Kim et al., 2018).

The Arab World sits on the cusp of creating a humane society within each of its respective nations and in the region at large. In creating a system in which entrepreneurs can evolve to reach their full potential, we might just be able to capture this opportune moment in history and further uplift the MENA region and each and every individual who calls it home.

Appendix

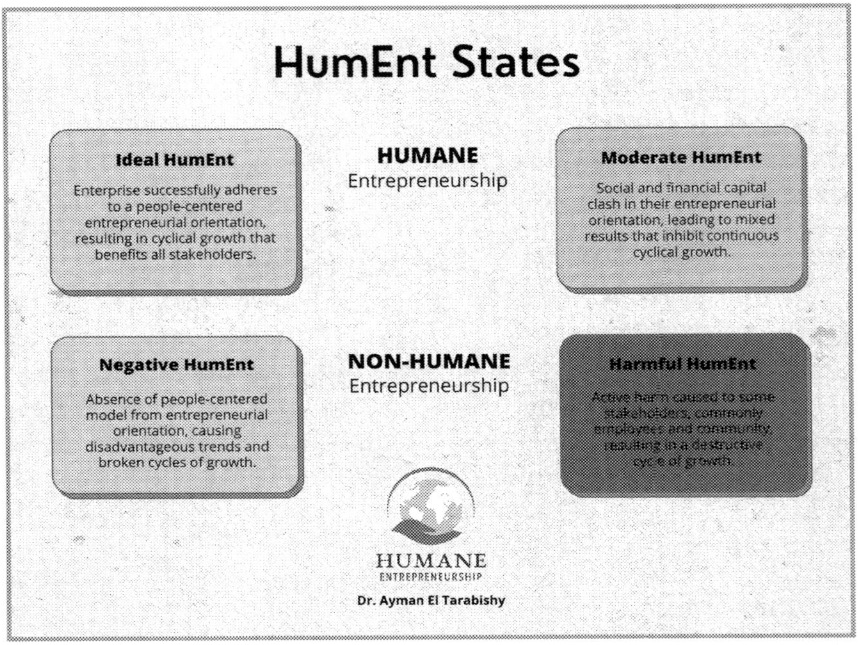
HumEnt States
Ideal HumEnt
Enterprise successfully adheres to a people-centered entrepreneurial orientation, resulting in cyclical growth that benefits all stakeholders.
HUMANE
Entrepreneurship
Moderate HumEnt
Social and financial capital clash in their entrepreneurial orientation, leading to mixed results that inhibit continuous cyclical growth.
Negative HumEnt
Absence of people-centered model from entrepreneurial orientation, causing disadvantageous trends and broken cycles of growth.
NON-HUMANE
Entrepreneurship
Harmful HumEnt
Active harm caused to some stakeholders, commonly employees and community, resulting in a destructive cycle of growth.
HUMANE
ENTREPRENEURSHIP
Dr. Ayman El Tarabishy

References

Abdou, E., Fahmy, A., Greenwald, D., & Nelson, J. (2010). *Social Entrepreneurship in the Middle East: Toward Sustainable Development for the Next Generation* (Rep.). Meyi-Silatech Social Entrepreneurship.

Aminova, M. (2019). *Entrepreneurship and Innovation Ecosystems in 22 Arab Countries: The Status Quo, Impediments and the Ways Forward* (Rep.). International Telecommunication Union.

Brown, T. (2008, June). Design Thinking. *Harvard Business Review*, 84–92.

Buy Uganda Build Uganda Policy (Rep.). (2014). The Republic of Uganda: Ministry of Trade, Industry and Cooperatives.

Choi, J. (2006). A Motivational Theory of Charismatic Leadership: Envisioning, Empathy, and Empowerment. *Journal of Leadership and Organizational Studies, 13*(1), 24–43.

El Tarabishy, A. (2008). *Moving Beyond Philanthropy and Corporate Social Responsibility in Egypt*. Unpublished Manuscript.

El Tarabishy, A. (2020a). Healing a Hurt Generation with Humane Entrepreneurship. *ICSB Annual Global Micro, Small, and Medium-Sized Enterprises Report*.

El Tarabishy, A. (2020b, October 3). *The Stakeholder Share: Entrepreneurship's Return to Its Roots*. Retrieved October 11, 2020, from https://icsb.org/stakeholdershare/

El Tarabishy, A., & Sashkin, M. (2008). Social Entrepreneurship at the Macro Level: Three Lessons for Success. *Innovations, 3*(3), 56–64.

El-Zein, A., Jabbour, S., Tekce, B., Zurayk, H., Nuwayhid, I., Khawaja, M., & Tell, T. (2014). Health and Ecological Sustainability in the Arab World. *The Lancet, 383*(9915).

Friedman, M. (1970). *The Social Responsibility of Business Is to Increase Its Profits*.

Global Entrepreneurship Model. (2017). *GEM 2017 Middle East and North Africa Report*. Retrieved October 11, 2020, from https://www.gemconsortium.org/report/gem-2017-middle-east-and-north-africa-report

Ickes, W., & Simpson, J. (1997). Managing Empathic Accuracy in Close Relationships. In W. Ickes (Ed.), *Empathic Accuracy* (pp. 218–250). Guilford Press.

Khouri, R. (2019). *How Poverty and Inequality Are Devastating the Middle East: Arab Region Transitions*. Retrieved October 11, 2020, from https://www.carnegie.org/topics/topic-articles/arab-region-transitions/why-mass-poverty-so-dangerous-middle-east/

Kim, K., El Tarabishy, A., & Bae, Z. (2018). Humane Entrepreneurship: How Focusing on People Can Drive a New Era of Wealth and Quality Job Creation in a Sustainable World. *Journal of Small Business Management, 56*(S1), 10–29.

Melé, D. (2003). The Challenge of Humanistic Management. *Journal of Business Ethics, 44*, 77–88.

Middle East and North Africa: Youth Facts. (2020). Retrieved October 12, 2020, from https://www.youthpolicy.org/mappings/regionalyouthscenes/mena/facts/

Pfeffer, J. (1998). *The Human Equation: Building Profits by Putting People First*. Harvard Business School Press.

Rangan, V. K., Chu, M., & Petkoski, D. (2011). Segmenting the Base of the Pyramid. *Harvard Business Review, 89*(6).

Schumpeter, J. (1934). *The Theory of Economic Development*. Cambridge, MA: Harvard University Press.

What Is Social Entrepreneurship? (2017, November 14). Retrieved October 11, 2020, from https://ironline.american.edu/blog/social-entrepreneurship-degree/

2

Entrepreneurship: Social Entrepreneurship in the Arab World—Innovation and Entrepreneurship

Sung Joo Park

What Is Entrepreneurship?

Entrepreneurship is the state of being an entrepreneur, or the activities associated with being an entrepreneur. Entrepreneur, as Joseph Schumpeter outlined in 1911, brings creative destruction through innovation. In other words, entrepreneurship is ultimately about innovation and entrepreneur is an executor of innovation or innovator. A French word, "entrepreneur" was coined by the French economist Jean-Baptiste Say in about 1800 from the word *entreprendre*, which can be translated as "undertaker" or "adventurer." The practice of entrepreneurship is not restricted to small businesses, as some people may think. It is important not only for the new ventures but also for the existing business (big or small) and the public-service institutions which include hospitals, schools, government, community agencies, religious institutions, and professional agencies. Since an entrepreneur is an individual who creates a new

S. J. Park (✉)
KAIST Business School, Seoul, Korea
e-mail: jpark@kaist.ac.kr

N. Azoury, T. Hafsi (eds.), *Entrepreneurship and Social Entrepreneurship in the MENA Region*, https://doi.org/10.1007/978-3-030-88447-5_2

business or society, bearing most of the risks and enjoying most of the rewards, many entrepreneurs have existed in history. Caravan merchants and traders along the tin road, silk road, tea road, and seafarers during the "Age of Exploration" were all entrepreneurs. In the modern days, famous entrepreneurs are mostly from America, since it was a new country and a land of venture, that include a great inventor and industrialist Thomas Edison, who founded General Electric; John D. Rockefeller of Standard Oil; Andrew Carnegie of Carnegie Steel Company; Henry Ford of Ford Motor Company; Charles Merrill of Merrill Lynch, an investment management company; Charles Schwab of Charles Schwab Corporation, a financial services company; Sam Walton of Walmart, a chain of supermarkets; Thomas Watson of IBM, a computer company; Bill Gates of Microsoft, a software company; Steve Jobs of Apple, a PC and mobile phone technology company; Mark Zuckerberg of Facebook, a social media company; Jeffrey Bezos of Amazon, an e-commerce and technology company; Elon Musk of Tesla, an electronic vehicle company; Jack Ma of Alibaba, an e-commerce and retail company in China; Konosuke Matsushita, who founded Panasonic, an electronics company in Japan; and Byung Chul Lee, who founded Samsung, an electronics and conglomerate in Korea. Social entrepreneurs seek to transform societies at large, rather than transforming their profit margin, as classic entrepreneurs typically seek to do. Muhamad Yanus is a well-known social entrepreneur who established Grameen Bank and started micro-finance in Bangladesh, and also those who conceived and established innovative hospitals and healthcare systems, schools, banks, insurance systems, and cooperatives were all social entrepreneurs. In short, throughout the whole history of human civilization, entrepreneurs emerged who led innovations to change the world towards growth and prosperity.

Innovation and Invention

Although there is no theory on innovation, it is about changes that create values. Innovation is not about the creation of new things but about a new way of doing existing things with the creation of meaningful values. On the other hand, invention is about creating a new thing, such as the invention of new theory, technology, materials and things both physical or biological. Many inventions, however, are discoveries of the nature, hence there are inventions that are not the creation of a totally new thing. Novel inventions may be entitled to receive the Nobel Prizes but most of them are discoveries of existing things in nature. In this regard, Newton's universal gravitation, Einstein's general relativity, Gregory Mendel's genetics, discovery of new virus (new to human but already existing in nature) and cures, DNAs, are not inventions but discoveries of already existing nature utilizing the inventions of tools such as space telescope or microscope. Invention is a new idea which can be used to make useful things. If anyone makes useful products using invention, that is the innovation since it is a new way of doing existing things. Again, innovation is the creation of any useful things utilizing existing ideas, inventions, or any things including existing innovations. For example, although many people misunderstand that steam engine is a great invention by James Watt in 1769 in Great Britain, in fact, he was not an inventor but an entrepreneur or innovator by improving apparatus from Newcomen's invention of steam engine in 1698. Hence, innovation is the creation or production of valuable things from the existing ideas of invention.

Innovation

After humans, homo sapiens, evolved to exist on earth and started to think or acquired cognitive capability, humankind started innovating—using fires, making tools, agriculture, writing and counting, law of nature or science, mathematics, education, mechanization, transportation, communication, nuclear power, electronics, computers, digitalization, and internet. In short, the humankind today exists through the evolution of innovations which are not natural things but man-made artifacts that are following artificial selections for existence. Innovations for human life span the whole spectrum of the necessities of life such as food, clothing, and shelter, and extend to work, business, society, entertainment, and religion.

Take food for example since it is the key ingredient for human survival; humankind started to plant and grow rice and wheat in about

6000–8000 BC in the southern part of current Turkey and began to cook to make hot food using fire. Ancient people used open fire initially but later innovated stoves to contain fire for the efficient use of fire. Food innovation was crucial for the evolution of humankind since it enabled the evolution of the brain of human to be able to think. With ground wheat or flour, humankind cooked bread, unleavened first but later leavened bread after accidentally discovered yeast and fermentation in about 4000 BC in Egypt. Bread making spread out to the neighboring regions of Central Asia and China. Along the course of spreading the bread making, people began to lengthened it and ended up with noodle. Chinese are dexterous people and could make noodle very thin, which was very special food for humankind, because noodle can be dried, stored, shipped, and cooked easily and safely; hence, it was the first fast food on earth. That means the noodle was very essential for the survival of humankind, and some people speculated that a big portion of the whole population on the earth would have died for hunger but for the innovation of noodle.

Innovations in Business

We live in the "Age of Innovation." Business competition is fierce and the life of business is shortening every year. To survive, companies should become the fittest in the battle grounds. Only thing that companies can do in the battle field to survive is innovation, which will make a company the fittest by artificial selection of market, and be sustainable. Innovation is imperative and a matter of survival for humankind and business.

Today, we are living in an environment surrounded by innovative products. Think about the innovative products you have—smartphone, notebook, TV, car, air conditioner to name a few. Lee Kwan Yew, the founder and former Prime Minister of Singapore, once mentioned that one of the most important success factors of Singapore is air conditioner, because Singapore would have remained as a small fishing village unless there was the innovation of air conditioner.

Although the longevity of a company cannot be guaranteed, there are some innovative companies who won the competition battles, temporarily at least, such as Apple, Amazon, Samsung, Toyota, Foxconn to name a few. They are successful for now but the future is uncertain and they are striving to innovate ceaselessly for survival. Innovation or perish is the mantra for the companies, current and future.

Categories of Business Innovation

There are different categories of business innovations—product and service, process, business model, and management idea. Product and service innovation includes innovative technology such as semiconductor, secondary battery, GPS, and internet, and innovative products, such as smartphone, digital camera, fintech, and MOOCs (massive open online courses). For process innovation, there are innovative manufacturing processes such as Ford's assembly line, material/manufacturing resource planning (MRP/MRPII), just in time (JIT) of Toyota, and supply chain management (SCM). Another innovation category is business models such as e-commerce and e-business, original equipment manufacturing (OEM), and contract manufacturing. Innovation of management ideas is also important such as GE's industrial research laboratory, DuPont's capital budgeting techniques, matrix organization, balanced score card (BSC), corporate social responsibility (CSR), and so on.

Approaches of Innovation

There are different approaches of innovation. Push innovation and pull innovation are based on the driving force whether it is pushed by technology or pulled by customer needs or demands. Depending on the subject, innovation can be divided by technology innovation vs. management innovation. In a sustainability aspect on the other hand, innovation can either be sustainable innovation or disruptive innovation. A good example of disruptive innovation is the case of mainframe computer vs. PC, where mainframe computer was innovated continuously with additional features to make it better and sustainable, whereas PC was created as a poor featured and low-quality product initially, but along the innovation path of growth, it disrupted stronger mainframe computer. Also, there is incremental innovation vs. radical innovation based on the magnitude of innovation effects whether innovation occurs in a small scale and incrementally or in a big scale and dramatically. Closed innovation vs. open innovation is another type of innovation approach depending on the boundary of innovation, whether it is closed R&D innovations within a company or open innovations such as crowdsourcing or user innovation.

Among the approaches of innovation, disruptive innovation is particularly important than ever since; fierce competition from the new venture companies and existing competitors disrupt the success of incumbents, and sustaining companies are continuously challenged to preemptively disrupt themselves, in other words, they will face the reality that "disrupt yourself, otherwise someone else will disrupt you."

Examples of Innovation

Product Innovation

There is a sea of innovative products surrounding human life these days—smartphone, smart watch, smart wallet, digital camera, smart TV, autonomous/smart vehicle, PC and computer. Among all the innovative products for the history of human civilization, there are no products other than computer which has impacted the world enormously and dramatically, and thus to create another world, a virtual world.

Computer is the greatest innovation of humankind by any means. Humans started to count long time ago, possibly from 1, 2 and many, then developed 10-digit number system, mimicking 10 fingers in hand, in ancient Egypt. Zero was a great innovation of number which was first conceived by an Indian, Brahmagupta in 628 AD. Early computing started from recording trade numbers on clay tablets in 4000–1200 BC in Babylonia, and then the first physical calculator Abacus was invented coincidentally in Sumeria and China in around 2500 BC. In the middle ages, there was John Napier's Logarithmic Bones in 1570–1580 AD, and Edmund Gunter's Slide Rule in 1620, both for computing numbers. A little after the slide rule, mechanical computing emerged, first with Blaise Pascal's Adder in 1642 and Gottfried Leibniz's Calculator in 1671, and then there was a more sophisticated concept of "Differential Engine" by Charles Babbage in 1823. Apart from the innovation of mechanical calculators, there was another critical innovation of number system, Boolean Algebra by George Boole in 1854. In his work "The Laws of Thought," Boole invented 0, 1, a two-number system for the algebra of logic which is the basic building block of binary computation of computer. The real innovation of computer came after the innovation of electricity; people electrified the mechanical calculator to make analog computer, which also led to the innovation of digital computer. Early digital computer represented binary number with on-off of vacuum tubes was the first general-purpose electronic digital computer ENIAC in 1964 which used 30 tons of 17,000 vacuum tubes and costed 6 million US dollars. The mechanical switch of on-off was electrified by vacuum tubes but still had the problem of reliable computing free from failures. This problem was solved by electronic on-off switch by solid-state transistor invented by William Shockley, John Bardeen, and Walter Brattain at Bell Laboratories of AT&T in 1947. This solid-state transistor invention led to the innovation of integrated circuits (ICs) which can be made in optoelectronics way by printing design mask on silicone wafer. That means we can make more integrated chips by drawing more dense design mask and just printing it on the silicone wafer. It was the fundamental innovation that led to very large-scale integration, ultra-large-scale integration, and exponential integration that followed the Moor's Law of doubling the number of transistors on a chip every two years, which also enabled the miniaturization of PCs, notebooks, tablets, and smartphones that we use now.

The first programming to operate computer was wired programming which connects computing components with wire. Then, Von Neuman proposed stored-program concept in 1945 with which computer can store not only numbers but also program instructions in the same computer and executes both program and number as it works today. Programming languages, software to control hardware computer, were developed along with the development of hardware. Machine language was the first programming language which directly instructs machine components, thus it was machine-specific and very complex to program. After the machine language, there was assembly language which was independent of machine but still very complex. Then the third-generation high-level languages emerged such as FORTRAN, COBOL, BASIC, and more advanced languages like C, C++, HTML, Java. Hardware and software complement each other to make a computer workable, applicable, and useful.

Computer communication network is another important innovation of computing. It started from packet switching idea, contrasts with circuit switching, of Leonard Kleinrock in 1964. When he was a doctoral student at MIT and flew on an airplane to other cities, he was hit upon an idea that, like a group of passengers on a plane, a stream of digital data of sentence may be broken down and grouped in a packet and sent from one place (computer) to another (computer) and regrouped to make an original sentence or information. This digital communication innovation revolutionized computer network on either wired or mobile channel, which enabled ubiquitous internet in the end. Internet innovation revolutionized the use of computer, mobile phones, and smart devices using internet of things (IoTs), which further drives home the concept of the 4th Industrial Revolution.

The implications of computer innovation are multi-faceted. First, it is a great fortune for humankind to be able to create, invent, and innovate all the necessary elements of computer—basic logics, devices, hardware, software, applications, and network; people have been able to integrate a wide variety of innovations into one, computer innovation. Second, it is a grand-scale industrial innovation that no other innovation can match. It is enabled by the rhythm of knowledge-based innovations that had a very long gestation period, from Boole's work on logic in 1854 until today, and also at some point in time, there was a sudden surge of convergence of innovations, which made computers a reality.

In some product innovations, complementary innovation is crucial. Take electric vehicle as an example. Electric vehicle is a great innovation and is environment friendly; it is fit for the world of environmental risks. However, there were many failures; companies such as Think, Aperta, Miles, Coda, Fisker, and Better Place, and the electric vehicle business on the whole, was undergoing a very long period of despair. About a decade ago, a rosy future of electric vehicle was predicted but the market did not bloom. There were problems of technology, including battery technology and higher price, but another real problem was charging stations, that is, without accessible charging stations, customers would not be willing to buy an electric vehicle. Hence, innovation of charging station was needed along with the innovation of electric vehicle. A great innovation alone cannot be guaranteed for success, and this type of complementary innovation is as important as the original product innovation.

Process Innovation

A typical early process innovation was the assembly line production of Ford's Model T in America in 1908. Prior to this process innovation, a car was made by craftsmanship style production where each craftsman worked on assembling a car at one place, fetching the parts needed. It was a "Eureka" moment when Henry Ford visited a slaughterhouse and got an idea of moving a car from the start stage and adding or assembling parts along a line on a conveyor belt just like meats flow along the upper steel bar. This rather simple idea of process innovation cut down the production time of a car from 12.5 hours to 93 minutes, 800% productivity improvement, which enabled Ford to sell a car much cheaper and made Model T a national public car. Ford Motor Company became very successful and the icon of business, of course, but the most important impact of the process innovation of assembly line was that it changed the whole country of America eventually—car owning and driving, the way of shopping and enjoying leisure, and the life and culture of American people.

Another important process innovation of automobile production and many other manufacturing processes as well, is a just in time (JIT) process. When an executive of Toyota Motor Company visited the US supermarket in the early 1970s, and saw how they restocked products on shelves, he got an idea of JIT, supplying parts in time when those are needed just like products are restocked when products are sold out or shelves are empty at the supermarket. It was developed and perfected in the Toyota manufacturing plants to become a rather philosophical Toyota Production System (TPS). It is a pull system of production and eliminates wastes like work-in-process, and later progressed as a lean production and management.

Business Model Innovation

In the year 2000, the year of new millennium, people witnessed the emergence of great revolution on the earth, digital revolution. Use of computer started from computing, so it was called computer, then it was used as logic analyzer, and applications for information and business. After the digital revolution, however, computer and internet replaced many things beginning from commerce, eCommerce and e-business, which brought a new business model innovation. Just before the new millennium, Jeff Bezos envisaged the potential of eCommerce and started a new business model, online book retailing as Amazon.com, because a book is a standardized commodity and orders can be linked directly with the publisher without any inventory on hand. But in fact, he was wrong. To meet the customer demands on time, he needed an inventory of books and there was a problem of matching and packing orders of multiple books. That drove Amazon.com in a grave situation that even Business Week published a cover article, “Can Amazon Make It?” in July 2000, when Amazon never made profits from the start and faced continued cash hemorrhage. Contrary to the zero inventory ideology of the New Economy, Jeff Bezos realized the key mistake and invested huge money on the automated warehouses, which ultimately saved the Amazon. As of 2020, Amazon is the biggest company in the world in terms of market capitalization of more than 1 trillion U.S. dollars, and Jeff Bezos became the richest man in the world as well.

Opportunities and Sources of Innovation

Along with the categories and approaches of innovation, people need to think about the wells or sources of innovation. There are many sources of innovation, such as gaps between existing products and customer wants/needs of either known or unknown, unsolved needs of reality and dream, information gaps, demographic change, environmental change, change in perception, and crisis including natural disaster. Against the common belief, continued success can be an important source of innovation as well. That is, every business or organization, either for-profit or non-profit, should consider how to innovate incessantly since no one can succeed forever and should be reproduced or renewed. An entrepreneur's important role is to look after and search for the innovation opportunities and try systematic innovation even though innovation may, often time, occur spontaneously on luck.

Gap between assumptions and realities is an important source of innovation. After the "Age of Exploration" in the fifteenth century, maritime transportation was the key transportation mode of commodities because of it being cheaper compared to land or air transportation. Currently maritime transportation accounts for more than 90% of the world's trade. Despite the growing importance of maritime transportation, shipping industry faced a great difficulty in mid-1900s and ocean freighters were dying because of the inherent inefficiency in loading and unloading of freights, and ships were idle for waiting in the ports. People tried to solve this problem by an assumption that developing faster ships would solve the problem but, in reality, it aggravated the situation. To solve the problem once and for all, an entrepreneur came up with an innovative idea of containerization system. Although standardized shipping containers existed separately, Malcom McLean of USA proposed a comprehensive containerization system in 1950s by having standard container box, container ship, container port, container truck which revolutionized the maritime transportation of goods, and contributed greatly to the globalization of trade in the following decades.

Gap of information speed is another source of innovation. We are in the age of affluent data and information. Tremendous amount of data is pouring toward people but humans cannot comprehend and digest the flood of data/information. The solution is an innovation of using AI and Big Data to digest data searching for valuable and meaningful information.

Crisis in Chinese character is the combination of "Danger" and "Opportunity," which means that danger and opportunity come together. If someone faces danger but cannot find opportunity, he or she will fail ultimately. Likewise, if a company faces danger in business but cannot find opportunity and turn around, it will be destined to fail. Many companies face danger and fail because they could not find opportunities for innovation. Kodak, Motorola, and Blockbuster in the USA failed in sensing the dangers approaching, could not find opportunities to turn around, and failed. In the face of danger, some, not all, companies succeeded in finding opportunity to innovate and turn around for the survival. A famous example is the crisis of IBM. After the long period of success of mainframe computer, IBM faced unprecedented crisis in the early 1990s since they could not sense the drowning of mainframe computer business and missed chances to innovate to prepare. They hired Lou Gerstner from outside and innovated management, and most importantly, innovated business model from hardware business to software business and IT services, which saved the nearly dead IBM. Another example is LG Electronics, which is a mobile devices and appliances company in Korea. LGE faced crisis of declining appliance market and labor disputes in late 1980s, and the top management decided to shut down and sell the home appliances (HA) unit of the company. After a long deliberation, however, they agreed with labor union and decided to try again, and started a crisis-initiated innovation called "tear down & redesign (TDR)." TDR aims to solve any one specific problem which intended to lead to new innovations with a clear goal in a fixed time duration of 6–12 months. TDR was the spring of innovations such as direct drive invert method, steam, 6-motion of drum washing machine, TROMM, which became the global top selling appliance and saved the home appliance unit of LG. In many cases, crisis has been one of the most important sources of innovation because crisis can be an opportunity.

Demographic change is critical in economy and brings a variety of markets and products—juvenile market, house market and related product market for the newly-weds, senior market, labor market—which can be an important source of innovation. One of the greatest burdens of today's society is "Aging." Fewer young generations need to support more senior generations. "How to innovate to solve this issue" is the key question for many countries, which is not only a business issue but also the social issue of innovation.

New knowledge—scientific, technological, and social—drives innovation as well. Telephone exchange, as an example, was carried out by manual service exchange for a long period of time. The number of telephone operators was exponentially increasing as telephone subscribers increased that caused headache inefficiency. New technology of electro-mechanical exchange and later electronic exchange were developed and solved the problem of manual exchange. Scientific discoveries and technological invention of electricity and computer, specifically, can lead to the innovation of the whole industries and society as we witnessed in the last several decades.

Social Innovations

Microfinancing of Bangladesh is a great social innovation of financing the poor. Another social innovation, Aravind Eye Hospitals, is revolutionizing the concept of efficient and sustainable eye care in India and across the developing world, which provide affordable, high-quality care for millions of individuals and also serve as a model example of sustainable health care business. Innovation of education is another important social innovation. Education has been evolved from the ancient times but formal education started from Christian monastic schools and Catholic schools in Europe in the Middle Ages. University was an educational innovation which played important roles in the development and prosperity of society. The oldest existing university in the world is the University of Karueein, founded in 859 AD in Fez, Morroco, and the first European university is the University of Bologna founded in 1088 in Italy. An important innovation of university was the Humboldtian model of German university, Humboldt University of Berlin established in 1820 based on the idea of research, thus a research university which impacted then new American universities. University education remained stagnated without major changes for a long period of time until it met with computer. MOOCs (Massive Open Online Courses) is another important social innovation which provides open, online, and free courses globally. The wide variety of changes in social systems are social innovations as well such as changes in health-care system, life-long training and education, social welfare system, future transportation system, food and drug administration system, public security and defense system, free trade system, climate accord, and economic communities like EU and African AEC.

Systematic Innovation

Entrepreneurs should search and analyze the sources of innovation using both the right and left brains, or conceptual and perceptual perspectives. Efforts of innovation need to start small and aim at the leadership of business such as Apple's platform strategy, which set the direction of future technology and industry. Talent, ingenuity, and knowledge can be the necessity of innovation but for sufficiency, you need hard, focused, and purposeful work for innovation.

For systematic innovation, every company needs to have an innovation strategy to do the following: (1) Search for opportunities and sources of innovation and try to find "Eureka" or "Aha" moment, (2) Synthesize the diverse ideas, (3) Select target projects with when and how, (4) Employ holistic approach to build innovation ecosystem, (5) Trade-off conflicting priorities, (6) Test in the consumer market and make final decision on the innovation. The final proof of innovation is always the "Market." Innovation efforts should be systematic, and continuous and intermittent; no company ever forgets to disrupt itself or self-disruption for eventual survival. Innovation culture is important as well to foster the mindset of never being fully satisfied with "status-quo," which is imperative for the survival and continued success.

Why Does Entrepreneurship Matter?

Everything changes; business changes, demography changes, people's perception changes, environment changes, political system changes, and society changes. The only eternal thing is the change. Changes are imperative and Darwin's evolutionary theory tells us that only those who can adapt to become the fittest can survive and thrive in nature by mutation, reproduction, and natural selection. Man-made artifacts, however, do not follow the natural selection evolutionary process apart from the natural beings. After human beings appeared on earth around 200,000 years ago, humans started making artifacts such as tools, agriculture, cities, and civilizations. The whole spectrum of artifacts is enormous, almost all things that are human made, and some artifacts survived not by natural selection but by artificial selection by market. We know the stories of success and failure of businesses, economies, and countries. For the survival of all the artifacts, there is no question that we need to understand and manage the changes.

Entrepreneurs take risks, and as Peter Drucker wrote, they see changes as the norm and as healthy, and always search for change, respond to it, and exploit it as an opportunity by systematic entrepreneurship. In other words, entrepreneurs innovate. Innovation is the specific instrument of entrepreneurship. Hence, for the business, society, and individuals, entrepreneurship and innovation matter for their survival and prosperity. With entrepreneurship, America succeeded. Entrepreneurship can expedite, like dynamite, the prosperity of the economy and country as a whole.

One remaining question may be, then, "Is entrepreneurship teachable or learnable?" Entrepreneurship is more of a personal character and is difficult to teach. However, it can be trained by the practice of business education, such as case study, role play, what-if simulation, project-based learning, and action learning. The practice of innovation and entrepreneurship is imperative, and should be learned systematically.

Why Entrepreneurship in the Arab World?

Arabs had been the birthplace, in the world, of agriculture, character, mathematics (algorithm), trade (early commerce), civilization, and entrepreneurship (camel-led caravan merchants) in ancient years. Since the middle ages, however, it lagged behind for long period of time in the development of economy and national wealth until oils were found in some part of the region. To be sure, natural resources are limited and can become a critical weakness, which often turns out to be a curse. Recognizing this limitation, the oil rich countries, let alone the oil-poor countries, are trying to change—a change from agrarian economy to industrial or knowledge economy—but most of them, if not all, are facing challenges. The biggest challenge is how to find something that can adapt itself (a country or business) to be the fittest for this fast-changing world and differentiate it from others—something different from the

Dubai's Future Mega Projects or NEOM Project in Saudi Arabia. Politics may matter the most but basically that's the question of entrepreneurship and the question of how to nurture entrepreneurs in this region. Eventually, entrepreneurship is important not only for the survival but also for the continued success and prosperity of business and country.

Part II

Entrepreneurship in the Arab World

3

Entrepreneurship and Social Entrepreneurship: A Trend or a Real Factor for a Prosperous Future?

Georges Yahchouchy and Vladimir Dzenopoljac

The Current Economic Situation in the Arab World

The Arab world consists of 22 countries, members of the Arab league. The countries included are (in alphabetical order): Algeria, Bahrain, Comoros, Djibouti, Egypt, Iraq, Jordan, Kuwait, Lebanon, Libya, Mauritania, Morocco, Oman, Palestine, Qatar, Saudi Arabia, Somalia, Sudan, Syrian Arab Republic, Tunisia, United Arab Emirates, West Bank and Gaza, and Yemen. According to the data published by the World

G. Yahchouchy (✉)
American University of the Middle East & College of Business and Economics, United Arab Emirates University, Kuwait City, United Arab Emirates
e-mail: georges.yahchouchi@aum.edu.kw

V. Dzenopoljac
College of Business and Economics, United Arab Emirates University, Kuwait City, United Arab Emirates
e-mail: vdzenopoljac@uaeu.ac.ae

N. Azoury, T. Hafsi (eds.), *Entrepreneurship and Social Entrepreneurship in the MENA Region*, https://doi.org/10.1007/978-3-030-88447-5_3

Bank (World Bank Data, 2020), the listed countries of the Arab world have seen significant update in the gross domestic product (GDP) over the last decade. Overall, all of the Arab League countries have $4739.60 billion in 2019, which represents 17.11% increase compared to 2010. The interesting fact about this growth is that the industrial and manufacturing growth was negative during this period (industry grew by -5.56%,

Table 3.1 GDP growth and structure, Arab world, 2020–2019 (World Bank Data, 2020)

	Gross domestic product		Agriculture		Industry		Manufacturing		Services	
	$ billions		% of GDP		% of GDP		% of GDP		% of GDP	
Country	2010	2019	2010	2019	2010	2019	2010	2019	2010	2019
Algeria	161.2	170	8	12	50	37	40	24	38.2	45.9
Bahrain	25.7	38.6	0	0	45	42	14	18	53.7	54.9
Comoros	0.9	1.2	30	33	12	9	n.a.	n.a.	53.2	53.5
Djibouti	1.1	3.3	n.a.	1	n.a.	17	n.a.	3	n.a.	75.2
Egypt, Arab Rep.	218.9	303.2	13	11	36	36	16	16	46.2	50.5
Iraq	138.5	234.1	5	2	56	56	2	n.a.	39	42.2
Jordan	26.8	43.7	4	6	29	28	20	19	60.2	61.8
Kuwait	115.4	134.8	0	0	66	60	6	7	47	54.1
Lebanon	38.4	53.4	4	5	14	13	8	8	71.9	75.9
Libya	74.8	52.1	2	n.a.	78	n.a.	4	n.a.	n.a.	n.a.
Mauritania	5.6	7.6	17	19	38	25	7	8	39.9	45.7
Morocco	93.2	118.7	13	11	26	26	16	16	51	50
Oman	57	77	1	3	66	47	58	38	28.2	52.6
Qatar	125.1	183.5	0	0	73	58	13	9	26.7	46.5
Saudi Arabia	528.2	793	3	2	58	47	11	13	39.2	50.4
Somalia	n.a.	n.a.	n.a.	n.a.	n.a.	n.a.	n.a.	n.a.	n.a.	n.a.
Sudan	61.7	18.9	34	28	23	31	8	12	41.1	32.3
Syrian Arab Republic	n.a.	n.a.	n.a.	n.a.	n.a.	n.a.	n.a.	n.a.	n.a.	n.a.
Tunisia	44.1	38.8	8	10	29	23	17	14	56.7	59.2
United Arab Emirates	289.8	421.1	1	1	53	46	8	9	46.7	53.1
Yemen, Rep.	30.9	27.6	8	4	44	30	8	n.a.	27.4	14.3

while manufacturing sector grew by -1.46%). Interestingly, the major contributor to the GDP growth was the services sector that increased on average by 5.79%. For more details, please refer to Table 3.1.

However, certain countries from the Arab world belong to high-income group of states, heavily dependent on oil. These countries include United Arab Emirates, Oman, Bahrain, Saudi Arabia, Oman, Qatar, and Kuwait. In this regard, these economies are going through some significant changes that are directly connected to the drop in oil prices that affected the entire region of Middle East. For the mentioned economies that are in many ways the economic growth leaders, the GDP growth rate reached its maximum value in 2012, coming to 6.6%, and then dropping to 2% in 2014. Furthermore, the exports of goods and services decreased with the simultaneous increase in the level of imports. Another indicator that is also relevant for entrepreneurship is that the unemployment rate increased to 11.5% on average in 2014 while the rest of the world experienced an average unemployment of 5.6% (Dzenopoljac et al., 2017).

According to El Namaki (2008), the small business sector, as a powerful tool for economic growth in the Arab region, does not play as important role as in some other parts of the world. Entrepreneurship and consequently the small business management are the source of employment; new business ideas adds value to the economy as a whole, it stimulates exports and replaces the needed import with domestically produced goods and service, and thus positively affects the international trade balance of the country. Unlike some other world economies (e.g., Ireland, Thailand, Japan) where this sector represents the foundation of many industries in the country, the Arab world on average does not seem to benefit from the entrepreneurship in that amount.

However, the government efforts in the Arab countries are significant towards boosting entrepreneurship and small business development. For example, in Kuwait, one of the richest oil-producing economies in the Arab world, the government tried to support individuals with innovative business ideas and initiated the creation of the Kuwait National Fund for Small and Medium Enterprise Development in 2013 with total invested capital of $6.1 billion in order to promote and support entrepreneurs (Dzenopoljac et al., 2021). On the other hand, the effects of such initiatives are not yet fully visible, nor do they create significant value for the economies in question. Overall, the sector of small- and medium-sized enterprises (SME) does not, unfortunately, play the same role and shows the similar value-creating features in Arab countries as it does in other parts of the world. One of the indicators of entrepreneurial activity is defined as the propensity to enterprise, which reflects the relationship between self-employment and the total number of economically active population within one country. When it comes to Arab countries, on average, this indicator has lower values than those elsewhere and it does not show the dynamic behavior in economies like South and East Asia, for example. In general, there are many reasons for this, but they can be categorized as pre-entry flaws, precarious existence of those who enter, lack of tools for survival, and not knowing how to exit (El Namaki, 2008). Additional factor is the specifics of the culture and individual's motivation to take risks, compared to the job security often offered by the government and public sectors in certain countries.

In line with the mentioned characteristics of economic development of countries in the Arab world, as well as with challenges that entrepreneurs face within these economies, the Global Entrepreneurship and Development Institute created their methodology (GEDI methodology) and Global Entrepreneurship Index (GEI) for ranking the countries in the world (currently 137 of them) in terms of the level of development of the entrepreneurship ecosystem. The GEDI methodology takes into account entrepreneurial attitudes, abilities, and aspirations of the local population, which are afterwards weighted against the prevailing social and economic "infrastructure" of the country. This infrastructure entails contemporary features like broadband connectivity and the transport links to external markets. The results of the process are 14 pillars, which are used to quantify and measure the health of the regional entrepreneurship ecosystem. These pillars include opportunity perception at national level, startup skills, risk acceptance, networking, cultural support, opportunity perception at individual level, technology absorption, human capital, competition, product innovation, process innovation, capacity for high growth, internationalization intentions, and availability of risk capital in the country (Acs et al., 2018). Table 3.2 shows the values of GEI for the countries in the Arab world, according to the latest available data

Table 3.2 Global entrepreneurship index ranking of Arab countries in 2018

No.	Country	Rank globally	GEI increase (%)
1	Qatar	22	55
2	United Arab Emirates	26	53
3	Oman	33	47
4	Bahrain	35	45
5	Kuwait	39	43
6	Tunisia	40	42
7	Saudi Arabia	45	40
8	Jordan	49	37
9	Lebanon	59	32
10	Morocco	65	29
11	Egypt	76	26
12	Algeria	80	25
13	Libya	104	19
14	Mauritania	136	11

Source: Acs et al. (2018)

from 2018. The data for Comoros, Djibouti, Iraq, Somalia, Sudan, and Syrian Arab Republic are not available in the GEDI database.

Among the countries who are regularly surveyed for the mentioned 14 criteria of quality entrepreneurship ecosystem, the countries from the Arab world have shown increase in two areas mostly, which are product innovation and risk capital. This increase is particularly visible in the countries from the Middle East and Northern Africa (MENA). The overall entrepreneurship activity of the MENA region economies shows improvements over the past decade, but this is far from enough for these countries to be able to strive and, in case of oil-dependent economies, to diversify their economies. One of the biggest challenges in the region is reducing the unemployment levels, which in some Arab countries have double digits. Yemen, for example, has 35% unemployment rate. Entrepreneurial activity and SME development are considered the biggest contributor to reducing unemployment. According to the World Economic Forum, the Arab countries and generally countries in the MENA region need to create 75 million jobs by the end of 2020 in order to only sustain the current unemployment rates. Ultimately, the entrepreneurship sectors should become and sustain their key roles as important GDP contributors (World Economic Forum, 2011). For comparison

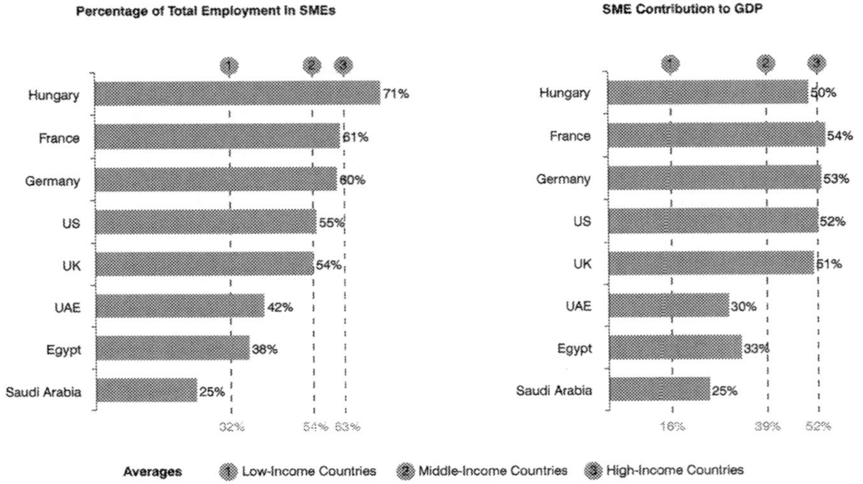

Fig. 3.1 SMEs contribution to employment and GDP. (Source: European Commission SME Performance Review; US Department of Statistics; OECD; UNECE; World Bank; Zawya; Booz & Company)

purposes, the total employment in SMEs and SME contribution to countries' GDP are shown in Fig. 3.1.

Figure 3.1 reveals the comparison between certain developed and developing countries in terms of SME performance and contribution to countries' GDP. What is noticeable here is that countries from the Arab world (like UAE, Egypt and Saudi Arabia) are ranked very low in areas of how many people are employed in the SME sector and in terms of SMEs' contribution to GDP. Saudi Arabia, for example, has SME performance that is ranked between low- and middle-income countries, although it is one of the wealthiest countries. This observation opens two avenues for future discussion. The first one is that there is evident need for these economies' diversification (mainly for oil dependent countries) and the second one is the fact that all these countries possess high latent potential for boosting entrepreneurship and SME development due to their still high income from oil production.

The current situation regarding entrepreneurship and small business development is twofold: on one side the situation is not positive since the entrepreneurs' and SMEs' performance are seen as the vital for economy due to certain internal and external obstacles. On the other hand, this same situation creates additional space and potential for development. One important note should be pointed out when discussing the need of richer economies in the Arab world to diversify and to turn more towards entrepreneurial ventures. This note revolves around the fact that the available financial resources and existing government support can be directed not only towards developing the SME sector but also towards a new trend in global business, which is labeled as social entrepreneurship.

Social entrepreneurship is a relatively new business model, defined by Gregory Dees (2001) as "a social entrepreneurial organization that places a social mission as the priority over creating profit or wealth, tackling social issues with a business-like approach." Similarly, Austin et al. (2006) define social entrepreneurship in a broader way as "innovative, social value creating activity that can occur within or across the nonprofit, business, or government sectors." In order to properly continue our debate regarding the value creation, justifications, and challenges, we need to assert the main philosophical and practical differences between the traditional way of viewing entrepreneurship, as seen by Schumpeter (1943), and the model of social entrepreneurship. There are two main distinctions between entrepreneurship and social entrepreneurship. The first distinction is related to the measure of success, or value creation indicator. For capitalism-oriented entrepreneurs, significant value is created when there is consistent growth in sales and when there is positive difference between costs and revenues, both in short and long term. When seeing social entrepreneurs as an actor of social change in a society, this measure of success is vague and often not visible. The business environment of social entrepreneur does not visibly reward the work. The markets rarely value social improvements clearly. The indicators that could show the success of social entrepreneurship are survival and growth of social enterprise. These two are far from good indicators of efficiency and effectiveness of socially oriented entrepreneurs. The second important difference is the organization and establishment of the market itself in which these two entrepreneurs exist. Usually, entrepreneurs can thrive in relatively secure, stable, and well-established product markets, where the rules of competition apply. On the other hand, social entrepreneurs often target economies and markets that fail to provide stability for business ventures. These markets do not possess the right discipline, and social entrepreneurs need to rely on donations, volunteers, and other sorts of external support (Dees, 2001).

This definition of social entrepreneurship reveals the potential of it being implemented successfully in the rich Arab countries. These countries possess the adequate resources to support this business model more than certain low-income Arab countries, which can ultimately lead towards creativity, innovation, and wealth spill-over in the region. This rather sounds as a utopia, which is why this chapter seeks to find the answers to what extent the concept of social entrepreneurship is seen as viable business approach in the region. In other words, we seek to reveal whether social entrepreneurship is merely a trend or a real factor for a prosperous future in the Arab world and beyond.

Entrepreneurship and Social Entrepreneurship as Trends

The interest in social entrepreneurship in the regions of Middle East and Northern Africa (MENA) has grown significantly in recent years. However, it is rather questionable to what extent this interest is rooted in real understanding and knowledge of the concept. It is clear and evident that the region covered by the countries of Arab world possesses enormous potential for successful application of social entrepreneurship philosophy. There are two main reasons for this, as mentioned earlier. The first one is the fact that many Arab countries are underdeveloped, with very high unemployment rates that in certain cases surpass 30% of economically active individuals. On the other hand, countries like Qatar and United Arab Emirates experience high economic growth and create surplus in their national budgets that could fuel the growth of entrepreneurship and social entrepreneurship in particular.

The consequences of Arab Spring revealed some of the deeply rooted socio-economic problems that have existed in the MENA region for decades. The entire region has an approximate population of over 345 million people where around 50% are people under the age of 25.

However, the number of unemployed people in the region reaches around 20 million. Nevertheless, this abundance of young but unemployed people in the region represents a noteworthy demographic challenge and an opportunity at the same time. In line with this, the logical and chosen path for the future development of these economies harnessing this entrepreneurial youth energy is the basis for future added value and source of innovation and new job creation across MENA (Jamali & Lanteri, 2015).

Besides the issue of unemployment, MENA region possesses many other diverse problems and challenges that are within social and economic areas. These include scattered poverty areas throughout the MENA region, while on the other side there are countries whose people enjoy elitist access to quality health care and education. Finally, in many parts of the region, certain gender inequalities exist. Among all Arab countries, excluding rich, oil-producing economies, between 30 and 40% are heavily affected by poverty. For example, statistical data from 2014 reveal that 23% of people in the entire MENA region live on less than $2 per day. In countries that are not rich with oil, only one-third of population on average can afford public health services. The percentage of employed women reaches only around 26%, which is one of the lowest globally. For comparison purposes, the world average in terms of female labor is 51% (Jamali & Lanteri, 2015). As shown in Table 3.1, there are obvious economic inequalities among the Arab world countries. Additionally, when observing GDP per capita in the region (Fig. 3.2), one can clearly see the discrepancies between the oil-rich countries (Bahrain, Kuwait, Oman, Qatar, and Saudi Arabia) and the rest of the countries in the region.

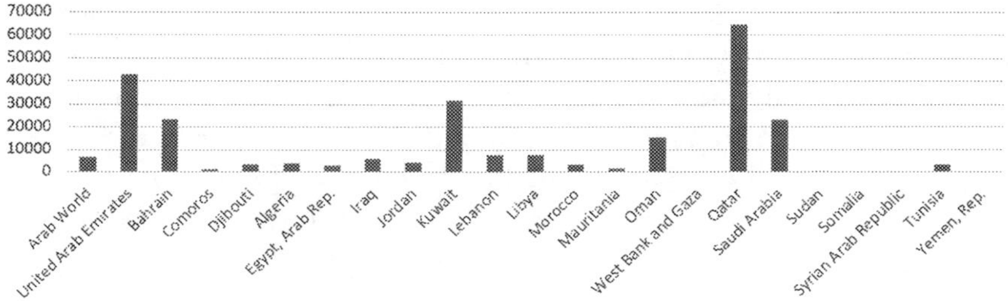

Fig. 3.2 GDP per capita in Arab World, 2019. (Source: World Bank Data (2020))

Data for several countries are not available for 2019 (West Bank and Gaza, Sudan, Somalia, Syria, and Yemen), but it is estimated that, for example, GDP per capita in Qatar is around 30 times higher than in Yemen. These discrepancies between the Arab countries create additional opportunities for social entrepreneurship initiatives. Through social entrepreneurship, economies would significantly benefit, together with government efforts, civil society organizations, and many evident corporate social responsibility activities by many large corporations in the region. According to the latest available data in regard to social entrepreneurship, currently there are 78 recognized social entrepreneurs in the Arab region who are between 35 and 44 years of age and usually hold post-secondary degree. Interestingly, the areas in which these social entrepreneurs operate are education, talent development, health care, and women empowerment. What is also important to denote is the fact, as mentioned earlier, that the main source of social entrepreneurship activities originate from stable economies, like the ones in the Gulf area, while the main recipients of social entrepreneurship initiatives are turbulent environment like Libya and Syria. It is noticed that many of the mentioned Gulf countries are riding on this new trend and try to create partnerships with recognized international institutions in order to foster the development of entrepreneurial ventures (Jamali & Lanteri, 2015). However, it is sometimes not easy to establish whether certain social entrepreneurship efforts really make change, or they are rather a passing trend, since lately social entrepreneurship narratives are "being broadcasted on television and published in newspapers, practitioner books and scientific journals as one of the very latest fashion trends that has penetrated researchers', politicians', and journalists' discourse in equal measure" (Dey, 2006).

The current discussion on social entrepreneurship is in line with a broader initiative that requires to transform from capitalism into a more ethical and socially inclusive framework. This means that the consumers are increasingly concerned with the way the products are manufactured, they look for ethical practices in business while the corporate social responsibility is expected from big companies. Additionally, there is evident pressure on politicians to develop and apply policies that are promoting social equality and socially responsible behavior of businesses. All these factors led to a wide array of research in the area of social entrepreneurship that does not properly focus on the issue it tries to solve, but rather on academic debates about proper definitions. In addition, the research published in this area is mainly conceptual and not empirical, which ultimately means that this academic approach will not produce a valid approach towards social entrepreneurship that could actually be followed. It is worth mentioning that the current research domain of social entrepreneurship suffers from certain biases that limit its potential and validity. Firstly, social entrepreneurs are mainly pictured as individuals, with heroic characteristics, which usually focuses on individual successes of these entrepreneurs. This approach limits their ability to learn from failure. Secondly, the focus on social entrepreneurs as heroes ignores the role that certain social enterprises play in this regard. Finally, these individual heroes are seen as persons who will somehow save the world, who are altruistic and put social goals above profitability. While this concept of goals in social entrepreneurship is perceived as a valid point, it neglects those entrepreneurs who are also driven by economic motives (Dacin et al., 2011). All these elements mentioned above make it difficult to assess the true effect on economy, social equality, and better allocation of resources of one country.

The problematic part of social entrepreneurship compared to traditional view of entrepreneurship, where the financial goals, like profitability, are the main measure of entrepreneur's success, is measuring its benefits on society. In other words, how can one measure the social impact of social entrepreneurship on people, economy, or society as a whole? (Ebrashi, 2013). In the Arab countries, more specifically in the MENA region, the main motives for social entrepreneurship are considered to be reducing high unemployment among young people in the region, solving issues like resource allocation and environmental challenges, equal accessibility to services in a country, and promoting good governance (Greenwald & Constant, 2015). After the Arab Spring, there was an optimistic view of the region's future, in both economic and social aspects. One of the ways that was seen as a possible avenue through which the regional challenges can be addressed was social entrepreneurship. The region was flooded with investment conferences and social entrepreneurship startup competitions, which started the creation of social entrepreneurship ecosystem. This ecosystem combined the social mission with principles of doing business, trying to make it a sustainable option that could restore and build social and economic equality. This was especially important and urgent, bearing in mind that several countries in the Arab world suffered a great deal after the Arab Spring. For example, Egypt encountered immense losses in the tourism industry when revenues in this area dropped by 43% in 2014 and caused many people to lose their jobs and turn to other forms of unregistered businesses. These issues are further reinforced by the fact that several countries (e.g., Egypt, Morocco, and Yemen) have high illiteracy rates, reaching 50%. Additionally, illiteracy rates are about 20% higher within female population. These reasons were seen at the time as the main driver for social entrepreneurship. For example, after these unrests in the region, certain countries showed more than usual interest in entrepreneurship activities. In Tunisia, for example, according to Global Entrepreneurship Monitor data, around 88% of people saw entrepreneurship as a viable and attractive mode of employment and career path (Zanganehpour, 2015).

To what extent these entrepreneurial in social area have yielded actual social and economic benefits is a different question. The need for a different approach was evident since the global non-profit sector lost its credibility in the region. Additionally, the traditional social institutions, like public social organizations, religious organizations, and non-governmental organizations, were either unwilling or incapable of coping with the new social challenges that rose after the political and social unrests at the time. This gave an opening to social entrepreneurship as an attractive modus operandi. This approach "seeks to transform society through revolutionary and disruptive experiments in ownership, human/user-centered design, open-sourced operating platforms, equitable decision-making and governance structures, fair incentives, and distributed responsibilities traditionally at the heart of the activities in either the public or private realm" (Zanganehpour, 2015).

With everything said, it is extremely hard to see whether social entrepreneurship is a trend or a real factor of economic growth and social equality advocate. On one side, there have been burning issues in the region that require a different approach compared to the traditional Schumpeterian entrepreneurship. On the other, it is questionable whether the region is ready to understand and properly engage in social entrepreneurship activities. In this sense, one might conclude that social entrepreneurship is an evolving scientific discipline, still young and underexplored when viewed academically. Furthermore, the concept is even newer in the Arab World countries and needs proper guidance and government support, which ironically represents another challenge. The irony of social entrepreneurship stems from the clash between the ideas of funding, ways of operations, and expected outcomes. Like it will be presented in the next segment of this manuscript, the majority of social enterprises is still dependent on public funding, grants, and donations. These still heavily depend on Schumpeterian ways of doing business. Funds received in this way later need to be managed in a business-like manner in order to achieve expected financial outcomes. Finally, we expect that social entrepreneurship yields social benefits, often not related to financial outcomes. Here lies the irony of this concept: how to create sustainable, self-sufficient model of socially responsible entrepreneurship, whose mission should be society benefits above the financial ones? As this is a complex and yet not fully investigated area, the conclusion can be set in this way, when discussing the Arab World: the social entrepreneurship approach in this region at early stages does represent the trend currently. However, this trend has a promising future, if properly nurtured by the main stakeholders, like government and non-profit organizations. It is up to the regional players to not let social entrepreneurship wind up merely as a fashionable trend but rather as the agent of change.

Entrepreneurship and Social Entrepreneurship as a Real Factor of Growth

The social enterprises have seen significant development in the UK, which is often seen as the pioneer in the areas of social enterprise development, applied practices, investment, and social value in general. According to the State of Social Enterprise Survey 2017 (Temple, 2017), there are around 70,000 social enterprises registered in the UK, with £24 billion contribution to the GDP of economy and employing nearly one million people. Although the added value from social enterprises may seem high, we must note that the UK's GDP in 2017 reached £2,115,296 million or

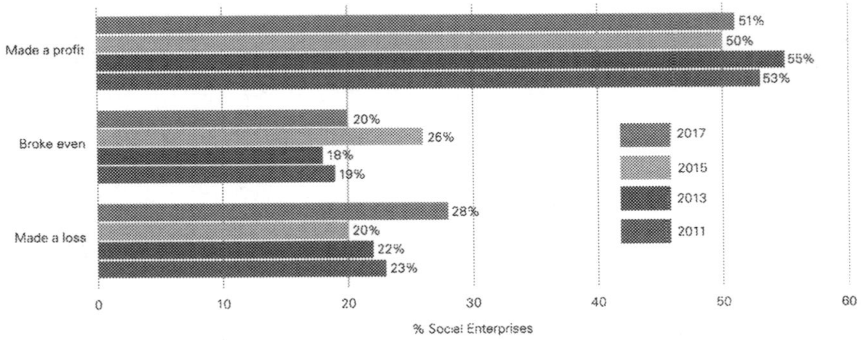

Fig. 3.3 Profitability of social enterprises in the UK in 2017

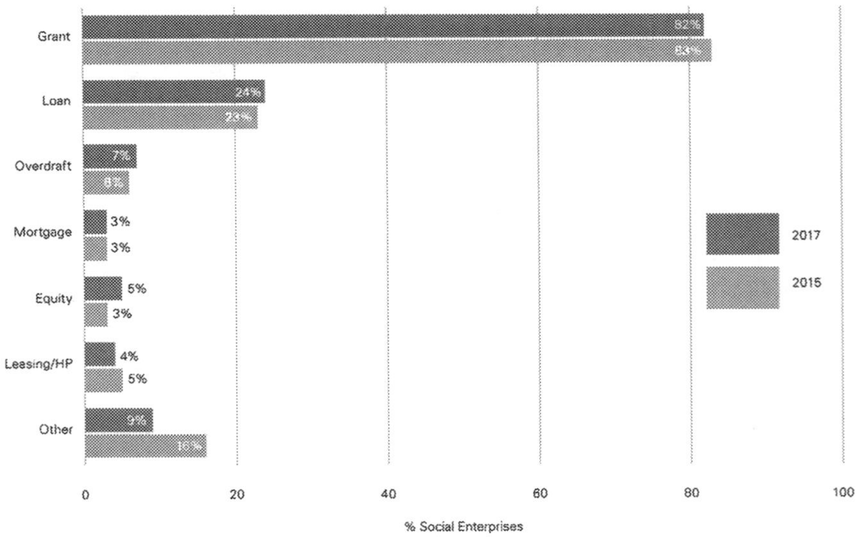

Fig. 3.4 Form of finance sought for in social enterprises in the UK in 2017

around £2.1 trillion (Statista, 2020). This means that the effective contribution of social enterprises in the UK is around 1.13%. The social enterprise survey in the UK revealed some interesting facts about the state-of-the art in this country. For example, the survey showed that this sector has outperformed traditional SMEs in several areas, like turnover growth, innovation, business optimism, start-up rates, and diversity in leadership. On the other hand, 70% of these enterprises were able to break even, leaving one-third of enterprises in loss (Fig. 3.3). The main pressure comes from the need to establish stable cash flow because of the need for working capital. Additionally, the sector showed decline in recruitment and level of optimism in general.

There is also an issue of finding the finance source at the right time, which limits growth significantly (Fig. 3.4). The additional challenge is the fact that these enterprises are mainly funded through various grants (82% of them sought this type of funding in 2017). This is a big obstacle for social enterprises in the Arab World as well. The public sector in the UK is the main source of income for social enterprises (59% of social enterprises that has turnover more than £5 million are funded by the public sector). The mentioned survey also showed that one in eight of those with public sector income is getting funded by various European programs (Temple, 2017). Although some might say that the social enterprises are showing growing and even promising outlook, the level of actual contribution is far from expectations, especially seeing the level of dependence on external public funding and grants. Also, globally, the proportion of sustainable investing in most developed regions in the world (Europe, United States, Canada, Australia/New Zealand, and Japan) has been increasing in the past decade, according to the Global Sustainable Investment Review (2018).

In the Arab World, there is still a long way to go in terms of understanding and getting engaged in social entrepreneurship. The study published by the Moroccan Centre for Innovation and Social Entrepreneurship (MCISE) revealed that the concept of social entrepreneurship is trendy in Morocco and that is only known to a certain class of people, who are usually with higher levels of education and have significant exposure to international trends. On the other hand, the majority of people in the country are hardly familiar with this term. Additionally, research showed that the main sources of funding of social enterprises are personal funds, membership fees, and government funding. Apart from the financial constraints, these enterprises are significantly limited by the lack of knowledge, experience, and the organizational culture needed to run such an enterprise, as well as required mindset. As pointed out in the report prepared by

Monitor Group and Acumen Fund, the social enterprises, regarded as impact investing, were assessed to have profit potential between $183 and $667 billion between 2012 and 2022. However, the main limiting factors include very modest profit margins (10 to 15% at the best), long time to scale their operations, and high risks. These constraints cause only one-third out of 439 promising social enterprises in Africa to be commercially feasible, while only 13% were able to scale their operations to that extent to justify the investments (Koh et al., 2012).

There are positive views on social entrepreneurship as it has the potential for growth and social impact in the Arab World as well. This positivism is again intertwined with strategic philanthropy, corporate social responsibility, and public–private partnerships in the Arab region. The authors with this point of view (Hill & Nocentini, 2015) base their stand on the notion that social enterprises are essential for creating a sustainable impact on society because philanthropy and economic growth and development failed in this regard. Also, the authors claim that these enterprises possess high business potential and significant resilience in volatile markets. Social entrepreneurship is seen as the main option that can deal with major identified social issues in the MENA region. These issues include population growth and pressure on the economy, poverty rates (14% of the population has less than $2 a day), high unemployment rates, climate changes that are caused by global warming, waste management sector has funding and innovation issues, water scarcity, food security is in question, healthcare issues (where significant portion of the population lives below poverty line, while some countries in the Gulf suffer from obesity), quality of education is considered low in majority of countries in the Arab World (except Qatar, Lebanon, and UAE. All these issues that exist in the Arab World are recognized by the governments, which in turn try to support entrepreneurship and small business development. There are many positive examples in the region showing that entrepreneurial ecosystems are in the making and that system thinking and successful business models are accepted. These initiatives include reforms of educational systems, provision of adequate business regulation and licensing, availability of various financing modes, appearance and support of seed funding (business angels, entrepreneurship incubators and accelerators), promotion of knowledge sharing, business culture change, and the like (Hill &

Table 3.3 Selected social enterprise accelerators in the region

Sector	Examples
Education	www.imaginek12.com
Clean energy	www.greenstart.com
	www.foresightcac.com
	www.cleantechopen.org
Social enterprise	www.vilcap.com
	www.agorapartnerships.org
	www.thefsegroup.com
In the MENA region	Nabad (Lebanon; mixed cohorts of for-profit and non-profit groups; www.nabadassociation.org)
	Nahdet Mahrousa (Egypt; mixed cohorts of for-profit and non-profit groups; www.nahdetelmahrousa.org)
	AltCity (Lebanon; mixed cohorts of for-profit and non-profit groups; www.altcity.me)
	Sustaincubator (Egypt; focus on food, renewable energy, and water; www.sustaincubator.com)

Source: Nabti (2015)

Nocentini, 2015). Some of the noticeable social enterprise incubator initiatives in the region are presented in Table 3.3.

Apart from these, some countries, like United Arab Emirates, have gone even further. In the UAE, the government announced the National Innovation Strategy in 2015 in order to promote innovation, entrepreneurship, and sustainability. This initiative is in line with the findings that, among the countries in the Gulf region, UAE has very high level of entrepreneurial awareness, most likely due to the government's resolve to diversify its oil-dependent economy (Abdo & Paris, 2017). As a result of this approach, the UAE's small- and medium-sized enterprises contribute 53% to the national GDP (Zawya, 2019). Ultimately, initiatives like this and the mindset that supports entrepreneurship in all of its forms make the UAE a very promising terrain for the development of social entrepreneurship, whose effects can produce spillover effects throughout the Arab region. The emergence of social entrepreneurship would mainly address the relatively high unemployment rate in UAE, which was 23.9% in 2012 (Abdo & Paris, 2017).

Social entrepreneurship is often related to impact investing, although the two concepts are not exactly synonyms. Impact investing is seen as the tool for supporting social entrepreneurship and it represents a type of investing with the primary aim of creating social impact, with financial returns. As an addition, it is important to note the concept of patient capital, which represents a related investment in the social enterprise that will bring the significant social impact in the long run, but with below-market financial returns. All these investment approaches are relatively unknown and not much investigated in the Arab World, and thus it is needed to address them. One of the possible sources of funding of social enterprises is zakat, which is the obligatory annual payment of Muslims and represents one of the key pillars of Islam. Zakat is a special type of tax where Muslims are required to pay 2.5% of their wealth, which will be forwarded to certain social causes. However, there is extensive debate whether zakat is actually allowed to be used for the purposes of social entrepreneurship, although its nature is very much consistent with the idea of social enterprise (Abdo & Paris, 2017).

In the last segment of assessing the social entrepreneurship's impact on growth, we will present two possible approaches to measuring the performance of social enterprises. Two interesting approaches are based on traditional measures of performance (like return on investment, ROI) and scorecard models of tracking performance. In terms of ROI, a more suitable model of performance was proposed as the Social return on Investment (SROI). The measure differs from traditional ROI approach in a way that it seeks to estimate the direct cost of actions and predict future outcomes, directly linking the metrics to the social value created. However, this measure is far from perfect and suffers from many limitations. For example, one is the fact that when calculating SROI, the costs and paybacks are often quite arbitrarily estimated, which dramatically affects the final calculated value. Additionally, the important limitation is the lagged effect between investment and actual payback, which is usually longer than in normal financial investments (Mulgan, 2010).

Another useful approach in measuring the social value of social ventures is based on the balanced scorecard approach (Kaplan & Norton, 1992). This model requires significant adaptations to the framework of social impact. The model developed by Kaplan and Norton (1992) focuses on private sector companies and manages performance of those companies by simultaneously assessing financial, customer, internal

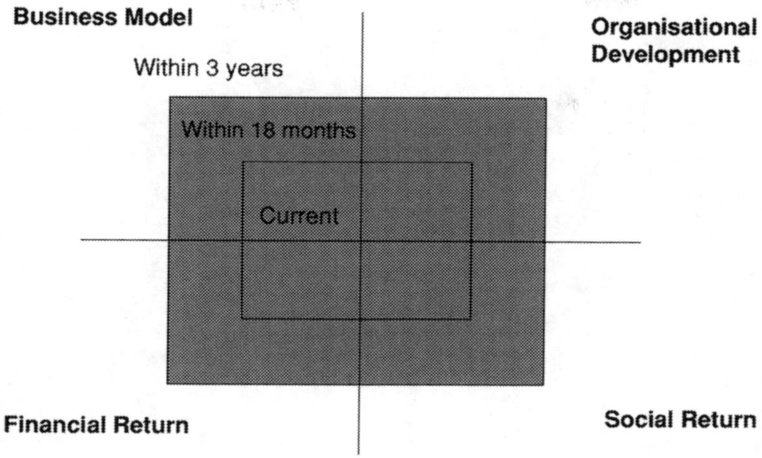

Fig. 3.5 The balanced scorecard model for social enterprise. (Source: Meadows and Pike (2010))

processes, and learning potential measures. In order for the approach to be applied to social enterprise, the dimensions are updated accordingly, with inclusion of the time variable, as seen in Fig. 3.5.

The important practical side of applying the balanced scorecard approach to social enterprise is seeing what performance indicators and measures can be used for tracking the performance of such venture. As an illustrative example, a case study of Adventure Capital Fund (ACF) from the UK that was established in December 2002 by the third sector partners, together with three government departments and five regional development agencies.

This type of organization was the first in the country and was created with the goal of trying to move away from grants and donations towards proper investment in social enterprise, with expected social and financial gains. The social enterprises apply for funding from ACF and ACF creates a balanced scorecard with clear performance indicators (Fig. 3.6). In order for social enterprises to be able to achieve sustainable competitive advantage, an example from Fig. 3.6 could serve as a benchmark for the ways in which performance can be monitored in short and long run.

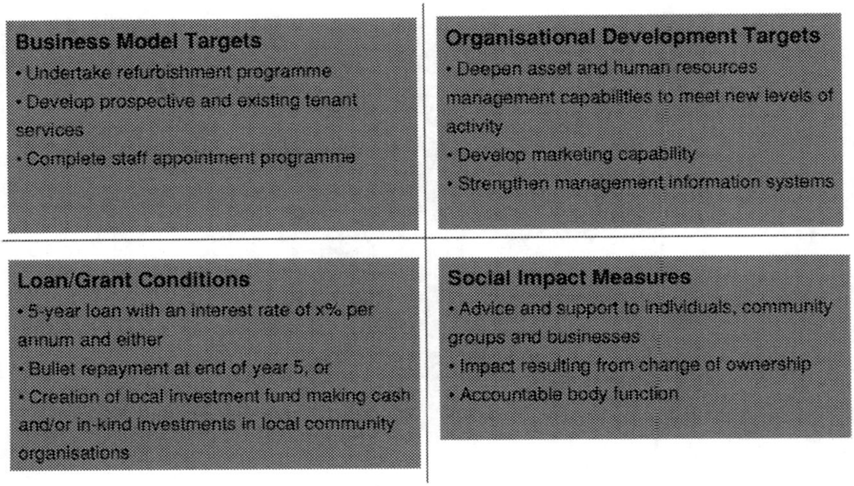
Business Model Targets
• Undertake refurbishment programme
• Develop prospective and existing tenant services
• Complete staff appointment programme
Organisational Development Targets
• Deepen asset and human resources management capabilities to meet new levels of activity
• Develop marketing capability
• Strengthen management information systems
Loan/Grant Conditions
• 5-year loan with an interest rate of x% per annum and either
• Bullet repayment at end of year 5, or
• Creation of local investment fund making cash and/or in-kind investments in local community organisations
Social Impact Measures
• Advice and support to individuals, community groups and businesses
• Impact resulting from change of ownership
• Accountable body function

Fig. 3.6 Example of performance measures in a social enterprise operating in business center housing, small businesses, and community organizations. (Source: Meadows and Pike (2010))

All of the proposed research avenues, performance measures and indicators should serve as the basis for proper development of social enterprises in the Arab World. We believe that quality approaches from the UK can serve as a good starting for understanding the potential impact on the region. Considering that the region of the Middle East (data currently only available for this segment of Arab World) is usually the recipient of approximately 10% of globally placed impact investments and that the MENA region is seen as the most challenging for identifying social enterprises opportunities (Wyne, 2015), it is rather difficult to properly assess whether social entrepreneurship really plays a significant role on the economic growth and wealth distribution and re-distribution in the Arab World.

Entrepreneurship and Social Entrepreneurship as Actors for Better Future

One of the main motivating factors for entrepreneurs in general to start their new ventures is considered to be also social good, which means that they are motivated by certain identified social problem for which they consider themselves able to use entrepreneurial principles and create a venture that would benefit this certain target group. When the motivation is seen as social, their main performance indicators include not only revenues and profit but also the social impact of the undertaking (World Economic Forum, 2011). In other words, social entrepreneurs seek to create sustainable change in people's lives whereas this change should affect the community level, not just individual level (Ebrashi, 2013). In order for social entrepreneurship to thrive and attain the needed change in society, certain prerequisites must be met (ElHidri & Baassoussi, 2018):

1. The first and foremost, certain and regulatory frameworks must be enacted or updated in collaboration with the government and various civil society representatives, business and workers' unions.
2. Besides this legal and political framework, a fiscal change should support the development of these enterprises. The fiscal policy should take into account the mixed nature of social enterprises, which at the same time act as private sector entities but also have an important role as public service provider.
3. The policy makers and social enterprises should agree on the selected measures of performance that social enterprises should rely on in their operations. These mutually agreed upon measures would also serve the policy makers in assessing the social impact and strategic decision making in this area in the future.
4. A general institutional body can be established to monitor, suggest, and direct current and future development of the social enterprises sector in certain economy. The body would use the global good practices and would try to adapt to local conditions in order to maximize the positive impact on the country and its development.

5. Educational institutions in the country should focus more on promoting and encouraging the area of social entrepreneurship, through different educational programs, activities, and formal degrees. Furthermore, these institutions, preferably public ones, would significantly encourage research on this topic and targeting the Arab countries in particular.
6. As a special form of support, governments should establish social entrepreneurship incubators that would serve as a starting point for young people with prospective social enterprise ideas. This incubator could serve as a local or regional hub for networking and idea exchange, from which the entire region could significantly benefit.
7. Impact investments should be promoted through official programs, government support through tax incentives and the like. In this way, this type of investment would draw larger corporate investors that could accept this patient investing in the long run.
8. Established social enterprises should receive support in terms of market exposure and penetration, through various trade fairs, exhibitions, and international collaborations. Additionally, these enterprises should be encouraged to use information technologies to their fullest potential.
9. The government can take certain steps towards encouraging all types of corporate social responsibility, which will be focused on environment protection awareness as well as a more balanced distribution of wealth.
10. A very stimulating step towards embracing and supporting social entrepreneurship can consist of establishing legislative in regard to microfinance institutions that would specialize in providing financial support to micro enterprises, which are one of the most common startup forms of social enterprises.
11. Finally, the regulations towards the import and export practices, which could incentivize the social enterprises, should lower the barriers towards international expansion.

The recommendations above will have significant positive implications on the society as a whole. However, all these recommendations represent the optimum scenario, which is difficult to attain but good to aim for.

The difficulties can come from many different sources. For example, the countries might take a long time to enact any of those changes. Also, the society consensus is required for big changes, like regulatory ones. Additionally, establishing different mindset in education also requires huge effort and time. At the end, we must ask ourselves whether the expected impact will ultimately justify all of the investments listed so far. This task requires that policy makers and business owners possess long-term orientation and sense for greater good. Well, something similar to our heroes from the beginning of this chapter.

Conclusion

Social entrepreneurship is often seen as an act of entrepreneurship with more noble intentions than the ones promoted by Schumpeter (1943). This in no way means that entrepreneurship is a less valuable endeavor. However, the social entrepreneur is somebody who initiates the new venture with primary focus on solving an existing social problem, with financial returns being secondary in his mind. Also, we have seen that social entrepreneurs are often referred to as a hero, who is individualistic in his/her efforts towards achieving their company's social mission. Since the Arab World has seen a lot of political and economic unrest in the recent past, it is expected that social entrepreneurship could successfully cope with these challenges. But one must practice extreme caution here. In order for one scientific field to produce quality outputs in terms of good practices, expected outcomes, practical measures of success, it needs significant time and extensive research efforts. Social entrepreneurship has not yet received this attention and therefore the literature is often scarce. Even more, the literature is scarce when assessing the economic effect of social entrepreneurship in the Arab World.

The economic effect of social entrepreneurship on national economies is currently very limited and, in the UK, which is considered one of the pioneers in this area, this activity contributed only about one percent to national GDP in 2019. On the other hand, bearing in mind long-term orientation of social entrepreneurship, this is to be expected. The dilemma in the Arab World is: do those burning issues in the region, like high unemployment, decrease in revenues from industries like tourism and oil, and prevailing mindset that might still not be ready to accept the novelty of social entrepreneurship, have time to wait for long term positive effects?

Finally, the need for more just society is in everyone's mind. This question was further deepened with the ongoing global pandemic of COVID-19 that revealed these global inequalities even more and made current economic situation even harder on policy makers, business owners, and general population. This is why social entrepreneurship as a concept is extremely appealing but yet not well understood and researched enough. Governments and all other stakeholders need more tangible proof of its positive effect on economy and society as a whole. The paradox of social entrepreneurship is also seen in the situation that the more issues societies face, the higher the need for such approach. This is especially true for many of the Arab countries that suffer from high rates of unemployment, low levels of literacy and education, and have limited access to public services. Their counterpart countries that enjoy benefits created from oil-producing business, should start considering giving back to the society through social enterprises, corporate social responsibility activities, and impact investment in less fortunate regions. Because the challenging times in which society is currently in require social approach to business. Finally, one interesting question is in the air: if the world did not have mentioned inequalities and societal problems, would social entrepreneurship emerge as an attractive field of study? Probably not. In this regard, social entrepreneurship is needed for society to heal, and afterwards it can transform back into its regular, Schumpeterian form.

References

Abdo, D., & Paris, C. M. (2017). Social Entrepreneurship in the United Arab Emirates: Challenges and Recommendations. *International Journal of Sustainable Society, 9*(1), 41–60. https://doi.org/10.1504/IJSSOC.2017.10006593

Acs, Z., Szerb, L., & Lloyd, A. (2018). Global Entrepreneurship Index. https://doi.org/10.1007/978-3-319-63844-7_3

Austin, J., Stevenson, H., & Wei-Skillern, J. (2006). Social and Commercial Entrepreneurship: Same, Different, or Both? *Entrepreneurship: Theory and Practice, 30*(1), 1–22. https://doi.org/10.1111/j.1540-6520.2006.00107.x

Dacin, M. T., Dacin, P. A., & Tracey, P. (2011). Social Entrepreneurship: A Critique and Future Directions. *Organization Science, 22*(5), 1203–1213. https://doi.org/10.1287/orsc.1100.0620

Dees, J. G. (2001). The Meaning of "Social Entrepreneurship". https://centers.fuqua.duke.edu/case/wp-content/uploads/sites/7/2015/03/Article_Dees_MeaningofSocialEntrepreneurship_2001.pdf

Dey, P. (2006). The Rhetoric of Social Entrepreneurship: Paralogy and New Language Games in Academic Discourse. In C. Steyaert & D. Hjorth (Eds.), *Entrepreneurship as Social Change: A Third Movements in Entrepreneurship Book* (pp. 121–144). Edward Elgar. https://doi.org/10.4337/9781847204424.00015

Dzenopoljac, V., Gerguri-Rashiti, S., Ramadani, V., & Dana, L.-P. (2021). The Context for Business in Kuwait. Forthcoming.

Dzenopoljac, V., Yaacoub, C., Elkanj, N., & Bontis, N. (2017). Impact of Intellectual Capital on Corporate Performance: Evidence from the Arab Region. *Journal of Intellectual Capital, 18*(4), 884–903. https://doi.org/10.1108/JIC-01-2017-0014

Ebrashi, R. E. (2013). Social Entrepreneurship Theory and Sustainable Social Impact. *Social Responsibility Journal.* https://doi.org/10.1108/SRJ-07-2011-0013

El Namaki, M. S. S. (2008). Strategy and Entrepreneurship in Arab Countries. In *Strategy and Entrepreneurship in Arab Countries.* Palgrave Macmillan. https://doi.org/10.1057/9780230288652

ElHidri, D., & Baassoussi, N. (2018). Social Entrepreneurship in the MENA Region: For Inclusion and Sustainable Development. https://www.cap-lmu.de/download/2018/CAPerspectives-Tunisia-2018-01.pdf?m=1542891062&

Global Sustainable Investment Alliance. (2018). Global Sustainable Investment Review 2018. Retrieved December 4, 2020, from http://www.gsi-alliance.org/wp-content/uploads/2019/03/GSIR_Review2018.3.28.pdf

Greenwald, D., & Constant, S. (2015). The Context for Social Entrepreneurship in the Middle East. In D. Jamali & A. Lanteri (Eds.), *Social Entrepreneurship in the Middle East: Volume 1* (pp. 39–66). Palgrave Macmillan. https://doi.org/10.1057/9781137395368_3

Hill, R., & Nocentini, M. (2015). Social Enterprise in the MENA Region: False Hope or New Dawn? In D. Jamali & A. Lanteri (Eds.), *Social Entrepreneurship in the Middle East: Volume 1* (pp. 84–106). Palgrave Macmillan. https://doi.org/10.1057/9781137395368_5

Jamali, D., & Lanteri, A. (2015). *Social Entrepreneurship in the Middle East: Volume 1* (D. Jamali & A. Lanteri, Eds.). Palgrave Macmillan.

Kaplan, R. S., & Norton, D. P. (1992). The Balanced Scorecard—Measures that Drive Performance. *Harvard Business Review, 70*(1), 71–79.

Koh, H., Karamchandani, A., & Katz, R. (2012). From Blueprint to Scale: The Case for Philanthropy in Impact Investing. https://acumen.org/wp-content/uploads/2017/09/From-Blueprint-to-Scale-Case-for-Philanthropy-in-Impact-Investing_Full-report.pdf

Meadows, M., & Pike, M. (2010). Performance Management for Social Enterprises. *Systemic Practice and Action Research, 23*, 127–141. https://doi.org/10.1007/s11213-009-9149-5

Mulgan, G. (2010). Measuring Social Value. *Stanford Social Innovation Review.*

Nabti, D. M. (2015). Scaling Social Enterprises and Scaling Impact in the Middle East. In D. Jamali & A. Lanteri (Eds.), *Social Entrepreneurship in the Middle East: Volume 1*. Palgrave Macmillan. https://doi.org/10.1057/9781137395368_7

Schumpeter, J. A. (1943). Capitalism, Socialism and Democracy. In *Capitalism, Socialism and Democracy.* Routledge Publishing. https://doi.org/10.4324/9780203857090

Statista. (2020). Annual Gross Domestic Product (GDP) of the United Kingdom from 1948 to 2019.

Temple, N. (2017). The Future of Business: State of Social Enterprise Survey.

World Bank Data. (2020). GDP (Current US$)—Arab World. Retrieved December 10, 2020, from https://data.worldbank.org/indicator/NY.GDP.MKTP.CD?locations=1A

World Economic Forum. (2011). Accelerating Entrepreneurship in the Arab World. A World Economic Forum Report in Collaboration with Booz & Company. Retrieved December 5, 2020, from http://www3.weforum.org/docs/WEF_YGL_AcceleratingEntrepreneurshipArabWorld_Report_2011.pdf

Wyne, J. (2015). Bridging Impact and Investment in MENA. In D. Jamali & A. Lanteri (Eds.), *Social Entrepreneurship in the Middle East: Volume 1.* Palgrave Macmillan. https://doi.org/10.1057/9781137395368_8

Zanganehpour, S. (2015). The Rise of Social Entrepreneurship in the Middle East: A Pathway for Inclusive Growth or an Alluring Mirage? In D. Jamali & A. Lanteri (Eds.), *Social Entrepreneurship in the Middle East: Volume 1* (pp. 67–83). Palgrave Macmillan. https://doi.org/10.1057/9781137395368_4

Zawya. (2019). SME Contribution to UAE's GDP Seen at 53% in 2019. Trade Arabia.

4

A Review and Research Agenda on the Determinants of Entrepreneurial Orientation and its Implications on Firm Performance: Tackling SMEs in Emerging Economies

Yara Harb

Introduction

Firms constantly face complex environments manifested by increased competition, and fast-paced changes in technologies and the lifecycle of deliverables. This reality triggers them to foster and sustain entrepreneurship, considered as a permanent attitude that firms must develop (Dess et al., 2008) and an objective for them to advance their alertness to a globalized and dynamic environment (Aloulou, 2002). Actually, the wealth and economic expansion of a country is a result of its entrepreneurial function reflected in the competitiveness and performance of its operating firms. Despite the many attempts by classical and neoclassical theorists to agree on a single definition of entrepreneurship, it seems to depend on the perspective of the party describing it. All related

Y. Harb (✉)
Holy Spirit University of Kaslik (USEK), Jounieh, Lebanon
e-mail: yara.h.harb@net.usek.edu.lb

N. Azoury, T. Hafsi (eds.), *Entrepreneurship and Social Entrepreneurship in the MENA Region*, https://doi.org/10.1007/978-3-030-88447-5_4

definitions however, have commonly emphasized the role of opportunities: their recognition, their evaluation and their exploitation in managing the opportunity development process.

Therefore, the field of entrepreneurship has occupied an extensive part of strategic management literature as of late, given that the scholarly conversation over this field doesn't concern the firm creation only, but outspreads to discuss entrepreneurship within an existing firm (adapting and managing a venture as per Aloulou, 2002), known in other terms as Corporate Entrepreneurship (Zahra & Covin, 1995; Covin & Miles, 1999). In fact, Schumpeter (1942) has been one of the first to shift attention from the individual entrepreneur to entrepreneurial firms, seeing their capability in dedicating more resources to innovation. Entrepreneurial Orientation (EO) emerged out of this field, and is considered as the construct that best describes the firm's entrepreneurial strategic orientation (Wiklund & Shepherd, 2003, 2005) that holds the methods, practices and decision-making processes that firms rely on to act in an entrepreneurial manner (Lumpkin & Dess, 1996).

On the one hand, the most-studied dependent variable in strategy and entrepreneurship research is firm performance (Covin & Slevin, 1991). Therefore, there is an everlasting concern to encourage firms to become more entrepreneurial in ways that enhance their performance and their international competitiveness. EO has been broadly acknowledged as a strong predictor of firm performance, though results in this field still appear to be contradictory, which incites researchers to thoroughly investigate this relationship especially in a developing country such as Lebanon, considering that EO doesn't function in the same way within different environments (Covin & Slevin, 1989). Actually, developing economies have lately witnessed an upsurge in entrepreneurship where private businesses are perceived to be less growth-oriented when compared to their Western counterparts (Manev et al., 2005). Since the majority of entrepreneurship research studies are conducted in developed Western countries, the assumption is that entrepreneurship barely exists in developing economies (Ratten, 2014).

However, criticism over the relationship between EO and firm performance focussed on the investigation of companies where a prominence of the role of EO in smaller firms had been advocated (Aloulou & Fayolle,

2005; Rauch et al., 2009). This prominence is due first to the increasing number of Small and Medium Enterprises (SMEs) that surpass the number of any other type of firm among different countries. Indeed, SMEs account for more than 95% of Lebanese companies (Koldertsova, 2006) which gives Lebanon a reputation as an exciting entrepreneurial landscape for SMEs. The country has been focusing on the existence of SMEs and their development as part of a reconstruction plan that aims to advance the economy and improve its wealth. Second, this prominence is perceived to be due to the changing environment that these SMEs face, and the acknowledged need of elaborating an entrepreneurship framework adapted exclusively for them, seeing the difference that exists between SMEs and large enterprises (Aloulou, 2002).

On the other hand, there have been few attempts to understand the factors that nurture EO, and its origins remain unclear, therefore this constitutes a fertile area that requires further development (Covin & Lumpkin, 2011; Miller, 2011; Wales, 2016). The role that internal factors play within EO is perceived to be accorded much importance when emphasizing the relationship between EO and firm performance. Thus, a complementarity between the firm's resources and its decision-making exists in the aim to attain profitability (Miller, 2003), and a connection between EO and theories from different disciplines occurs (Miller, 2011). This chapter builds on this work to attain both of its goals. The first goal considers the influence that firm resources, dynamic capabilities (DCs), social capital (SC) and additional internal factors have on EO, whereas the second goal elaborates the relationship between EO and firm performance while pertaining to the context of SMEs in both goals.

In this context, Resource-Based View (RBV) has been defined as the theory of competitive advantage, where to be productive, firms' resources must collaborate. This theory also explains that what lies behind the firm's competitive advantage relies on the firm's capability to provide the optimum use of its resources (Barney, 1986, 1991). DCs are considered as the ability of the firm to persistently adapt and reconfigure its resource base to address fast-moving environments and attain a competitive advantage, whereas SC depicts the social interaction and network of relationships in which the firm is disposed to get access to useful information and additional resources and knowledge, thus facilitating the entrepreneurial activity. Additional internal factors that consider both the organization and the entrepreneur running it, are perceived to fit on some theoretical lenses that exist to enhance the literature on EO's antecedents. These factors pertain to the previous skills and experience of the entrepreneur (known as the subjectivist theory of entrepreneurship), their self-efficacy, the entrepreneurial Dominant Logic (DL), and the organization's culture and structure considered as intangible resources that are hard to imitate. An additional part will be reserved to pass by these theoretical lenses.

Entrepreneurship and SMEs' Contribution to Developing Economies

Seeing that research on entrepreneurship has roots in economics, Cantillon (1755) was the first economist to introduce entrepreneurship and recognize the entrepreneur as a significant economic factor responsible for all the exchange in the economy. Afterward, world economies started to consider entrepreneurship among their individuals and firms. This is because entrepreneurship is considered and acknowledged to be a main engine and a vital source of economic growth and expansion (Henderson, 2002). Indeed, Henderson (2002) perceived entrepreneurs as an added value to local economies that create entrepreneurial development strategies. This added value has implications at both local and national levels. Locally, economies with frequent entrepreneurship actions witness a serious increase in Gross Domestic Product (GDP), whereas nationally, entrepreneurs are capable of creating new employment opportunities as well as leading to exceptional wealth increase. In fact, both entrepreneurship and the attainments of entrepreneurial societies contribute to the competitiveness and efficiency of global markets (Audretsch, 2007). From this viewpoint, both policymakers and entrepreneurs are considered to be engaged in entrepreneurship, despite the differences that exist in their aims. Policymakers focus on entrepreneurship as the source of job opportunities, causing structural change and generating a competitive advantage especially in global markets; while entrepreneurs perceive it as an opportunity of exploitation, generating a lifetime career and further high gains (Kuckertz & Wagner, 2010).

However, the growing interest in the field of entrepreneurship is accompanied with a prominence attributed to SMEs thought of as a source of innovation and competitiveness (Milovanovic & Wittine, 2014) for the role they play in stimulating entrepreneurial skills. The interest in SMEs has been renewed due to major enhancements performed in both industries and markets (Caner, 2010). Indeed, the economy of today is different from the economy of the nineteenth century and globalization accentuates the role of SMEs in providing a healthy climate in which to operate businesses. This is because they are considered to foster income growth, international exchange and economic development. The economic importance of SMEs has been much witnessed as of late, especially that larger firms have been performing mass layoffs (Van Stel et al., 2005) and SMEs offer new job opportunities and provide new products and services to the market (Henderson, 2002). In this context, Bouri et al. (2011) have presented the implications of SMEs' growth on the domestic economic development when they stated that an increase in the growth of an SME leads to both a direct and indirect increase in GDP. The direct increase occurs through the increased profits and the added value accompanied accordingly, while the indirect increase is produced by the innovation and macro-economic resilience of the economy.

Most importantly, since the early 1980s SMEs began looking for innovation mechanisms and ways of diminishing their costs. This had the aim of opting for a more competitive offering than large corporations (Caner, 2010). In this context, SMEs are perceived to have a competitive structure that makes them respond promptly to the newest demands, technologies and market improvements as well as having the ability to resist economic crises (Schumacher, 1973). Also, they constitute the best workplace for potential and skilled employees further to the training programs they offer to their actors (Yılmaz, 2004). SMEs are capable of employing more than 60% of a country's labor force as well as contributing to almost 50% of the productivity of a given sector (Hill, 2001), for around 85% of new jobs in the US are provided by small businesses (Audretsch, 2002). However, constituting specifically the emerging markets and economies with "weak institutions" such as the Middle Eastern countries, it's found that most of these countries have recently started to adopt free-market systems. In fact, SMEs' contribution to total employment is up to 60%, and up to 40% of the GDP in emerging countries as stated by the World Bank, excluding the existence of informal SMEs. As present, approximately 400 million Microenterprises and SMEs (MSMEs) exist in emerging economies, in which the majority are informal. The difference in the number of formal SMEs that exist between emerging economies and developed ones urges on the importance of the role that governments play in enhancing their economies through SMEs (Ndiaye et al., 2018). Nevertheless, in an estimation projection for the coming fifteen years made by the World Bank for the Asian and Sub-Saharan African countries, over 600 million workers are estimated to be joining the workforce worldwide, which eventually leads to an estimate that four out of five new jobs will be generated by SMEs. On this same note, and in a report prepared for an agenda workshop concerning Lebanon National Investment improvement, it has been stated that SMEs constitute 99% of companies in the MENA (Middle East and North Africa) region (Koldertsova, 2006).

SMEs are perceived to be the rescue plan for the majority of struggling economies. Both regulatory as well as financing initiatives can lead the path to better employment opportunities and higher GDP. Seeing this, the MENA region has started to pay attention to the emergence and growth of SMEs, although the competitiveness of these SMEs is still considered low compared to their regional and international counterparts. One of the main reasons behind this is the minimal access to external financing granted to these firms. In this context, Aloulou and Fayolle (2005) stated that when a small firm is compared to a large firm, it's noticed that the small firms are lacking in resources and capabilities compared to the large firms. This has been in line with Storey (1994) arguing that small firms face difficulties in having access to financial capital which may impede their growth potential. However, and despite the existence of a considerable number of banks and financial institutions in the MENA region, only 2% of the Gulf banks' loans are provided to SMEs, which is perceived to be due to the unavailability of a credit history for these SMEs, thus leading to a lack of sufficient information to provide the banks with (Bouri et al., 2011). Therefore, it has been argued that governments must interfere to close the financing gap and contribute to developing SMEs' institutional environment (Ratten, 2014). This is another brick in the many initiatives that governments of most emerging economies, especially the Middle Eastern ones, must accomplish to keep up with the expectations of their people, the young leaders and the nascent entrepreneurs as well as to ensure long-term sustainability and development. Thus, this has been emphasized during the Arab Spring movements that aroused resistance against all forms of corruption that exist in the Arab countries and the inequality in employment opportunities. Against this background, Lebanon has been noted for its energetic entrepreneurial background, depending on SMEs to contribute to its economy. This began two to three decades agpo, when Lebanon started leveraging efforts to develop its ecosystem for SMEs' emergence and development, allowing innovative and creative entrepreneurs to venture and initiate their ideas. However, and due to the continuous political and economic instability that the country has experienced, SMEs in Lebanon face many challenges. With an aim to overcome these challenges (Miles et al., 1978) and to have the ability to thrive in highly competitive or unstable economic environments, these SMEs need to adopt a suitable strategic response (Covin & Slevin, 1989) such as EO for long-term success.

Entrepreneurial Orientation and Interrelationship with Firm Performance

EO has been initially captured as the construct that holds the factors that are essential and relevant for making a firm entrepreneurial (Lumpkin & Dess, 1996; Miller, 1983). It concerns the processes, methods and decision-making activities that lead to a new entry (Lumpkin & Dess, 1996) and constitutes the process of entrepreneurial strategy-making that entrepreneurs rely on to ensure the firm's well-being and competitive advantage (Rauch et al., 2009). Moreover, Morris et al. (1996) perceived the entrepreneurial business activity as opportunity-driven and based on an opportunity-driven mindset, which is further translated as the discovery and exploitation of new opportunities that may further affect change. The perception, discovery and exploitation of opportunities are perceived to happen at the firm level, and therefore Lumpkin and Dess (1996) defined EO as a firm-level phenomenon considering the small firm as an extension of the leader individual. Indeed, management scholars have been much interested in entrepreneurship research to a point where the focus of their studies has shifted from the entrepreneurs themselves to the growth of their firms (Aloulou, 2002).

The origins of EO go back to the work of both Mintzberg (1973) and Khandwalla (1976/1977). However, its definition as a concept in the literature has been first acknowledged by Miller (1983) who considered EO (without mentioning it as a term) as a composite dimension including innovativeness, risk-taking and proactiveness. Similarly, Covin and Slevin (1989) considered EO as a unidimensional construct in a way such that when all three dimensions exist collectively and work concurrently, the firm will be considered to have an EO, and thus be entrepreneurial (Covin & Wales, 2012). However, a decade later, another operationalization of EO appeared, suggested by Lumpkin and Dess (1996) that added two other dimensions: autonomy and competitive aggressiveness. Within this view, emphasis has been laid on the practicality of viewing EO as a multidimensional construct, yielding the possibility that only some of the dimensions exist in the case of a successful new entry, which in other terms means that these dimensions may vary independently rather than co-vary. This eventually has underscored the independent effect of each of the dimensions, treated as separate constructs.

On a complementary note, the unidimensional view of EO has already been proved in previous research to have a relationship with firm performance. Therefore, it is recommended to assess the unique effects of each of the five dimensions on firm performance. Besides, many researchers (e.g., Awang et al., 2009; Hughes & Morgan, 2007; Kreiser et al., 2002) have led studies adopting and defending the multidimensional conceptualization. Therefore, we describe each dimension individually. Starting with *Autonomy*, it is argued to be split into two different directions as per Lumpkin and Dess (1996). Within the first direction, autonomy is perceived to be autocratic and characterized by strong leaders, especially in smaller firms. The second direction describes the firm's actors' tendency to act autonomously from strong leaders and to pursue opportunities independently. Dess and Lumpkin (2005) emphasized the importance of motivating entrepreneurial thinking within a firm, recognizing it as a driver of competitive advantage. Indeed, a person may have a solid aspiration in having the freedom to develop and implement ideas (Li et al., 2009). In their turn, Hughes and Morgan (2007) perceived autonomy as a main driver of flexibility, permitting the firm to respond rapidly to changes in its environment and markets. Many studies have defended the positive influence that autonomy has on firm performance, and argued that displaying autonomy in a firm inspires its actors to act more entrepreneurially, leading to superior competitiveness and enhanced firm performance (Awang et al., 2009; Coulthard, 2007; Frese et al., 2002; Prottas, 2008). Second, talking about *Competitive Aggressiveness*, this is the strength of the posture that a firm takes when threats from its rivals appear. By this posture, the firm aims to challenge and undo its competitors. According to Lumpkin and Dess (1996), being competitively aggressive can secure and improve market positioning. Similarly, Dess and Lumpkin (2005) expounded how companies with competitive aggressiveness are ready to "do battle" with competitors either to gain market share or to keep the share they already have. In other terms, companies may cut their prices or even sacrifice profitability in favor of market share. Lumpkin and Dess (1996) argued that improvement in firm performance can be achieved by using aggressiveness, since the firm's competitiveness at the expense of rivals will increase by discouraging competitors in the market. Later, Lumpkin and Dess (2001) found that a positive relationship between competitive aggressiveness and firm performance exists, and which was later confirmed in the study performed by Frese et al. (2002). Moving to *Innovativeness*, it was first recognized as entrepreneurial innovation (Schumpeter, 1934, 1942) and considered as the core of entrepreneurship (Covin & Miles, 1999; Drucker, 1985; Henderson, 2002). It is the implementation of new and creative methods that ensure a firm's survival in highly competitive markets (O'Regan & Ghobadian, 2005) and yield new products, services and processes (Aloulou & Fayolle, 2005; Pittino et al., 2017; Schumpeter, 1934). Innovativeness is a key component of entrepreneurship, seeing that it reflects a way in which firms pursue new opportunities (Lumpkin & Dess, 1996), build differentiation and improve solutions that challenge those of its competitors (Hughes & Morgan, 2007) as well as to overcome challenges and attain profitability (Hult et al., 2004). Previous research emphasized the role that innovation plays in achieving a firm's competitiveness and attaining a higher firm performance (Coulthard, 2007; Hameed & Ali, 2011; Hughes & Morgan, 2007). Indeed, innovativeness has proved to lead to the firm's success (Awang et al., 2009; Frese et al., 2002). Considering *Proactiveness*, it has been given little attention in scholarly articles, while it encompasses the most important perspective. It concerns the active and continuous search of the firm to pursue promising opportunities (Stevenson & Jarillo, 1990; Venkatraman, 1989) and to anticipate future demands and trends in the market. The pursuit of opportunities is vital in entrepreneurship (Stevenson & Jarillo, 1990; Shane & Venkataraman, 2000). A proactive firm is the one that looks in advance of the competition, and is keen to introduce newness to the market. Indeed, Jalali et al. (2014) disclosed that proactiveness is essential for firms that are in the process of innovating and looking to attain a competitive advantage. Proactiveness incorporates the firm's alertness to customers' needs and its openness to market indications (Hughes & Morgan, 2007). Both Coulthard (2007) and Hughes and Morgan (2007) were among the researchers that studied proactiveness in regard to the developmental stage of the firm, stating that higher levels of proactiveness were associated with higher levels of performance. Also, in a study on Indonesian SMEs, Kusumawardhani (2013) found that proactiveness is the only dimension of EO that is positively related to firm performance. Finally, coming to *Risk-Taking*, this refers to bearing the risk of venturing into the unknown and taking bold actions in some undefined situations such as committing resources for uncertain returns. The concept of risk-taking, used frequently to describe entrepreneurship (Aloulou & Fayolle, 2005), actually refers to the adoption of calculated business risks that entrepreneurs make (Brockhaus, 1980). Without risk-taking (constructive risk-taking as per Miller, 1983), firms tend to be conservative when facing market changes and tend to refrain from introducing innovations. Consequently, this can result in weaker performance (Hughes & Morgan, 2007). However, previous findings (Frese et al., 2002; Hameed & Ali,

2011) revealed a direct positive impact that risk-taking has on the firm performance.

Most entrepreneurship scholars have tended to explain firm performance by investigating the firm's EO (Wiklund & Shepherd, 2003), which accredited performance to be one of the most dependent variables examined in the EO literature. Firm performance is the best indicator of how a company's operations and activities are being handled and how successfully the firm is operating. Notwithstanding this interest, studies observing this relationship have been crowned with mixed results. While some have been able to find a positive correlation between EO and firm performance (e.g., Awang et al., 2009; Frese et al., 2002; Hameed & Ali, 2011; Hughes & Morgan, 2007; Wiklund & Shepherd, 2003, 2005), other studies did not succeed in finding any correlation (e.g., Covin et al., 1994; Lee et al., 2001) or have found at least that this relationship is not linear (Zahra & Garvis, 2000). In this context, Bhuian et al. (2005) have shown that the EO-performance relationship is an inverted U-shape, for in the case of some markets or conditions, higher levels of EO are not essentially needed for a firm to perform better. However, Rauch et al. (2009) have attributed these differences in results to the adoption of different methodologies and research samples.

Moreover, and on a complementary note, the historical perception of small businesses has been different from that of today. Birley and Norburn (1985) stated that small businesses were viewed as "country cousins" and mainly patronized by larger firms when undertaking a heavy business. Accordingly, studies conducted on large firms have been more visible than those concerning SMEs in the EO literature. In this context, Aloulou and Fayolle (2005) stated that the vast majority of studies that investigated the relationship between EO and firm performance were conducted in the framework of large companies rather than SMEs. However, the cases when EO is investigated in large firms operating in developed countries can't be generalized to the case of smaller firms that are mainly centered on their CEOs/founders (Fini et al., 2012; Wiklund, 1998). Therefore, many scholarly conversations focussed on the presence of EO in SMEs (e.g., Aloulou, 2002; Aloulou & Fayolle, 2005), and acknowledged its importance in enhancing SMEs' performance (Rauch et al., 2009).

Firm Resources, Dynamic Capabilities (DCs) and Entrepreneurial Orientation

The existence of entrepreneurial opportunities emerges from the difference in value attributed to resources when these resources are converted from inputs to outputs, considering that this attribution varies according to the individual's beliefs (Shane & Venkataraman, 2000). Haynie et al. (2009) have suggested that reflecting on both existing and future resources surrounds the process of opportunity development, i.e., discovery, evaluation and exploitation. They argued in this context that when entrepreneurs evaluate an opportunity, they focus on their current firm resources and the resources that they may have in the future to decide whether to exploit this opportunity or not. Moreover, Cai et al. (2018) argued that both opportunity development and resource development are main topics in entrepreneurship because the entrepreneurial process is opportunity-based, whereas resources can secure it. Therefore, an integrated view of the convergence of both opportunity development and resource development has occurred, believing that the entrepreneurial behavior is a series of actions by which the entrepreneur acquires resources in order to pursue opportunities. Indeed, Haynie et al. (2009) argued that existing resource recognition is primordial in opportunity evaluation, whereas Haugh (2005) highlighted the importance of both resource acquisition and integration in the whole opportunity development process, and particularly in the opportunity exploitation phase. Besides, Sirmon et al. (2007) argued that resource management is core in building a firm's resources portfolio, bundling these resources in order to build capabilities and further create value and the business sustainment.

Firm-level entrepreneurial activity and resources are appropriately related through RBV specifically with the case of high-tech venturing (Miller, 2011) where a shortage of resources can harm the entrepreneurial activity of top key persons in the organization. Indeed, much of entrepreneurship literature focusses on the difficulty encountered in obtaining resources, especially financial accessibility, for it is seen that even highly entrepreneurial firms are hindered in achieving their optimum performance when there is unavailability of adequate internal resources.

Entrepreneurship has its share in the resource-based framework (Conner, 1991) since resource-based theory discusses new visions in entrepreneurial decision-making (Alvarez & Busenitz, 2001). Indeed, Alvarez and Busenitz (2001) state that RBV emphasizes the heterogeneity of resources, whereas entrepreneurship emphasizes the heterogeneity in beliefs about these resources' value. Irava and Moores (2010) stated however, that the heterogeneity of beliefs may grow into a robust resource, thus making the connection between RBV and entrepreneurship as a value-added proposition. In fact, Penrose (1959) has been the first to introduce the concept of resources in the literature, and RBV has been primarily defined as the theory of competitive advantage, where to be productive, firms' resources must collaborate. It explains that what lies behind the firm's competitive advantage does not concern the industry composition, but instead relies on the firm's capability to provide the optimum use of its resources (Barney, 1986, 1991) by developing internal strengths and acquiring complementary resources. In this context, Chandler and Hanks (1994) argued that the perception of resource availability is related to entrepreneurs' beliefs in acquiring resources. These beliefs relate to the individual's self-efficacy (Bandura, 1977, 1989) that has its effect on resources' acquisition and the whole entrepreneurial activity of the firm particularly in the case of an SME. Similarly, a framework has been developed to show CEOs' decisions on resources allowance driving their firms to engage in entrepreneurial behavior. This is because due to their size, these SMEs encounter challenges in attaining and combining the appropriate resources that allow them to formulate competitive strategies (Aloulou, 2002).

However, many researchers have tried to derive resource categorization schemes (Miller & Shamsie, 1996). Based on the perception of Wernerfelt (1984), resources are considered as anything that can be thought of as a strength or a weakness of the firm, defined as the tangible and intangible assets that semi-permanently exist. Thus, firm-specific internal factors are of great importance when considered within the RBV framework, and strategy selection is based on the careful evaluation of these bundles of tangible and intangible resources (Galbreath & Galvin, 2008). Indeed, Barney (1991) affirmed that all of a firm's resources (i.e., physical, human and capital) can be used by the firm to implement strategies that expand both its efficiency and effectiveness.

On the one hand, tangible resources encompass both physical and financial resources (Das & Teng, 2000). While physical resources are thought of as the technology undertaken by the firm, its plant and equipment, or even its geographic location (Barney, 1991), financial resources (Grant, 1991) are considered of critical importance especially for the case of small firms (Wiklund & Shepherd, 2005). Indeed, financial resources are the basis of all other resources, seeing that they can be easily converted into other types of resources (Dollinger, 1999). Within RBV, tangible resources are perceived to be easily imitated by competitors (Barney, 1991) for they are easily obtained in the factor markets (Teece, 1998). However, small firms still face many challenges when considering their access to financial capital and this has implications on their growth potential (Malhotra et al., 2007; Storey, 1994).

On the other hand, intangible resources are of great importance due to their influence on increasing the firm's adaptability to the market's expectations and needs, thus yielding a competitive offering (Miller & Shamsie, 1996). Knowledge-based resources specifically, are considered as a source of the firm's ability to discover and exploit new opportunities (Wiklund & Shepherd, 2003). This chapter considers different types of intangible resources since recent approaches to firm resources focus on a wide variety of them. First, we perceive the top management team (Barney, 1991) as having the main influence on the firm's well-being through the skills and capabilities of key people operating in the organization that hold specific managerial and technical knowledge (Manev et al., 2005). The complementarity of their skills and capabilities is essential (Carmeli & Tishler, 2004). Second, we are concerned with the firm's employees, their creativity, innovativeness and expertise, considered as a source of competitive advantage. In fact, research on EO and its relationship with firm performance looks into human capital and interrelates it with many EO facets. On this same note comes the organizational reputation (Grant, 1991; Teece et al., 1997) that constitutes the information and response that different stakeholders present to reflect a given firm (Teece et al., 1997). Moreover, an emphasis is accorded to the Human Resource Management policies. Indeed, the recruiting criteria employed to grant individuals to join organizations in addition to the empowerment and training programs offered to the firm's actors are considered of crucial importance. Finally, there exists the labor relations and open internal communications that grant a mixture of skills and sharing of function-specific knowledge among different areas within the organization (De Clercq et al., 2013) to effectively cooperate on innovative ideas (Miller, 1983). Reflecting on this, many EO scholars claim that a lack of resources impedes the entrepreneurial activity that leads to a firm's growth, for the access to significant resources is the basis of strategic orientation (Covin & Slevin, 1991) and both organizational resources and EO are mutually correlated (Chen et al., 2007). Indeed, financial capital allows firms to pursue new opportunities (Shane & Venkataraman, 2000; Wiklund & Shepherd, 2005), encourages the firm's innovativeness (Lumpkin & Dess, 1996) specifically its product innovations (Lee et al., 2001; Wiklund & Shepherd, 2005; Zahra, 1991), and favors its risk-taking propensity (Tsai & Luan, 2016; Wiklund & Shepherd, 2005). In addition, both intangible assets and capabilities considered as intangible resources are perceived to affect the firm's innovativeness (Bakar & Ahmad, 2010). More specifically, knowledge and prior experience are found to be positively related to proactiveness (Farmer et al., 2011; Shane, 2000) and professional decision-making (Pennings et al., 1998) which favors actors' autonomy within a firm. In this context, Barney (1991, from Hambrick, 1987) argued that managerial talent is the essential firm resource leading to the employment of almost all firm's strategies. Besides, other researchers (e.g., Ferrier, 2001; Grimm et al., 2006; Ndofor et al., 2011) have acknowledged the importance of resources in competitive behavior. These relationships addressed to specific EO components when tackling their antecedents is favored in terms of expanding and advancing the EO-related academic conversation (Anderson et al., 2015) seeing that these components are separate constructs and must be individually examined, for they aren't supposed to share all antecedents and consequences (Covin & Wales, 2012; George & Marino, 2011).

However, a further development of RBV into a dynamic recipe has taken place to explain the process by which these resources should be employed. The research on DCs has been evolving for more than a decade, and papers conducting them have been recently populating in the aim to change the static perspective of RBV. In Barney's (1991) view, firms have the freedom as well as the ability to choose the bundle of resources that best fit their purpose, or even change on the bundle they have already chosen in order to achieve the desired competitive advantage. In this context, Teece et al. (1997) have developed the "Dynamic Capabilities" approach to understand the sources of wealth creation and the methods with which firms achieve and most importantly sustain a competitive advantage. Teece et al. (1997) have argued that dynamic and demanding environments often require firms to develop DCs to attain a competitive advantage, gain market shares and undo competitors in the industry, specifically considering those that are technology-based. Therefore, it has been defined by Zahra et al. (2006) that DC is the capability of the firm to extend or modify its resources in a way approved by its main decision-makers. By this, firms intend to create opportunities by reconfiguring their existent asset and resource bases. In their attempt to demonstrate the necessary fundamentals of DCs, Teece et al. (1997) have contrasted the concept to other models of strategy from which RBV has been considered.

In their turn, Jantunen et al. (2005) argued that in terms of grasping the right opportunities, having a value-added resource combination and enduring a competitive advantage, a firm must develop its DCs. They viewed that endorsing different and innovative organizational strategies and practices can enhance firm performance, and that their implementation can lead the firm to successfully reconfigure its asset base in a way to respond to its environment. Ambrosini and Bowman (2009) have tried to attribute DCs to real examples when they argued that the managerial processes are the main developers of DCs that convert the static type of resources into dynamic resources. By static resources, researchers meant both tangible and intangible resources. This has been similarly argued by Helfat and Martin (2015), who state that DCs are the tools that managers rely on to create, change and extend the firms' decisions. In this context, it has been perceived that some capabilities in a firm may lead to a higher EO or affect the relationship between EO and its implications. Indeed, Zahra et al. (2006) argued that what encourages or stimulates the presence of EO in a firm is sometimes related to its DCs developed through operations. Similarly, Rodrigo-Alarcón et al. (2018) have found in their turn that DCs have a positive effect on EO as well as to mediate the relationship between social capital and EO. In contrast, it has also been argued in the academic conversation that EO can in its turn enhance the existence of capabilities and resources in any given firm.

By reconfiguring their asset base, it is actually easier for firms to profit from opportunities. However, when it's the case of a rapidly changing environment known by its dynamism and hostility, it becomes more difficult for a firm performing in such an environment to attain and sustain a competitive advantage; therefore, the ability to effectively combine resources and build new capabilities are perceived primordial for this objective to be attained (Teece et al., 1997).

Social Capital and Entrepreneurial Orientation

In their study on Chinese new state-owned firms, Cai et al. (2018) found that entrepreneurial firms first discover opportunities based on their resources and then exploit the opportunity when integrating external resources that come from their social networks. Similarly, it has been argued by Baron (2002), that the capability of entrepreneurs to accumulate different resources required to initiate any kind of venture is facilitated and encouraged by the entrepreneurs' SC. In fact, and besides the role of financial capital and other capital attributes, ongoing research in entrepreneurship has shed light on the importance of SC in triggering the ability to engage with effective entrepreneurial activities (Davidsson & Honig, 2003), highlighting on the impact that SC has on entrepreneurial behavior (Davidsson, 2006).

Over the last decades, SC theory has been occupying the scholarly conversation as its discussion has become increasingly complex in management. SC depicts the social interaction and network of relationships that firms position into, in order to get access to useful information and resources. When it's the case of SMEs, they may face scarcity in internal resources and thus acknowledge the necessity to interact with the external environment. Nahapiet and Ghoshal (1998) defined SC as the sum of the resources that an individual or a social unit has or "may have" due to their network of relationships. Coleman (1988), one of the first scholars to initiate the concept of SC to the literature, has argued that it is similar to human capital and physical capital because it is both productive and defined by its function. Thus, SC can be reflected as a strategic intangible resource due to its uniqueness and invisibility to competitors (Coleman, 1988; Rodrigo-Alarcón et al., 2018; Stam & Elfring, 2008). Indeed, social networks supplement the effects of financial capital, prior experience and education (Bourdieu, 2011; Coleman, 1988). Further to a long debate concerning its operationalization, this concept has been proved and agreed on to be multidimensional, allowing researchers to focus on one or two components of its multidimensionality that they perceive to facilitate or improve EO (Stam & Elfring, 2008) and that serve the scope of their study. The relationship between SC and EO is especially critical in developing economies (Manev et al., 2005). In this context, Foss (2011) elaborated and acknowledged the existence of the "strategic entrepreneurship" field on which opportunity-seeking (considered as the dominant focus of the entrepreneurial field) and advantage-seeking (considered as the dominant focus of the strategic management field) should be cooperatively considered for the benefit of both processes and this is through "organizational networks."

We build on the identification of Nahapiet and Ghoshal (1998) who recognized three components of SC; namely structural, relational and cognitive. The structural dimension refers to the connection's configuration between a firm and others involved in the structure of a network, including the social interaction produced. The relational dimension involves the characteristics of personal relationships that actors have established with time (Granovetter, 1992). Finally, the cognitive dimension of SC represents the resources that offer understandings and meanings within groups (Nahapiet & Ghoshal, 1998). It reveals the extent to which actors within a social network understand each other and share the same goals and culture (Chang & Chuang, 2011). Indeed, shared culture refers to the degree to which relationships are ruled by norms of behavior (Inkpen & Tsang, 2005). Besides, these actors are considered valuable resources because they ease the creation of intellectual capital (Nahapiet & Ghoshal, 1998).

Focussing on the structural aspects of SC, social networks considered as the source of information, helps in sharing information that leads to both proactiveness and creativity. Proactive thinking is a result of the density of this network that takes place through direct interactions (Okafor & Ameh, 2017). In fact, Okafor and Ameh (2017) have stated that proactiveness is somehow related to the strength of the network that builds interaction between the network actors. Ferris et al. (2017) found that SC positively affects risk-taking. Similarly, Rodriguez and Romero (2015) found that structural SC is a determinant of the risk-taking attitude, whereas other researchers concluded that a higher level of structural SC may lead to knowledge redundancy or internal block and blindness (Inkpen & Tsang, 2005; Koka & Prescott, 2002), which reduce both innovativeness and proactiveness. Others researchers found no significant effect of structural SC on EO (e.g., Rodrigo-Alarcón et al., 2018). In the same study conducted by Rodrigo-Alarcón et al. (2018) on the Spanish agri-food industry, it was found that cognitive SC has a positive and significant effect on the EO of the firm. It's considered to help in growing the entrepreneurs' efficiency by letting them seize exclusive opportunities (Batjargal, 2003) and thus, increase firm innovation (Doh & Acs, 2010; Jawahar & Nigama, 2011) and proactiveness (Tang, 2010) due to the valuable information it provides. Indeed, cognitive SC plays a crucial role in nurturing and facilitating the transmission of all kinds of transactions, especially when it considers the dispersion of information (Birley, 1985). This is consistent with the "information channels" of Coleman (1988) that network actors keep because of the flow of useful information they grant to them and their role as facilitators for any subsequent action. In this context and under uncertain environmental conditions, the information gathered from social networks enhances opportunity identification (Manev et al., 2005; Shane & Venkataraman, 2000) and exploitation (Aldrich & Zimmer, 1986). In fact, entrepreneurship entails the profiting of such privileged information to practice decision-making over resources' usage in favor of markets' servicing and opportunity exploitation (Foss, 2011). Similarly, Batjargal (2003) argued on the role that SC and generated resources play to assist entrepreneurs in mobilizing resources.

Additional Theoretical Lenses

Self-Efficacy

Since a small business is perceived as the extension of the running individual/CEO (Lumpkin & Dess, 1996) and since the entrepreneur that runs the firm has a huge effect on its entrepreneurial posture and overall culture (Becherer & Maurer, 1997) especially when it's the case of an SME, we perceive a lack of research to see what drives business owners to choose among the entrepreneurial orientations. In this context, *Self-Efficacy* is considered as a widely employed term when coming to entrepreneurship, explained as the belief of a person in their capabilities and skills to perform a given task or behavior (Ajzen, 1987; Bandura, 1997). It is defined as a self-appraisal of one's ability to accomplish a task and one's confidence in possessing the skills needed to perform this task (Garcia et al., 1991). As its name indicates, self-efficacy accelerates the pursuit of goals because it drives a positive view of self. Bandura (1997) argued that an individual's self-efficacy concerning a given task makes them undertake the task as well as persist in it. Similarly, self-confidence turns out to be considered as self-efficacy only in the case when it's task-centered, considering an individual with high self-efficacy to be more perseverant and more consistent on the goals they set (McShane & Von Glinow, 2008).

Self-efficacy as a term has been initially proposed in the social learning theory of Bandura (1977, 1989). According to Bandura (1989), an individual with high self-efficacy gets to positively perceive any challenge they face, shows a higher level of interest, commitment and perseverance for a given behavior, and stands back up directly in case of any frustration. Besides, widely dispersed intentional models explain and elaborate the entrepreneurial activity by incorporating the concept of self-efficacy (Krueger et al., 2000) in addition to social and psychological theories (e.g., Ajzen, 1991 [Perceived Behavioral Control]; Boyd & Vozikis, 1994 [Self-Efficacy]; Shapero & Sokol, 1982 [Perceived Feasibility]). In this context, Bandura (1986) has argued that human functioning and action is best explained by incorporating the concept of self-efficacy and theories that have a broad range of applicability. Boyd and Vozikis (1994) argued that self-efficacy doesn't influence entrepreneurial intentions only, but extends to affect entrepreneurial behavior as well. In their refinement on Bird's intentional model (1988), Boyd and Vozikis (1994) have suggested that both attitudes and self-efficacy beliefs influence entrepreneurial intentions, whereas self-efficacy moderates the relationship between intentions and the subsequent entrepreneurial behavior. In fact, the individual's judgment on their self-efficacy in fulfilling the entrepreneurial behavior is what leads to their judgment on the feasibility of this behavior (Krueger & Brazeal, 1994). Therefore, self-efficacy is perceived to play a primordial role in the success or the failure of any venture.

An extension of the self-efficacy construct has been acknowledged through "Entrepreneurial Self-Efficacy" (ESE) (Chen et al., 1998). ESE, as described, refers to a person's own beliefs in their ability to successfully perform and achieve the entrepreneur's role and tasks. People with high ESE are opportunistic in nature and tend to prioritize opportunities over risk. They believe that their attitude influences what results from their actions, and they don't count failure as an option (Chen et al., 1998). Self-efficacy as a concept is perceived to be at lower levels in disadvantaged economies where many skilled individuals don't pursue desired entrepreneurial activities mainly because they lack self-efficacy. This was much emphasized by Krueger and Dickson (1994) who acknowledged the role of self-efficacy in opportunity recognition. Also, in their study on Malay entrepreneurs, Mohd et al. (2014) found that self-efficacy is also related to EO, specifically affecting innovativeness. In turn, Kumar (2007) found a positive correlation between self-efficacy and innovativeness. However, and despite the criticality of self-efficacy in general and in the entrepreneurship field and the subsequent behavior, entrepreneurship scholars didn't accord much importance to its conceptualization in their scholarly conversations (Krueger et al. 2000).

Subjectivist Theory of Entrepreneurship

There have been many academic attempts that aim to understand what differentiates people who discover opportunities from others who don't.

Venkataraman (1997) argued about the reasons behind these people having the ability to recognize current market problems and gaps and fitting to them suitable offerings, while stating that it all refers to the information that these people have and that in its turn, is based on their own life experiences. Both Covin and Lumpkin (2011) and Wales (2016) linked EO to many theoretical lenses that are found to be triggering it and shaping its scholarly research. One of these theories is the "Subjectivist Theory of Entrepreneurship" proposed by Kor et al. (2007) and that concerns the entrepreneurs themselves.

This theory suggests that the prior experience and knowledge of the entrepreneur are responsible for opportunity recognition and some particular leverage of resources. In addition, this theory is advanced in terms of tackling the existence of EO as a phenomenon while considering both its antecedents and its consequences (Covin & Lumpkin, 2011). Kor et al. (2007) have introduced this theory to focus on the individuals themselves and what concerns their skills and knowledge along with keeping the same focus on the role that subjectivity plays in both the creativity and the discovery processes. In fact, they have emphasized that entrepreneurship can be subjectively perceived and handled. This is because different entrepreneurs have different combinations of knowledge where each combination has its own interpretation. The unique bundle of knowledge and life experiences that the entrepreneur owns will effectively enhance entrepreneurial activity and further affect the competitiveness and growth of its firm. In this context, Shane (2000) argued that the entrepreneur discovers opportunities that are related to their prior knowledge and gathered information, stated as the "knowledge corridor" by Venkataraman (1997). Such information varies among entrepreneurs, being contingent on specific and unique life experiences. Moreover, Kor et al. (2007) have described how someone's knowledge bundle changes over time, and how this change is accompanied by many disclosures capable of enhancing entrepreneurial discovery. By entrepreneurial discovery, the theorists didn't mean the discovery of existing opportunities only, but encompassing creativity and opportunity creation, as being a result of interactions between entrepreneurs and different stakeholders. Those entrepreneurs who are driven by creativity don't settle only on responding to the changes that happen in the market, but instead aim to create change, to innovate and to affect demand (Kor et al., 2007).

One of the main stand-up points of this theory was the focus on the firm-specific knowledge that the entrepreneurs gather and by which they earn a superior quality over managers, key persons and executives of the same firm. This gathered knowledge is mainly tactical, concerns all firm levels, and originates from specific experiences within the firm. Consequently, it seems evident that those entrepreneurs with broad knowledge and experience will be capable of perfectly fitting between an opportunity offered from their surrounding environment and the firm's insights into its own strengths and weaknesses. In addition to that, the subjectivist theory tackles the team-specific experience and the industry-specific experience as well. The former, as its name indicates, is capable of making the entrepreneur better understood by each member of the team and their attributes. The skills, personality traits and relationships that individuals have with others reflect these personal attributes on which the entrepreneur can rely to assess the overall productivity of the team. Indeed, these attitudes play a major role in the whole team decision-making process and thus affect the firm's overall performance. Now, moving to the industry-specific experience, the entrepreneur has an interaction with many stakeholders in the industry such as customers, suppliers, lenders and many others, and on which they can build an industry-specific knowledge affecting their subjective perception on different opportunities accordingly. In fact, the ability to recognize and evaluate opportunities highly depends on industry-related knowledge and experiences, as this theory suggests. An opportunity discovery can be well achieved when information on industry actors, behavioral patterns of customers as well as unmet needs is gathered. The subjective perception of the individual entrepreneur is consequently built upon this information, and favors the growth and prosperity of the firm.

Entrepreneurial Dominant Logic (DL)

The concept of Dominant Logic (DL) was first introduced by Prahalad and Bettis (1986) and defined as the managers' approach of conceptualizing the business and deciding on resource distribution. The cognitive orientation of top decision-makers reflects the way they engage in strategic decisions in their organization. This cognitive orientation is a resultant of the individual's previous experience and knowledge. The concept of entrepreneurial DL has been later elaborated by Meyer and Heppard (2000) to be considered as a more employed concept when connecting to EO research and its scholarly conversation (Covin & Lumpkin, 2011). In their book, Meyer and Heppard (2000) presented the idea of entrepreneurship as a DL that drives the creation of firms' entrepreneurial strategies. They perceived the entrepreneurial DL as a stimulus for the continuous information search and filtering in order to bring on innovations to the firm and further profit from these innovations.

In their later work, thought on DL has rotated, and thus Bettis and Prahalad (1995) redefined DL as a level of strategic analysis and an information filter through which strategists consider important data and information. This filter has control over what these strategists find important or not, since they select data that fit to their cognitive filter mechanism. Considering this, and as per the conceptualization of DL described above, any current or future structural and strategic decisions made by managers will be based on their DL which is the only factor capable of diminishing some choices or to motivate undertaking others accordingly. Along with this, Covin and Lumpkin (2011) have attributed the difference between EO patterns in firms performing in similar environments to DL considering its high influence on the entrepreneurial posture of a given firm and its ability to differentiate between one firm and another. In this context, and within a study performed on Mexican manufacturing ventures, it was found that DL mediates the EO-performance relationship, and risk-taking, aggressiveness and innovativeness had the highest correlations with DL (Campos et al., 2012).

Organizational Culture and Structure

With the aim of not narrowing the discussion of internal factors on entrepreneurs and decision-makers only, though they are the ones having the most influence on the firm's strategic orientation and its entrepreneurial posture, especially when it considers the case of SMEs, one must consider the organizational context that differentiates a firm from its rivals and that can be considered as a valuable type of intangible resources. In this context, "Culture" as a term has its roots in the anthropology discipline. When this term is used, anthropologists usually aim to show the uniqueness of a certain community and the extent to which it differs from other communities in its behavior transmitted to the subsequent generations. However, four decades ago, "culture" as a term started being attributed to the "organization" term to then be combined as "organizational culture" that is mostly employed to differ an organization from others. In fact, the rewarded behaviors in an organization as well as the most valued manners belong to the organizational culture. This culture is transferred from one generation of employees to another and is defined as the set of shared values, attitudes and business principles that outline accepted behaviors in a given firm. Therefore, within the aim to be entrepreneurially active, a firm must hold a positive culture that favors proactiveness and innovativeness. Defending this point of view, Covin and Slevin (1991) within their investigation on internal variables, have talked about both the culture and the structure of an organization and how both can affect the firm's entrepreneurial posture by enhancing its innovativeness, its proactive search for opportunities and its risk-taking tendency. Moreover, in their study on the factors that produce EO, Fayolle et al. (2010) proposed corporate culture to enhance the firm's EO. Within this same perspective, Abdullah et al. (2017) argued that organizational culture defines the behavior of the organization through the influence it has on the attitudes and behaviors of its members. Indeed, the thoughts and actions of an organization's members are shaped by the existing corporate culture and the strength of this culture is measured by the extent to which the organization's members believe in it and manifest it. In fact, it has been perceived that when relationships and interactions between the organization's members are fostered, many dimensions of EO get affected, specifically innovativeness and risk-taking (Miller, 2011).

Also, Denison (1990) has shown in a study that the culture of an organization has four main characteristics which are: involvement, consistency, adaptability and mission, and it's through these characteristics that the organizational culture has implications on the efficiency of the firm.

Involvement is considered as the level to which members of an organization have a say in the decision-making process. This involvement diffuses a sense of responsibility and is capable of fostering the firm's actors' creativity and innovativeness since they start to feel that they have a real impact on the organization and its goals' achievement process (Abdullah et al., 2017). Similarly, Schein (1983) perceived entrepreneurial leaders as the ones that set the corporate culture in an organization through promoting autonomy between members and units and stimulating innovation. Consistent however, is the level to which those members accept the essential and fundamental values of the organization. By accepting the values, members get more integrated into the organization and start to coordinate activities which in turn has implications on the organization's effectiveness. Adaptability (having common characteristics of DCs as per the researcher's judgment) is how an organization leads to internal changes as a response to environmental changes. Adaptability is a tool for organizations to serve customers with the best value possible by making necessary changes internally. Mission, and as its name indicates, is defined as the most important purpose of why the organization exists. Therefore, the organization's mission should be well-defined in order to facilitate the relationship with the external environment and thus structure an effective future vision (Abdullah et al., 2017).

Moving to "Organizational Structure", this is more about how communication and authority relationships are settled within the organization (Covin & Slevin, 1991) where differences in structure exist, defined as either organic or mechanistic (Covin & Slevin, 1991). In both cases, the structure influences the entrepreneurial activity and posture of the firm. However, flexibility in the structure of the firm is needed for it to take decisions promptly especially in response to its rivals (Covin & Slevin, 1988). So there is always a call for a suitable organizational structure (flattening hierarchies and assigning authority as per Lumpkin & Dess, 1996) that includes mainly an easy flow of information and communication with the minimum number of layers possible. Miller (2011) added that many contingency theorists in the literature have asserted that a looser and more organic structure is capable of enhancing innovation.

Eventually, one must know that when it's a mechanistic structure, authority has higher prominence than expertise in the firm, and information concerning the business is only accessible to picked top-notch individuals inside the organization. In this kind of structure, job descriptions are very rigid and procedures of operations are formalized. Instead, when it's an organic structure, expertise has a higher prominence than authority, and information is easily accessed and shared among different members of the organization; also existing procedures have little importance when confronted with a goal to be attained. In this context, decentralized decision-making is considered as an important asset for a firm. Miller and Friesen (1982) argued about the relationship between structural variables and entrepreneurial firms' innovativeness. In their turn, Lumpkin and Dess (1996) argued that when the decision-making is decentralized, the performance of the firm is enhanced, especially when this firm displays EO. In contrast, bureaucracy has been perceived differently by another group of scholars, who have perceived routines to positively serve innovation, and proactiveness of the firm seen as their ability to gather and monitor resources.

Conclusion

EO has occupied the scholarly conversation within the entrepreneurship domain for decades (Covin & Lumpkin, 2011). Therefore, and for the construct research to advance, this chapter acknowledges the gaps within the EO theory and adds valuable theoretical and practical ramifications to the body of knowledge of EO. This review has followed the suggestions of many scholars and aimed to bring on to the academic conversation what has been thought of as a promising path in the EO research that concerns its antecedents. Thus, according to the previous emphasis put on different firm attributes in facilitating exhibition of entrepreneurial activity and strategic action, in this chapter, we exhibited the role of firm resources, DCs, the conditions of a firm's network and some additional internal factors that consider both the firm and the entrepreneur in fostering EO within SMEs. In addition, as this review has considered the context of SMEs operating in emerging economies, it raises the hope of motivating further exploration of EO in this context, seeing the low incorporation of such frameworks within entrepreneurship studies.

On a theoretical level, this study is based those rare ones that tackled the EO construct-antecedents-and-consequences-relationship and illustrated a theoretical framework based on this exploration. On a practical level, the analysis of the literature review highlighted some recommendations to SMEs to reconsider the dispositions of EO aspects within their firms and reconfigure what triggers their attitudes and behaviors. However, other recommendations are addressed to the parties concerned with formulating strategies that foster the existence of SMEs and enhance their capabilities. They must tailor their strategies and policies to meet the needs of SMEs and ease their environment, specifically those competing in both national and regional economies. As for the recommendations addressed to scholars, this chapter inspires further exploration in investigating the EO construct and the context where it occurs. Also, a recommendation maintains on proposing a longitudinal study design in EO where the relationship between the dimensions of the construct and firm performance can be tracked over time and among different stages of the firm's development.

References

Abdullah, S., Musa, C. I., & Azis, M. (2017). The Effect of Organizational Culture on Entrepreneurship Characteristics and Competitive Advantage of Small and Medium Catering Enterprises in Makassar. *International Review of Management and Marketing, 7*(2), 409–414.

Ajzen, I. (1987). Attitudes, Traits, and Actions: Dispositional Prediction of Behavior in Personality and Social Psychology. *Advances in Experimental Social Psychology, 20*, 1–63.

Ajzen, I. (1991). The Theory of Planned Behavior. *Organizational Behavior and Human Decision Processes, 50*(2), 179–211.

Aldrich, H. Z., & Zimmer, C. C. (1986). Entrepreneurship through Social Networks. *Ballinger. Cambridge, MA.*

Aloulou, W. (2002). Entrepreneurial Orientation Diagnosis in SMEs: Some Conceptual and Methodological Dimensions. *Entrepreneurship Research in Europe; Specificities and Prospectives, INPG-ESISAR Valence (France).*

Aloulou, W., & Fayolle, A. (2005). A Conceptual Approach of Entrepreneurial Orientation within Small Business Context. *Journal of Enterprising Culture, 13*(1), 21–45.

Alvarez, S. A., & Busenitz, L. W. (2001). The Entrepreneurship of Resource-based Theory. *Journal of Management, 27*(6), 755–775.

Ambrosini, V., & Bowman, C. (2009). What are Dynamic Capabilities and are They a Useful Construct in Strategic Management? *International Journal of Management Reviews, 11*(1), 29–49.

Anderson, B. S., Kreiser, P. M., Kuratko, D. F., Hornsby, J. S., & Eshima, Y. (2015). Reconceptualizing Entrepreneurial Orientation. *Strategic Management Journal, 36*(10), 1579–1596.

Audretsch, D. B. (2002). The Dynamic Role of Small Firms: Evidence from the US. *Small Business Economics, 18*(1–3), 13–40.

Audretsch, D. B. (2007). *The Entrepreneurial Society*. Oxford University Press.

Awang, A., Khalid, S. A., Yusof, A. A., Kassim, K. M., Ismail, M., Zain, R. S., & Madar, A. R. S. (2009). Entrepreneurial Orientation and Performance Relations of Malaysian Bumiputera SMEs: The Impact of Some Perceived Environmental Factors. *International Journal of Business and Management, 4*(9), 84–96.

Bakar, L. J. A., & Ahmad, H. (2010). Assessing the Relationship between Firm Resources and Product Innovation Performance. *Business Process Management Journal, 16*(3), 420–435.

Bandura, A. (1977). Self-efficacy: Toward a Unifying Theory of Behavioral Change. *Psychological Review, 84*(2), 191–215.

Bandura, A. (1986). The Explanatory and Predictive Scope of Self-Efficacy Theory. *Journal of Social and Clinical Psychology, 4*(3), 359–373.

Bandura, A. (1989). Human Agency in Social Cognitive Theory. *American Psychologist, 44*(9), 1175–1184.

Bandura, A. (1997). *Self-efficacy: The Exercise of Control*. Macmillan.

Barney, J. B. (1986). Strategic Factor Markets: Expectations, Luck, and Business Strategy. *Management Science, 32*(10), 1231–1241.

Barney, J. B. (1991). Firm Resources and Sustained Competitive Advantage. *Journal of Management, 17*(1), 99–120.

Baron, R. A. (2002). OB and Entrepreneurship: The Reciprocal Benefits of Closer Conceptual Links. *Research in Organizational Behavior, 24*, 225–269.

Batjargal, B. (2003). Social Capital and Entrepreneurial Performance in Russia: A Longitudinal Study. *Organization Studies, 24*(4), 535–556.

Becherer, R. C., & Maurer, J. G. (1997). The Moderating Effect of Environmental Variables on the Entrepreneurial and Marketing Orientation of Entrepreneur-Led Firms. *Entrepreneurship Theory and Practice, 22*(1), 47–58.

Bettis, R. A., & Prahalad, C. K. (1995). The Dominant Logic: Retrospective and Extension. *Strategic Management Journal, 16*(1), 5–14.

Bhuian, S. N., Menguc, B., & Bell, S. J. (2005). Just Entrepreneurial Enough: The Moderating Effect of Entrepreneurship on the Relationship between Market Orientation and Performance. *Journal of Business Research, 58*(1), 9–17.

Birley, S. (1985). The Role of Networks in the Entrepreneurial Process. *Journal of Business Venturing, 1*(1), 107–117.

Birley, S., & Norburn, D. (1985). Small Vs. Large Companies: The Entrepreneurial Conundrum. *Journal of Business Strategy, 6*(1), 81–87.

Bourdieu, P. (2011). The Forms of Capital. (1986). *Cultural Theory: An Anthology, 1*, 81–93.

Bouri, A., Breij, M., Diop, M., Kempner, R., Klinger, B., & Stevenson, K. (2011). *Report on Support to SMEs in Developing Countries through Financial Intermediaries*. Dalberg, November.

Boyd, N. G., & Vozikis, G. S. (1994). The Influence of Self-efficacy on the Development of Entrepreneurial Intentions and Actions. *Entrepreneurship Theory and Practice, 18*(4), 63–77.

Brockhaus, R. H., Sr. (1980). Risk Taking Propensity of Entrepreneurs. *Academy of Management Journal, 23*(3), 509–520.

Cai, L., Peng, X., & Wang, L. (2018). The Characteristics and Influencing Factors of Entrepreneurial Behaviour: The Case of New State-Owned Firms in the New Energy Automobile Industry in an Emerging Economy. *Technological Forecasting and Social Change, 135*, 112–120.

Campos, H. M., la Parra, J. P. N. D., & Parellada, F. S. (2012). The Entrepreneurial Orientation-Dominant Logic-Performance Relationship in New Ventures: An Exploratory Quantitative Study. *BAR-Brazilian Administration Review, 9*(SPE), 60–77.

Caner, S. (2010, April). The Role of Small and Medium Size Enterprises in Economic Development. In *HSE Conference*.

Carmeli, A., & Tishler, A. (2004). The Relationships between Intangible Organizational Elements and Organizational Performance. *Strategic Management Journal, 25*(13), 1257–1278.

Chandler, G. N., & Hanks, S. H. (1994). Market Attractiveness, Resource-based Capabilities, Venture Strategies, and Venture Performance. *Journal of Business Venturing, 9*(4), 331–349.

Chang, H. H., & Chuang, S. S. (2011). Social Capital and Individual Motivations on Knowledge Sharing: Participant Involvement as a Moderator. *Information & Management, 48*(1), 9–18.

Chen, C. C., Greene, P. G., & Crick, A. (1998). Does Entrepreneurial Self-efficacy Distinguish Entrepreneurs from Managers? *Journal of Business Venturing, 13*(4), 295–316.

Chen, C. N., Tzeng, L. C., Ou, W. M., & Chang, K. T. (2007). The Relationship Among Docial Capital, Entrepreneurial Orientation, Organizational Resources and Entrepreneurial Performance for New Ventures. *Contemporary Management Research, 3*(3), 213–232.

Coleman, J. S. (1988). Social Capital in the Creation of Human Capital. *American Journal of Sociology, 94*, S95–S120.

Conner, K. R. (1991). A Historical Comparison of Resource-based Theory and Five Schools of Thought within Industrial Organization Economics: Do We have a New Theory of the Firm? *Journal of Management, 17*(1), 121–154.

Coulthard, M. (2007). The Role of Entrepreneurial Orientation on Firm Performance and the Potential Influence of Relational Dynamism. *Journal of Global Business & Technology, 3*(1), 29–39.

Covin, J. G., & Lumpkin, G. T. (2011). Entrepreneurial Orientation Theory and Research: Reflections on a Needed Construct. *Entrepreneurship Theory and Practice, 35*(5), 855–872.

Covin, J. G., & Miles, M. P. (1999). Corporate Entrepreneurship and the Pursuit of Competitive Advantage. *Entrepreneurship Theory and Practice, 23*(3), 47–63.

Covin, J. G., & Slevin, D. P. (1988). The Influence of Organization Structure on the Utility of an Entrepreneurial Top Management Style. *Journal of Management Studies, 25*(3), 217–234.

Covin, J. G., & Slevin, D. P. (1989). Strategic Management of Small Firms in Hostile and Benign Environments. *Strategic Management Journal, 10*(1), 75–87.

Covin, J. G., & Slevin, D. P. (1991). A Conceptual Model of Entrepreneurship as Firm Behavior. *Entrepreneurship Theory and Practice, 16*(1), 7–26.

Covin, J. G., Slevin, D. P., & Schultz, R. L. (1994). Implementing Strategic Missions: Effective Strategic, Structural and Tactical Choices. *Journal of Management Studies, 31*(4), 481–506.

Covin, J. G., & Wales, W. J. (2012). The Measurement of Entrepreneurial Orientation. *Entrepreneurship Theory and Practice, 36*(4), 677–702.

Das, T. K., & Teng, B. S. (2000). A Resource-based Theory of Strategic Alliances. *Journal of Management, 26*(1), 31–61.

Davidsson, P. (2006). Nascent Entrepreneurship: Empirical Studies and Developments. *Foundations and Trends® in Entrepreneurship, 2*(1), 1–76.

Davidsson, P., & Honig, B. (2003). The Role of Social and Human Capital among Nascent Entrepreneurs. *Journal of Business Venturing, 18*(3), 301–331.

De Clercq, D., Dimov, D., & Thongpapanl, N. (2013). Organizational Social Capital, Formalization, and Internal Knowledge Sharing in Entrepreneurial Orientation Formation. *Entrepreneurship Theory and Practice, 37*(3), 505–537.

Denison, D. R. (1990). *Corporate Culture and Organizational Effectiveness*. John Wiley & Sons.

Dess, G. G., & Lumpkin, G. T. (2005). The Role of Entrepreneurial Orientation in Stimulating Effective Corporate Entrepreneurship. *Academy of Management Perspectives, 19*(1), 147–156.

Dess, G. G., Lumpkin, G. T., & Eisner, A. B. (2008). *Strategic Management—Creating Competitive Advantage* (4th ed.). McGraw-Hill/Irwin.

Doh, S., & Acs, Z. J. (2010). Innovation and Social Capital: A Cross-Country Investigation. *Industry and Innovation, 17*(3), 241–262.

Dollinger, M. J. (1999). *Entrepreneurship: Strategies and Resources*. Prentice-Hall.

Drucker, P. F. (1985). The Discipline of Innovation. *Harvard Business Review, 63*(3), 67–72.

Farmer, S. M., Yao, X., & Kung-Mcintyre, K. (2011). The Behavioral Impact of Entrepreneur Identity Aspiration and Prior Entrepreneurial Experience. *Entrepreneurship Theory and Practice, 35*(2), 245–273.

Fayolle, A., Basso, O., & Bouchard, V. (2010). Three Levels of Culture and Firms' Entrepreneurial Orientation: A Research Agenda. *Entrepreneurship and Regional Development, 22*(7–8), 707–730.

Ferrier, W. J. (2001). Navigating the Competitive Landscape: The Drivers and Consequences of Competitive Aggressiveness. *Academy of Management Journal, 44*(4), 858–877.

Ferris, S. P., Javakhadze, D., & Rajkovic, T. (2017). CEO Social Capital, Risk-Taking and Corporate Policies. *Journal of Corporate Finance*, 47, 46–71.

Fini, R., Grimaldi, R., Marzocchi, G. L., & Sobrero, M. (2012). The Determinants of Corporate Entrepreneurial Intention within Small and Newly Established Firms. *Entrepreneurship Theory and Practice, 36*(2), 387–414.

Foss, N. J. (2011). Entrepreneurship in the Context of the Resource-based View of the Firm. *Perspectives in Entrepreneurship: a critical approach,* Palgrave Macmillan, UK.

Frese, M., Brantjes, A., & Hoorn, R. (2002). Psychological Success Factors of Small Scale Businesses in Namibia: The Roles of Strategy Process, Entrepreneurial Orientation and the Environment. *Journal of Developmental Entrepreneurship, 7*(3), 259–282.

Galbreath, J., & Galvin, P. (2008). Firm Factors, Industry Structure and Performance Variation: New Empirical Evidence to a Classic Debate. *Journal of Business Research, 61*(2), 109–117.

Garcia, T., McKeachie, W. J., Pintrich, P. R., & Smith, D. A. (1991). A Manual for the Use of the Motivated Strategies for Learning Questionnaire. Ann Arbor: The University of Michigan, School of Education.

George, B. A., & Marino, L. (2011). The Epistemology of Entrepreneurial Orientation: Conceptual Formation, Modeling, and Operationalization. *Entrepreneurship Theory and Practice, 35*(5), 989–1024.

Granovetter, M. (1992). Problems of Explanation in Economic Sociology. In *Networks and Organizations: Structure, Form, and Action* Boston: Harvard Business School Press.

Grant, R. M. (1991). The Resource-based Theory of Competitive Advantage: Implications for Strategy Formulation. *California Management Review, 33*(3), 114–135.

Grimm, C. M., Lee, H., & Smith, K. G. (Eds.). (2006). *Strategy as Action: Competitive Dynamics and Competitive Advantage*. Oxford University Press.

Hambrick, D. (1987). Top Management Teams: Key to Strategic Success. *California Management Review, 30*, 88–108.

Hameed, I., & Ali, B. (2011). Impact of Entrepreneurial Orientation, Entrepreneurial Management and Environmental Dynamism on Firms' Financial Performance. *Journal of Economics and Behavioral Studies, 3*(2), 101–114.

Haugh, H. (2005). A Research Agenda for Social Entrepreneurship. *Social Enterprise Journal, 1*(1), 1–12.

Haynie, J. M., Shepherd, D. A., & McMullen, J. S. (2009). An Opportunity for Me? The Role of Resources in Opportunity Evaluation Decisions. *Journal of Management Studies, 46*(3), 337–361.

Helfat, C. E., & Martin, J. A. (2015). Dynamic Managerial Capabilities: Review and Assessment of Managerial Impact on Strategic Change. *Journal of Management, 41*(5), 1281–1312.

Henderson, J. (2002). Building the Rural Economy with High-growth Entrepreneurs. *Economic Review-Federal Reserve Bank of Kansas City, 87*(3), 45–75.

Hill, H. (2001). Small and Medium Enterprises in Indonesia: Old Policy Challenges for a New Administration. *Asian Survey, 41*(2), 248–270.

Hughes, M., & Morgan, R. E. (2007). Deconstructing the Relationship between Entrepreneurial Orientation and Business Performance at the Embryonic Stage of Firm Growth. *Industrial Marketing Management, 36*(5), 651–661.

Hult, G. T. M., Hurley, R. F., & Knight, G. A. (2004). Innovativeness: Its Antecedents and Impact on Business Performance. *Industrial Marketing Management, 33*(5), 429–438.

Inkpen, A. C., & Tsang, E. W. (2005). Social Capital, Networks, and Knowledge Transfer. *Academy of Management Review, 30*(1), 146–165.

Irava, W., & Moores, K. (2010). Resources Supporting Entrepreneurial Orientation in Multigenerational Family Firms. *International Journal of Entrepreneurial Venturing, 2*(3/4), 222–245.

Jalali, A., Jaafar, M., & Ramayah, T. (2014). Entrepreneurial Orientation and Performance: The Interaction Effect of Customer Capital. *World Journal of Entrepreneurship, Management and Sustainable Development, 10*(1), 46–68.

Jantunen, A., Puumalainen, K., Saarenketo, S., & Kyläheiko, K. (2005). Entrepreneurial Orientation, Dynamic Capabilities and International Performance. *Journal of International Entrepreneurship, 3*(3), 223–243.

Jawahar, D., & Nigama. (2011). The Influence of Social Capital on Entrepreneurial Opportunity Recognition Behaviour. *International Journal of Economics and Management, 5*(1), 351–368.

Khandwalla, P. N. (1976/1977). Some Top Management Styles, their Context and Performance. *Organization and Administrative Sciences, 7*(4), 21–51.

Koka, B. R., & Prescott, J. E. (2002). Strategic Alliances as Social Capital: A Multidimensional View. *Strategic Management Journal, 23*(9), 795–816.

Koldertsova, A. (2006). Lebanon National Investment Reform Agenda Workshop Background Paper for Session IV Improving the Entrepreneurial Finance: Venture Capital and Access to Credit for SMEs, OECD.

Kor, Y. Y., Mahoney, J. T., & Michael, S. C. (2007). Resources, Capabilities and Entrepreneurial Perceptions. *Journal of Management Studies, 44*(7), 1187–1212.

Kreiser, P. M., Marino, L. D., & Weaver, K. M. (2002). Assessing the Psychometric Properties of the Entrepreneurial Orientation Scale: A Multi-country Analysis. *Entrepreneurship Theory and Practice, 26*(4), 71–93.

Krueger, N. F., Jr., & Brazeal, D. V. (1994). Entrepreneurial Potential and Potential Entrepreneurs. *Entrepreneurship Theory and Practice, 18*(3), 91–104.

Krueger, N. F., Jr., & Dickson, P. R. (1994). How Believing in Ourselves Increases Risk Taking: Perceived Self-efficacy and Opportunity Recognition. *Decision Sciences, 25*(3), 385–400.

Krueger, N. F., Jr., Reilly, M. D., & Carsrud, A. L. (2000). Competing Models of Entrepreneurial Intentions. *Journal of Business Venturing, 15*(5–6), 411–432.

Kuckertz, A., & Wagner, M. (2010). The Influence of Sustainability Orientation on Entrepreneurial Intentions: Investigating the Role of Business Experience. *Journal of Business Venturing, 25*(5), 524–539.

Kumar, M. (2007). Explaining Entrepreneurial Success: A Conceptual Model. *Academy of Entrepreneurship Journal, 13*(1), 57–77.

Kusumawardhani, A. (2013). The Role of Entrepreneurial Orientation in Firm Performance: A Study of Indonesian SMEs in the Furniture Industry in Central Java (PhD Thesis). University of Wollongong Thesis Collections.

Lee, C., Lee, K., & Pennings, J. M. (2001). Internal Capabilities, External Networks, and Performance: A Study on Technology-based Ventures. *Strategic Management Journal, 22*(6/7), 615–640.

Li, Y. H., Huang, J. W., & Tsai, M. T. (2009). Entrepreneurial Orientation and Firm Performance: The Role of Knowledge Creation Process. *Industrial Marketing Management, 38*(4), 440–449.

Lumpkin, G. T., & Dess, G. G. (1996). Clarifying the Entrepreneurial Orientation Construct and Linking it to Performance. *Academy of Management Review, 21*(1), 135–172.

Lumpkin, G. T., & Dess, G. G. (2001). Linking two Dimensions of Entrepreneurial Orientation to Firm Performance: The Moderating Role of Environment and Industry Life Cycle. *Journal of Business Venturing, 16*(5), 429–451.

Malhotra, M., Chen, Y., Criscuolo, A., Fan, Q., Hamel, I. I., & Savchenko, Y. (2007). *Expanding Access to Finance: Good Practices and Policies for Micro, Small, and Medium Enterprises.* The World Bank.

Manev, I. M., Gyoshev, B. S., & Manolova, T. S. (2005). The Role of Human and Social Capital and Entrepreneurial Orientation for Small Business Performance in a Transitional Economy. *International Journal of Entrepreneurship and Innovation Management, 5*(3–4), 298–318.

McShane, S. L., & Von Glinow, M. A. (2008). Perception and Learning in Organizations. *Organizational Behavior, 4*, 68–100.

Meyer, G. D., & Heppard, K. A. (2000). *Entrepreneurship as Strategy: Competing on the Entrepreneurial Edge*. Sage Publications.
Miles, R. E., Snow, C. C., Meyer, A. D., & Coleman, H. J., Jr. (1978). Organizational Strategy, Structure, and Process. *Academy of Management Review, 3*(3), 546–562.
Miller, D. (1983). The Correlates of Entrepreneurship in Three Types of Firms. *Management Science, 29*(7), 770–791.
Miller, D. (2003). An Asymmetry-based View of Advantage: Towards an Attainable Sustainability. *Strategic Management Journal, 24*(10), 961–976.
Miller, D. (2011). Miller (1983) Revisited: A Reflection on EO Research and Some Suggestions for the Future. *Entrepreneurship Theory and Practice, 35*(5), 873–894.
Miller, D., & Friesen, P. H. (1982). Innovation in Conservative and Entrepreneurial Firms: Two Models of Strategic Momentum. *Strategic Management Journal, 3*(1), 1–25.
Miller, D., & Shamsie, J. (1996). The Resource-based View of the Firm in Two Environments: The Hollywood Film Studios from 1936 to 1965. *Academy of Management Journal, 39*(3), 519–543.
Milovanovic, B. M., & Wittine, Z. (2014). Analysis of External Environment's Moderating Role on the Entrepreneurial Orientation and Business Performance Relationship among Italian Small Enterprises. *International Journal of Trade, Economics and Finance, 5*(3), 224–229.
Mintzberg, H. (1973). Strategy-making in Three Modes. *California Management Review, 16*(2), 44–53.
Mohd, R., Kamaruddin, B. H., Hassan, S., Muda, M., & Yahya, K. K. (2014). The Important Role of Self-Efficacy in Determining Entrepreneurial Orientations of Malay Small Scale Entrepreneurs in Malaysia. *International Journal of Management Studies, 20*(1), 61–82.
Morris, M. H., Pitt, L. F., & Berthon, P. (1996). Entrepreneurial Activity in the Third World Informal Sector: The View from Khayelitsha. *International Journal of Entrepreneurial Behavior & Research, 2*(1), 59–76.
Nahapiet, J., & Ghoshal, S. (1998). Social Capital, Intellectual Capital, and the Organizational Advantage. *Academy of Management Review, 23*(2), 242–266.
Ndiaye, N., Razak, L. A., Nagayev, R., & Ng, A. (2018). Demystifying Small and Medium Enterprises' (SMEs) Performance in Emerging and Developing Economies. *Borsa Istanbul Review, 18*(4), 269–281.
Ndofor, H. A., Sirmon, D. G., & He, X. (2011). Firm Resources, Competitive Actions and Performance: Investigating a Mediated Model with Evidence

from the In-vitro Diagnostics Industry. *Strategic Management Journal, 32*(6), 640–657.

O'Regan, N., & Ghobadian, A. (2005). Innovation in SMEs: The Impact of Strategic Orientation and Environmental Perceptions. *International Journal of Productivity and Performance Management, 54*(2), 81–97.

Okafor, L. C., & Ameh, A. A. (2017). Social Networks and Entrepreneurship Orientation among Students in Nigerian Universities: A Study of Social Network Density and Proactiveness. *International Journal of Business and Management Invention, 6*(7), 33–41.

Pennings, J. M., Lee, K., & Witteloostuijn, A. V. (1998). Human Capital, Social Capital, and Firm Dissolution. *Academy of Management Journal, 41*(4), 425–440.

Penrose, E. T. (1959) 'The Theory of the Growth of the Firm', Basil Blackwell, Oxford, UK.

Pittino, D., Visintin, F., & Lauto, G. (2017). A Configurational Analysis of the Antecedents of Entrepreneurial Orientation. *European Management Journal, 35*(2), 224–237.

Prahalad, C. K., & Bettis, R. A. (1986). The Dominant Logic: A New Linkage between Diversity and Performance. *Strategic Management Journal, 7*(6), 485–501.

Prottas, D. (2008). Do the Self-employed Value Autonomy More than Employees? Research across Four Samples. *Career Development International, 13*(1), 33–45.

Ratten, V. (2014). Future Research Directions for Collective Entrepreneurship in Developing Countries: A Small and Medium-sized Enterprise Perspective. *International Journal of Entrepreneurship and Small Business, 22*(2), 266–274.

Rauch, A., Wiklund, J., Lumpkin, G. T., & Frese, M. (2009). Entrepreneurial Orientation and Business Performance: An Assessment of Past Research and Suggestions for the Future. *Entrepreneurship Theory and Practice, 33*(3), 761–787.

Rodrigo-Alarcón, J., García-Villaverde, P. M., Ruiz-Ortega, M. J., & Parra-Requena, G. (2018). From Social Capital to Entrepreneurial Orientation: The Mediating Role of Dynamic Capabilities. *European Management Journal, 36*(2), 195–209.

Rodríguez Gutiérrez, M. J., & Romero Luna, I. (2015). The Influence of Social Capital on Risk-Taking Propensity. A Study on Chinese Immigrant Entrepreneurs. *International Conference on Regional Science*, Spain.

Schein, E. H. (1983). The Role of the Founder in Creating Organizational Culture. *Organizational Dynamics, 12*(1), 13–28.
Schumacher, E. F. (1973). *Small is Beautiful: A Study of Economics as if People Mattered.* Blond & Briggs.
Schumpeter, J. A. (1934). Change and the Entrepreneur. *Essays of JA Schumpeter.*
Schumpeter, J. A. (1942). Creative Destruction. *Capitalism, Socialism and Democracy, 825*, 82–85.
Shane, S. (2000). Prior Knowledge and the Discovery of Entrepreneurial Opportunities. *Organization Science, 11*(4), 448–469.
Shane, S., & Venkataraman, S. (2000). The Promise of Entrepreneurship as a Field of Research. *Academy of Management Review, 25*(1), 217–226.
Shapero, A., & Sokol, L. (1982). The Social Dimensions of Entrepreneurship. In *Encyclopedia of Entrepreneurship.*
Sirmon, D. G., Hitt, M. A., & Ireland, R. D. (2007). Managing Firm Resources in Dynamic Environments to Create Value: Looking Inside the Black Box. *Academy of Management Review, 32*(1), 273–292.
Stam, W., & Elfring, T. (2008). Entrepreneurial Orientation and New Venture Performance: The Moderating Role of Intra-and Extra-industry Social Capital. *Academy of Management Journal, 51*(1), 97–111.
Stevenson, H. H., & Jarillo, J. C. (1990). A Paradigm of Entrepreneurship: Entrepreneurial Management. *Strategic Management Journal, 11*, 17–27.
Storey, D. J. (1994). The Role of Legal Status in Influencing Bank Financing and New Firm Growth. *Applied Economics, 26*(2), 129–136.
Tang, J. (2010). How Entrepreneurs Discover Opportunities in China: An Institutional View. *Asia Pacific Journal of Management, 27*(3), 461–479.
Teece, D. J. (1998). Capturing Value from Knowledge Assets: The New Economy, Markets for Know-how, and Intangible Assets. *California Management Review, 40*(3), 55–79.
Teece, D. J., Pisano, G., & Shuen, A. (1997). Dynamic Capabilities and Strategic Management. *Strategic Management Journal, 18*(7), 509–533.
Tsai, H. F., & Luan, C. J. (2016). What Makes Firms Embrace Risks? A Risk-Taking Capability Perspective. *BRQ Business Research Quarterly, 19*(3), 219–231.
Van Stel, A., Carree, M., & Thurik, R. (2005). The Effect of Entrepreneurial Activity on National Economic Growth. *Small Business Economics, 24*(3), 311–321.

Venkataraman, S. (1997). The Distinctive Domain of Entrepreneurship Research. *Advances in Entrepreneurship, Firm Emergence and Growth, 3*(1), 119–138.

Venkatraman, N. (1989). Strategic Orientation of Business Enterprises: The Construct, Dimensionality, and Measurement. *Management Science, 35*(8), 942–962.

Wales, W. J. (2016). Entrepreneurial Orientation: A Review and Synthesis of Promising Research Directions. *International Small Business Journal, 34*(1), 3–15.

Wernerfelt, B. (1984). A Resource-based View of the Firm. *Strategic Management Journal, 5*(2), 171–180.

Wiklund, J. (1998). *Small Firm Growth and Performance: Entrepreneurship and Beyond* (Doctoral dissertation, Internationella Handelshögskolan).

Wiklund, J., & Shepherd, D. (2003). Knowledge-based Resources, Entrepreneurial Orientation, and the Performance of Small and Medium-Sized Businesses. *Strategic Management Journal, 24*(13), 1307–1314.

Wiklund, J., & Shepherd, D. (2005). Entrepreneurial Orientation and Small Business Performance: A Configurational Approach. *Journal of Business Venturing, 20*(1), 71–91.

Yılmaz, B. (2004). Küçük ve orta büyüklükteki işletmelerin toplumda üstlendikleri roller bakımından analizi. *Dış Ticaret Dergisi, 9*(30), 141–179.

Zahra, S. A. (1991). Predictors and Financial Outcomes of Corporate Entrepreneurship: An Exploratory Study. *Journal of Business Venturing, 6*(4), 259–285.

Zahra, S. A., & Covin, J. G. (1995). Contextual Influences on the Corporate Entrepreneurship-Performance Relationship: A Longitudinal Analysis. *Journal of Business Venturing, 10*(1), 43–58.

Zahra, S. A., & Garvis, D. M. (2000). International Corporate Entrepreneurship and Firm Performance: The Moderating Effect of International Environmental Hostility. *Journal of Business Venturing, 15*(5–6), 469–492.

Zahra, S. A., Sapienza, H. J., & Davidsson, P. (2006). Entrepreneurship and Dynamic Capabilities: A Review, Model and Research Agenda. *Journal of Management Studies, 43*(4), 917–955.

5

Women in Entrepreneurship and Social Entrepreneurship in the Arab World

Thami Ghorfi and Dora Jurd de Girancourt

Introduction

The Arab world has experienced significant social, political, and economic changes for two decades. More recently, the Covid crisis has shaken the whole world's paradigm and brought new forms of work leaderships globally and in the Arab countries, mainly. In this context, the status of women in the Arab world has changed dramatically. It is still continuously evolving among paradoxes and challenges but also new opportunities and great expectations.

Two dates were landmarks for women's rights in the Arab world: the Cairo Conference in 1995 and the Arab spring in 2011. These were both turning points where most governments in the region realized that increasing women's rights and consequently boosting female participation in the economy could highly benefit their country. But women still face strong social norms and unchanging traditional rules that don't

T. Ghorfi (✉) • D. Jurd de Girancourt
ESCA École de Management, Casablanca, Morocco
e-mail: tghorfi@esca.ma

N. Azoury, T. Hafsi (eds.), *Entrepreneurship and Social Entrepreneurship in the MENA Region*, https://doi.org/10.1007/978-3-030-88447-5_5

encourage them to work. Nevertheless, these challenges don't discourage them. On the contrary, they have never been so determined to enter the workforce and make their voice heard. They see entrepreneurship and social entrepreneurship as opportunities to empower and thrive professionally. Some Arab women are successful and committed to jump on the bandwagon of the digital revolution. Still, we will analyze in this chapter the challenges they have to tackle when starting new businesses and the innovative solutions they need to create to achieve their dream.

Before discussing the rationale of women in entrepreneurship and social entrepreneurship in the Arab world, we need to clearly define the scope and the concepts from the perspective of this chapter. By the Arab world, we mean countries from the MENA (Middle East and North Africa) zone with Arabic culture and language. This includes the GCC (Gulf Cooperation Council) countries: Bahrain, Kuwait, Oman, Qatar, Kingdom of Saudi Arabia (KSA), and the United Arab Emirates (UAE). In this chapter, we will focus on upper-income countries such as KSA, the UAE, Qatar, and Kuwait; upper-middle-income countries such as Turkey, Iran, Jordan, Lebanon, Oman, and Tunisia; and lower-middle-income economies such as Morocco, Algeria, and Egypt. The Arab countries, even though they may be studied as a whole because of the cultural and religious similarities, are not a homogeneous group. The states have all very different dynamics, different forms of demography, and other social norms. In particular, women's status varies significantly from one country to another. It is essential to observe that women's participation in the workforce, in particular, can be impacted by legal conditions such as freedom to work, and travel, equal legal rights, access to education, networks, technology, capital, social norms and values. Also, the lack of reliable data is a common feature affecting many Arab countries, even those belonging to the upper-income group. This issue is central to our subject as often women work in the informal economy.

By entrepreneurship, we mean the process of grasping an opportunity in a market or answering a necessity by introducing new products or services to be transformed into monetary value (Szycher, 2014). The scope of entrepreneurship is huge, embracing small and large, new, and old organizations. It applies to very different categories of people from poor rural dwellers to street vendors to doctorate graduates wanting to create their own business by exploiting cutting-edge scientific advances. Entrepreneurship is widely considered to stimulate competition, drive innovation, create employment, generate positive externalities, increase productivity by introducing technological change, and provide a route out of poverty (Audretsch & Thurik, 2001). It is a crucial element in fostering not only economic development but social growth as well. Bringing social growth by providing innovative solutions to social problems is known as social entrepreneurship. The social entrepreneur's primary purpose is to drive social change and generate social value.

If entrepreneurship and social entrepreneurship are crucial to fostering economic development, what's the place of women in these fields in the Arab world?

To answer this critical question, we first need to underline the two central paradoxes that structure the place of women in the Arab world. Despite impactful governmental measures and one of the highest girls' education levels globally, the female labor force participation rate remains one of the weakest in the world. Why?

The Paradoxes of the Arab World Regarding Women

Why, Despite Impactful Governmental Measures and One of the Highest Education Levels in the World, the Female Labour Force Participation Remains One of the Weakest in the World?

Most Arab country' governments have taken many political, educational, and juridical measures in favor of women for a few years. Often supported by the local elite and international organizations, these measures challenge the traditional social norms that remain strong in these countries where patriarchal rules regulate societies. To succeed professionally, women need to find their way between these norms that generally favor their domestic role as wives and children caregivers and governmental measures that encourage them to study and work outside of the domestic sphere.

Impactful Numerous Governmental Measures for Two Decades

Since the Cairo International Conference on Population and Development in 1995, which stands as a landmark for women empowerment in the Arab region, considerable improvements towards women's rights have been made by the governments of most Arab countries. First, "health indicators, including female life expectancy and maternal mortality (as well as under-five mortality), have improved notably in many countries. Also, the vast majority of countries in the region have ratified the Convention on the Elimination of all Forms of Discrimination Against Women (CEDAW)."[1]

In spring 2011, many Arab countries faced social uprisings and street riots to fight for more social and economic inclusion and equality. The uprisings have changed the populations' aspirations and brought a window of opportunities for change for women. The case of Tunisia, which was one of the earliest and most involved participants of the 2011 uprisings, is evocative: in 1956, the year of its independence, the country granted to women the right to vote, the right to divorce, and the government abolished polygamy. In 2017, five years after the protests, Tunisia adopted laws to sentence violence against women. In 2015, the Tunisian National Dialogue Quartet composed of four Tunisian associations received the Nobel Peace Prize for its contribution to the building of a pluralistic democracy. As a result, 2011 was a landmark in terms of women's rights in the region. First of all, female political participation at the ballot box and in government has grown in several countries, thanks to electoral quotas' implementation to promote women's political participation. In Morocco, for example, the new constitution of 2011 implemented for the first time full equality between men and women. In the parliament, 15% to 25% of seats are reserved for women. Egypt, which already has a 10% quota for women deputies, implemented a second quota of 25% for women in local councils. Algeria imposed equality between men and women for electoral lists. In KSA, 20% of seats were reserved for women in the Choura, the consultative assembly, and in the UAE, ministers increased the representation of women in the Cabinet in 2016.

Socially and economically speaking, governmental measures have also improved women's status since 2011. In 2015, Algeria, along with Tunisia, changed their law to sentence violence against women, and Lebanon adopted law 293 to protect women against four types of acts of violence: physical, sexual, psychological, and economic. In Oman, "women have the right to pursue any career under the Basic Law, which also guarantees protection against gender discrimination, the right to own property and equal pay for equal work."[2] Same for the UAE, which issued in 2018 "a draft law to ensure men and women receive equal pay and introduced three months' paid maternity leave for government employees."[3] But the most advanced Arab country in terms of economic rights for women is Morocco, thanks to its avant-gardist constitution of 2011. The Moroccan Constitution imposed a full parity in many fields. Morocco is one of the only Arab countries to have a law that punishes discrimination against financial credit access for women. Along with Djibouti, Algeria, and Oman, Morocco also has a law to guarantee an equal salary between men and women for equivalent work.

Social and economic measures in favor of women are more recent in KSA: in 2018, they were granted the right to drive their car, the right to apply for the Saudi military, and the right to open their businesses without a guardian's permission. Female participation in the workforce is part of the priorities of Vision 2030 of the country, and the target is to reach 30% by 2030 (at 22.3% in 2018 according to the World Bank).

The status of women in the region mainly differs from a country to another. Oman, UAE, and Morocco are leading the way in terms of women's rights. Egypt also has a long history of legislative advances for women's rights whereas KSA has just started to tackle the issue since 2018.

One of the Strongest Performances in Girls' Education in the World

For a few years, boosting girls' education has been the other priority of most Arab countries regarding women, and starts to pay off. From 1974 to 2016, the female alphabetization rate rose from 46% to 89% in the MENA region. The progress in girls' education has been phenomenal and rapid. The alphabetization rate improved drastically in forty years, but women have been granted access to high-quality education and secondary education. And they massively took this right. "In Morocco, the government's Tayssir program offers cash transfers worth about 5% of annual household consumption for families to spend on education. The scheme has been particularly successful in encouraging girls to stay in school and return to school after dropping out. The cash transfer offered to parents resulted in an increase of about 12% in re-enrolment".[4]

Nowadays, in most Arab countries, women account for the majority of university students. It starts early at school, where girls generally outperform their male peers. "In Saudi Arabia ten years ago, about 30% of university-age women attended university. Today, half of them go—a higher proportion than Mexico, China, Brazil, and India."[5] The result is that more than 60% of all Saudi women hold at least a graduate degree.[6] Not only has female literacy and attendance at school risen substantially, but, in some parts of the region, women now exceed men in terms of performance in secondary and post-secondary education. "In Jordan, for example, girls in school do better than boys in nearly all subjects and at every age level, from grade school to university."[7]

Science, technology, engineering, and mathematics (STEM) education for women is a particular success story, setting up women in the Arab world for the "fourth industrial revolution", meaning the digital revolution. "In Brunei and Kuwait, among students enrolled in STEM, women outnumber men […]. Women make up 40% or more of STEM students […] in Tunisia, Qatar, Algeria, Oman, Malaysia, Jordan, Bahrain, Azerbaijan, and the UAE. In Saudi Arabia, 38% of students in those fields are women, and in Iran, 34%. In UK, 36% are women, while in the USA, it's 30%."[8] But despite their success at school and the fact they hold advanced degrees, especially in STEM, Arab women still lay behind men in the job market. "Many of them choose to stay at home, either by choice or by cultural, social, or familial pressures."[9]

Despite These Significant Improvements in Women Rights and Status, the Arab World Scores One of the Lowest Female Labor Force Participation Rate in the World

The Arab world has one of the lowest rates of women labor force participation globally at 20.9% in 2017. "It had only marginally improved from its 19.7% value in 2000. Arab women's participation rate is 3.5 times lower than for men, which stood at 74.1% in 2017. This drags down the region's total labor force participation rate, which, at 49%, is the lowest among world regions and far below the world average of 62%. [...] In Maghreb Arab countries (Morocco, Algeria, and Tunisia), the percentage has even dropped between 1997 and 2007 (minus 21%)."[10]

By country, the female labor force participation rate is remarkably low in KSA at around 20%[11] despite a female literacy rate of 79%. This low percentage can partly be explained by a broad representation of women in the informal economy. Many women run informal businesses and are not included in the statistics. In KSA, "more than 63% of women have unofficial businesses running that are doing quite well. These kinds of businesses rely mainly on word of mouth and personal communication."[12] Egypt also has a low female labor force participation rate at 22%, even if a lot of progress has been made by the legislation to bring women at the forefront of society. Only in the UAE, the percentage has increased dramatically, reaching 40.6% in 2018 from 29.2% in 1990.[13] In the Arab Emirates, women make up 66% of public-sector workers, with 30% in leadership roles."[14]

What is interesting to underline is the gap between the female labor force participation rate at 49% and the men's one at 76% in the region. This is the highest gap globally, alongside South Asia, "though one could note a 12% improvement for Arab States (only 4.5% for North Africa) in 2017 over the 1997 value."[15] This gap is due to heavy social norms and traditional rules that regulate societies and legal and financial barriers that prevent women from entering the workforce. This gap also means that most job opportunities are reserved for men in the Arab world. The 2020 Arab Youth Survey underlines it: "although a majority (52%) of young Arab women cited equal opportunities, more than one-third (35%) said men have better professional opportunities than women." The World Economic Forum even predicts it will take 150 years to close the gender gap in the Middle East and North Africa if the current progress rate continues. Why such a gap?

A Mix of Structural and Contextual Reasons: Heavy Social Norms and High Unemployment Rate Undermine Women's Participation in the Workforce

The social norms in most Arab societies consider the men to be the leading providers for their family. Some of them feel more and more pressure in completing this role in today's economic uncertainty. "For young men in the region, social pressure to realize the "provider" model of manhood is a frequent source of tension. In a region where male employment is often a prerequisite for marriage, unemployment and poverty are often felt as emasculating. And men's unemployment is among one of the highest in the world. In Egypt,[16] economic uncertainty and women's low labor market participation mean that men face tremendous pressure to be providers. Almost 80% of men are the primary breadwinners for their families. More than half of men reported frequently feeling stressed due to lack of work and worried about not being able to meet their family's daily needs. More than 60% of male respondents worried about their ability to provide their families with daily necessities, among other concerns."[17] Therefore, it is understandable that men have mixed views regarding empowering women in the workforce. In a study conducted by UN Women, which analyzes masculinities in the Arab world in four countries (Egypt, Lebanon, Morocco, and Palestine), the results highlight this mix of opinions: "Two-thirds to more than three-quarters of men support the notion that a woman's most important role is to care for the household. Women often internalize these same inequitable views: about half or more women across the four countries support the same idea. [...] In some countries, majorities of women not only affirm but also appear to accept male guardianship; in others, they challenge the idea, in theory if not in practice. [...] Across the countries surveyed, about half of men—or fewer—believed a married woman should have the same right to work as a man. At the same time, a majority of men in all four countries would accept a woman as a boss, and were willing to work in gender-integrated workplaces. Much of this acceptance is theoretical, however; what emerges is that many men in the region support women working outside the home—as long, it seems, as he is still the main breadwinner and she is still the main caregiver and organizer of domestic life."[18] It appears that as long as women continue to take care of the domestic sphere and remain the principal caregiver for the children, men are favorable with women's work outside the home. In general opinion, women can work as long as they also take care of their family and home. In countries like KSA, though, many men are still resistant to the idea of women working outside the house, which partly explains why female labor force participation had changed little since 1990, when it was 21.3%.[19]

Social norms dictate not only the place of women in society and the workforce, but also the choice of an "appropriate" employment. Most of the time, working outside the feminized sectors like teaching or nursing is looked down upon by society. In the UAE, 75% of the workforce is female in the education and health sectors.[20] In general, in the Arab countries, "women are 'encouraged' to seek tertiary education in humanities, education-related specialties, and care."[21] Consequently, depending on the states and their cultural codes, women are more highly represented in some sectors than others. The ILO database,[22] which scans Algeria, Egypt, Kuwait, Morocco, Palestine, SA, Syria, Tunisia, and Yemen, indicates that agriculture employs more women than men in Morocco, Egypt, Yemen, and Syria. In contrast, it is the opposite in Algeria, Tunisia, and KSA. The industry attracts more men than women in all countries scanned, whereas services attract more women in all states except Morocco and Yemen. The industry is therefore not considered as a "feminine" sector, whereas service wins the score, expect in Morocco and Yemen.

Social norms are not the only explanation for the low female workforce participation rate in the Arab world. The high unemployment rate of the region, especially among young people, which has worsened with the Covid crisis, also has negatively impacted the female work participation. In 2020, the World Economic Forum issued edifying figures: the youth unemployment (15 to 24 years old) in the Middle East and North Africa is the highest in the world at 27.2% in the Middle East and 29% in North Africa, which is more than double the global average. Consequently, "nearly half of young Arabs have considered leaving their country and one third are more likely to leave their country due to the pandemic."[23] This extremely tough labor context undermines women to enter the workforce or to keep their job when they have one. Men feel highly challenged, and they consider themselves as the primary resource providers of their family, women need to prove even more that they deserve the jobs.

Despite these structural (social norms) and contextual (high youth unemployment rate) reasons that partly explain the low female workforce participation rate in this part of the world, most Arab countries are aware that women economic and social inclusion will be the engine of economic growth and development. They acknowledge that they can't develop with only one half of their population. To develop thoroughly and soundly, they know that they need to lean on both legs: men and women. The World Bank recently reminded us that we are losing globally $160 trillion in wealth because of the gender gap in earnings, including $3.1 trillion in the MENA region. According to many estimates from international organizations, "improving Arab women labor participation rates could significantly boost Arab countries' GDP from 20 to 40% depending on each country."[24] McKinsey predicted that full gender parity would add 32% to the GCC region's economy by 2025. For the UAE specifically, the International Monetary Fund calculated that closing the gender gap could increase UAE's GDP by 12%. Governments and local institutions in the Arab world agree on these projections and recognize that women represent untapped economic potential. KSA acknowledges that "a large part of Saudi Arabia's wealth is in the hands of its women totaling US$11.9 billion. [...] King Abdullah is focusing on building the required infrastructure and offering greater opportunities for education for the youth and women. The economic status of women is now accepted as an indicator of a society's stage of development. Therefore, it becomes imperative for the government to frame policies for the development of entrepreneurship among women. The long-term objectives of the development programs for women should aim to raise their economic and social status in order to bring them into the mainstream of national life and development. For this, due recognition has to be accorded to the role and contribution of women in the various social, economic, political, and cultural activities."[25] Also, governments of most Arab countries know that increasing the female labor force participation rate could help their economies, especially the GCC ones, to diversify in promising sectors and be less dependent on oil production because "oil-rich countries tend to have undiversified private sectors characterized by male-dominated employment and large public sectors."[26]

To empower women and give them the chance to become a real economic force, Arab governments have emphasized girls' education and implemented strong measures to provide women more social, juridical, and political rights. It is real progress but not enough to completely solve the economic problem of low women's labor force participation. As a result, entrepreneurship is more and more considered a good alternative for women to enter the labor force. And it is boosted by the digital era.

Women's Entrepreneurship

An Opportunity to Enter the Labor Force and to Thrive

The entrepreneurship spirit is relatively high in the Arab world, with 40% of young people wanting to start their own business in the next five years.[27] The highest score goes to the GCC countries with a percentage of 55%. This spirit is also driving women in the region who see entrepreneurship as a way to enter the formal labor force with relative freedom, without much financial capital, and to explore untapped and less male-dominated sectors. It is also an exciting way for them to avoid unemployment, which is as high as 34% in the region. Moreover, governments are supporting women entrepreneurship more and more because they know that the trend can be transformative for the area. Even though the rate of women entrepreneurship is still meager, the trend is encouraging, and the digital sector seems to lead the way.

Despite Low Figures in Female Entrepreneurship, Women-Owned and Led Businesses Stand Out in the Service Sector

According to McKinsey,[28] women-owned businesses in GCC account for ~24%, but only 9% of women are engaged actively in running companies, with ~1.7% in the CEO positions. In the wider MENA region, it is worse. Women in MENA have the lowest rates of Total Entrepreneurial Activity (TEA) a merely 4% of the population. The World Bank Enterprise Survey[29] data are on the same page: less than 23% of enterprises in the Arab world have female participation in ownership compared with almost 35% in the rest of the world. By country, only 1.4% of businesses are women-owned in KSA, while 3.3% in Egypt, 3% in Oman.[30] To explain these low figures, it seems that most Arab countries, mainly North African ones, do not have favorable conditions to develop women entrepreneurship. Based on a women entrepreneurs' survey run in four North African countries—Algeria, Egypt, Morocco, and Tunisia—by the ILO's WED (Women Entrepreneurship Development) framework,[31] it resulted that only Morocco and Egypt presented the six favorable conditions for the development of women's entrepreneurship: gender-sensitive legal and regulatory system, effective policy to promote women entrepreneurship, access to gender-sensitive financial services, access to gender business development services, access to markets and technology, representation of women entrepreneurs and participation to policy dialogue.

But figures are contradictory regarding women entrepreneurship in the Arab region. Many of them show that almost one in three startups in the area is founded by women, a higher percentage than in Silicon Valley! "More than 25% of startups in the Arab world are founded or led by women, compared to 17% in the USA."[32] When they create their own business, women prefer small- and medium-sized service companies employing one or two workers with minimal working capital. "In Oman, over 70% of women-owned businesses are in the service sector, mostly in education and childcare."[33] Women are paying close attention to innovation in their business and many of them are going into the digital and new technology sector because they start at the same level than men. Besides, the digital requires less financial capital and fewer entry barriers. For example, in Jordan, bio-scientist entrepreneur Penelope Shihab created MonoJo in 2005. Her team has filed UK and US patents for products that treat acne and acute digestive infections using camel milk antibodies. Shihab, who won the Ernst &Young's Jordan Emerging Entrepreneur of the Year in 2014, hopes her success will encourage more Jordanian women to consider a career in science. Successful women entrepreneurs want to inspire other women in the region and internationally. According to the Global Entrepreneurship Monitor (GEM) 2017 Women's entrepreneurship report, women entrepreneurs have high innovation levels and are 60% more likely than men to report that their products and services are innovative.

When they haven't created their own business, they sometimes take part in family businesses either by taking a piece of ownership or by managing the family company or both. But they are usually not granted full ownership, only part of it, and rarely hold prominent managerial positions inside the family business. A survey,[34] from ESCA École de Management in Casablanca on twenty Moroccan family-owned listed companies, showed that very few women are members of the family business' board of directors: of 159 members that count the 20 companies, only 10% are women from the family. To be independent and free, many women chose, therefore, to create their own business. We will see further in this article, their inner motivations.

Women Consider the Digital Field as a Tremendous Opportunity for Entrepreneurship, Where Everything is Possible

According to IPSOS She Speaks, a range of studies explicitly targeting women in the MENA region, Middle Eastern women's access to the internet is high, with an overall of 69% of women having access to the internet. "It ranges from 99% of Kuwaiti women down to 54% of those in Morocco. Across the region, 86% of women with internet access use social media. YouTube is the top social media platform, with three-quarters (75%) using it, but all the key social media platforms—Facebook (71%), Instagram (64%) and Snapchat (59%)—are used by a majority."[35]

Beyond only using the internet, women are more and more creating new businesses in the digital field. This field, in line with their successful scores in science, technology, and math education, is seen as untapped, less male-dominated, and more comfortable to access sector. An article from the International Finance Corporation (IFC)[36] says it clearly: "Because the tech industry is still relatively new in the Arab world, there is no legacy of it being a male-dominated field. Many entrepreneurs from the region believe that technology is one of the few spaces where everything is viewed as possible, including breaking gender norms, and is therefore, a very attractive industry for women. [...] Key to these efforts has been their ability to leverage the internet and engage through online platforms to reach new markets and be able to work from home if they wish. As Saadia Zahidi argues in her book *Fifty Million Rising*, these digital platforms allow women to be unimpeded by cultural constraints or safety issues and lowers the implicit and explicit transaction costs of transportation, child care, discrimination, and social censure." Therefore, the digital field seems to be the perfect place to empower women because it requires less capital, allows more flexibility, and allows women entrepreneurs to gather into digital platforms to make their voice heard and conduct business.

More and more Arab women are getting noticed as digital entrepreneurs in the region. Some have built real success stories that are known internationally, like Egypt's Raye7, which is a ride-sharing service created by entrepreneur Samira Negm, solving both traffic congestion in Cairo and safe transport. Women often start their business based on their personal experience and knowledge of the market, in this specific case, a safe women-friendly shared ride. In the case of Sarwa, an award-winning fintech proposing the first automated investment advisory platform in the Middle East founded by Nadine Mezher, this is the need to democratize investment and broaden it to women. The idea of Sarwa is to make investing more accessible to the masses, through minimum investment amounts and extremely low fees. On her side, Algerian-born and Dubai-based Ghizlan Guenez, founder and CEO of The Modist, created the world's first global e-commerce platform where luxury fashion brands are curated for women who dress modestly. "The need to empower women through choice of attire stemmed from Ghizlan's own needs: working fourteen years in private equity, she had to dress conservatively for years, but often struggled to find clothing that was also fashionable and contemporary".[37] In Morocco, Zineb Drissi Kaitouni co-founded in 2014 Dabadoc, the first digital platform on the African continent that eased access to doctors and medical treatments for the whole population. Dabadoc revolutionized health access in Morocco particularly in rural and remote areas. The same year, the Moroccan entrepreneur Niama El Bassunie founded WaystoCap, a B2B marketplace that eases trade in Africa. The platform, that received an award from the Davos forum in 2019, helps importers and exporters to find trading partners on the continent and to secure their transactions. These women entrepreneurs have all created breakthrough digital platforms answering unmet needs and relying on their desires and experiences. They have gone into digital not only because it allows them to reach a large consumer base but also because it offers many advantages for them as women entrepreneurs like working freely while staying in line with social norms and taking care of their families. In a survey conducted in 2016 in KSA on 200 Saudi women entrepreneurs, "it was understood that the reasons to start a business was to be an independent person, to get recognition in the society, to build a successful organization, to have innovativeness and to continue the family traditions."[38]

One of the main advantages of the digital field for women is its low entry barriers. No substantial financial capital is required. Women can get quick and reliable marketing information and start to sell their products and services without having to buy a store or rent expensive offices. Women can work from home with flexible hours to take care of their families. A study conducted by Accenture showed nearly 60% of women who are not currently employed believe that flexible hours and working from home, full or part-time, would help them find work, which digital technology can enable. Moreover, the digital reduces transaction costs, makes prices more transparent, improved competition, and facilitates learning of best practices. Indeed, digital platforms, often created by women entrepreneurs for women, allow to share content, and good practices in a virtual place where women share business information, identify new opportunities for their products or services, and solve new types of problems. These platforms represent stimulating environments and essential support for women who can naturally enhance their potential for innovation and entrepreneurship. These platforms are also the place where the private and public sectors meet. This is key for women entrepreneurs who can therefore have access to business opportunities from governments: "public procurement contracts when associated with policies targeting women's entrepreneurship particularly in the domain of ICT can be an essential tool for the development of women-led SMEs. They also allow linkages with large foreign and domestic enterprises as suppliers and subcontractors or distributors. Linkage with digital platforms plays a central role in allowing women-led enterprises integrate into these global supply chains."[39]

What are the Key Drivers that Push Women to Create Their Businesses?

In the Arab world, like anywhere else in the world, women entrepreneurs are pushed by a desire to fulfill professionally, to get financial independence, and to achieve something great. Some researchers differentiate the push and pull factors that drive women when they are about to create their own business. "The push factors such as a desire for 'self-fulfillment', 'achievement' and 'market opportunity' have embedded the vision in Saudi women to become entrepreneurs."[40]

The difference with other regions lies in the fact that female entrepreneurs are also driven by "pull factors" when starting a business in the Arab world. These factors can come from governments or partnerships, but most of the time from their own family. They help women to get a foot on the ladder. As seen before in this chapter, most women who have difficulties in getting financial credits, often ask the help of their family. Therefore, entrepreneurship in the Arab world is very often family entrepreneurship. "In the Middle East and Africa, more than three-fourths of entrepreneurs involve the family in the high-TEA (Total Entrepreneurial Activity) economies of Angola, Lebanon, and Sudan."[41] This is also true in Morocco where entrepreneurship and family entrepreneurship are tightly linked. In a research conducted by ESCA École de Management in Casablanca on the place of women in Moroccan family businesses,[42] women members of the family holding top positions in the family business are often driven by a strong entrepreneurial spirit when they take over. They act as entrepreneurs inside the company by developing, internationalizing, or diversifying it. Khalida Azbane for example, who took over Laboratoires Azabane from her founding father has worked on the internationalization of the famous cosmetic company. Sothema, a leading Moroccan pharmaceutical laboratory, opened several laboratories in Sub-Saharan Africa since Lamia Tazi, the daughter of the founder, took over. Zhor Kabbaj who leads Soft Group, one of the biggest real estate and textile Moroccan holdings, with her father Mohamed Kabbaj and her brothers, has diversified the activities of the family holding in business real estate.

As for Saudi women entrepreneurs, they often "take advantage of their families' strong position in the society. Such families' financial and moral support facilitated their businesses with regard to, for example, funding, licensing, and other business requirements. Other types of Saudi women entrepreneurs take advantage of their families' moral support. These families provide advice and encouragement that help Saudi women entrepreneurs to establish and succeed in their businesses."[43]

Since recent years, the Arab world has experienced a wave of entrepreneurship, illustrating the energy and vitality of most countries in the region. Women are increasingly taking part in this positive momentum by undertaking new ventures mostly in the digital field, considered more accessible and more flexible. Some women in the region have built real entrepreneurial success stories, inspiring other women to pursue their actions to achieve their dreams. Regarding social entrepreneurship, the field is still not fully developed in the Arab world, and women don't wholly involve in it for now.

Social Entrepreneurship for Women

A Potential That Still Remains Untapped

If women are more and more present in the entrepreneurship field in the Arab world, how about social entrepreneurship? Does it also attract women?

First of all, it is essential to recall that healthy economies need both social and business entrepreneurship. Social entrepreneurship improves the lives of many persons, tackles important social challenges, and is often ruled by business principles to succeed on a large scale. It fills gaps in emergent economies and answers critical needs of a substantial portion of the population. But for now, the field remains relatively unknown and untapped in the Arab world, making it difficult for women to enter it.

What matters for social entrepreneurs is a positive return to society thanks to broad social, cultural, and environmental goals. They work for the good of society, the environment, cohesion, and integration. Social entrepreneurship is often seen as an alternative social solution when governments or public organizations can't implement them. On a global level, social entrepreneurship has attracted enormous attention from various sectors and decision-makers in society. It is considered a promising mechanism for alleviating poverty, inequality, environmental degradation, and other societal problems. In the Arab world, social entrepreneurship is gaining attraction but is still very new. In particular, gathering reliable data on it is a real challenge. Nevertheless, an index has recently been developed to measure the social innovation's progress per country in the world. "The Regional Social Innovation Index (RESINDEX) was developed as a research project by SINNERGIAK Social Innovation (UPV/EHU). […] The social innovation index 2016 included 45 countries assessed across four pillars, namely policy and institutional framework, financing, civil society and entrepreneurship. The United States of America scored the highest in 2016, while South Korea (12th overall) was the leader in the Asia-Pacific region. From the Arab region the 2016 assessment included only Saudi Arabia with an overall ranking of 43. The country was ranked low in three of the pillars, namely policy and institutional framework (45), financing (41) and civil society (29). However, it was ranked 7th in its entrepreneurship potential."[44]

A Relatively Unknown Field Preempted by International Organizations and Donors

What is missing in the Arab world is a clear view of what type of value brings social entrepreneurship. The governments and populations don't grasp the added value this field can bring to countries' economies. As it is often linked with voluntary work or social responsibility, it gets almost unnoticed. However, it addresses key challenges that the region has to face, "including service delivery gaps, increasingly vulnerable social services, environmental degradation, and a restless younger generation. The growth in service demand often outstrips the government's financial and technical capacity to keep up or address these issues, and markets for them are often neither conducive to entrepreneurship nor profitable enough for traditional private sector players. Social entrepreneurs can address these problems by developing business models that solve these challenges, such as by developing skills for low-income youth, providing jobs platforms for refugees, recovering and recycling waste, increasing access to last-mile health services, and improving smallholder productivity through ICT."[45] But social entrepreneurs in the region find it hard to attract investors who are mainly interested in financial returns. Moreover, many of them have difficulties in dealing with the governments that don't consider them. In KSA, for example, "most social enterprises in the region are legally registered as non-profit organizations. Social entrepreneurs find themselves struggling with restrictive regulatory environments and bureaucratic procedures that often limit their ability to become sustainable or to scale up (Abdou et al., 2012)."[46]

However, the Arab world governments would highly benefit from encouraging the growth of social entrepreneurship. "On the regulatory side, recognition of social enterprises as a business type can help provide awareness, targeted assistance, and tax incentives that will ease an enterprise's growth. Public financing to support the growth of social enterprises and hence their social impact could also be provided through grants. For more advanced social enterprises, financing could be provided through public–private partnerships, social procurement preferences (by including the social impact of an enterprise as part of the selection criteria in addition to economic cost), or, as has been done more recently, social impact bonds (as is currently being developed in the West Bank and Gaza on job creation for youth). Governments can also provide legal frameworks and vehicles to impact investors and philanthropists that will incentivize them to invest in social entrepreneurs. The last few years have seen an increase in the number of non-governmental organizations trying to address societal challenges that governments have not been able to resolve. However, because of the absence of impact investors, these initiatives have been funded mostly by donors. This is a less sustainable model, and it has not been able to introduce many social enterprises to the ecosystem."[47]

The good news is that a new generation of young educated entrepreneurs in the region is increasingly interested in social entrepreneurship. "For now, Arab social entrepreneurs are overwhelmingly young, ambitious, and male, with over 70% of those interviewed under the age of 35 and only 28% female. It is striking that all have tertiary degrees (with 72% master and 9% doctorate).[48] This new type of entrepreneurs has different goals from older ones. They don't merely seek to innovate or make money but want to achieve a lasting impact on their businesses and the communities. Therefore, social entrepreneurship in the Arab world has been slowly growing in the past few years, even if it remains a new concept that people and even governments are still grasping.

A Field Led by the Success of Some Women-Led Digital Platforms with Massive Social Impact

Even if women are still underrepresented in the Arab social entrepreneurs' area, they gather on digital platforms to be more powerful, make their voice heard, and get high social impact. These platforms operate mainly in the health, transportation, or environmental sectors, sectors with which female entrepreneurs often feel familiar. Women social entrepreneurs offer female perspectives on familial, social problems they have faced or currently face. Some platforms are catching on the "women's market". Mumm foods in Egypt, for example, "is connecting skilled female cooks with thousands who want healthy, home-cooked meals delivered to their offices. Careem in Saudi Arabia has been training a new cohort of women drivers before the law authorizing women to drive in summer 2018. The gig economy is a new path to flexible, more secure livelihoods for women [...] unlike in the West where it is often synonymous with precarious work."[49] Other social entrepreneurial platforms focus on improving the health of populations who usually don't have easy nor cheap access to it. Proximie in Lebanon, for example, uses augmented reality to connect surgeons in developed countries with those operating under poorer conditions. It eases connections and knowledge transfer between two worlds, and the device is designed by doctors for doctors. Co-founded by surgeon Dr. Nadine Hachach-Haram, Proximie allows doctors to transport themselves virtually into any operating room anywhere in the world to visually and practically interact in an operation from start to finish. Another example in the health field is Affectiva founded by Egyptian entrepreneur Rana El Kaliouby. Thanks to a cutting-edge artificial intelligence technology she has developed, Rana El Kaliouby helps computers recognize human emotions based upon physiological responses and facial cues. "Nabbesh, the first Middle East's first freelance marketplace founded by Loulou Khazen Baz, helps on its side to tackle the region's youth unemployment challenge and was recognized as one the World Economic Forum's 100 Arab Startups Shaping the Fourth Industrial Revolution."[50] In Morocco, social entrepreneurship meets fashion with Amaz, an ethical handcrafted Moroccan sneakers brand with a social purpose, founded by Fadela Bennani. Fadela wants to "value the ancestral know-how of Moroccan craftsmen and contribute to improving access to education for girls in the landlocked regions of Morocco". At Amaz, one pair of sneakers bought is equivalent to one school day for a girl, because for Fadela, who partners with the NGO Education for All, "to educate a girl is to educate a whole nation", as a Senegalese proverb says. Another Moroccan, Aya Laraki founded Cuimer, a startup specialized in the transformation of fish skins into fine leather goods, thanks to an advanced technological know-how. Cuimer received the Women's prize of the Orange Social Venture Prize in Africa and the

Middle East (POESAM). Even in KSA, Saudi Women social entrepreneurs "have also led a number of pioneering efforts, especially in the health and environment. A number of women were working on creating awareness of women's health issue a holistic lifestyle services and affordable programs which satisfy the requirements of the full spectrum of women's health issues and the ways that science and technology be used to keep people healthy. They also offer online awareness campaigns tackling environmental issues such as preserving the environment and encouraging and assisting businesses to go green."[51]

Governments are aware that they should promote social entrepreneurship and, among it, women's social entrepreneurship. In KSA, "embedding social entrepreneurship within entrepreneurship education activities in schools, universities, vocational education and training and in non-formal education or across a number of disciplines and subjects, helping students develop the necessary skills to succeed in both business and social sphere are ways to foster social entrepreneurship. Both public and private agencies should promote and support the startup social enterprises in overcoming challenges along with finance, support services and regulatory frameworks to motivate the youth and emerging women social entrepreneurs to continue their various social programs and projects sustainably. There is a need for government and private sectors to collaborate towards strengthening the entire ecosystem for social entrepreneurship considering the challenges faced, for example, by Saudi women in starting and scaling their social enterprise activities and implementation. The government, educators, and corporate private organizations should consider reckoning and implementing the strategic measures identified by the study to foster and sustain the social entrepreneurship ventures of various enterprises on a sustainable basis."[52]

As a result, social entrepreneurship is currently mostly a male and young field gathering a handful of passionate entrepreneurs with social and long-term view for their countries. But women, digitally, are starting to invest in the area that naturally fits their skills and knowledge. Of course, entering a new field, be it social entrepreneurship or entrepreneurship, is not an easy task, especially for women who need to overcome many challenges.

Women Entrepreneurs Still Face Heavy and Various Challenges

Even though more and more women are getting noticed and succeed as entrepreneurs in the Arab world, most of them, and even the most successful ones, face multiple challenges to start their business and make it grow. Barriers are numerous, be they external, like social, economic, and legal barriers or internal, like psychological, that women sometimes put on themselves.

Social barriers are the most common in the Arab world and prevent many women from thriving professionally. Traditionally, society expects women to be devoted primarily to their families and children. Their dedication to the domestic sphere gives them less time to prepare for a job, less access to professional resources and information and less access to economic and market knowledge. It nevertheless differs by country, by age, and by the type of education girls received. The younger women are, and the more they have been educated in an equally gendered environment, the more they believe in gender equality and the more likely they are to thrive in their professional lives. From the women's point of view, "women with more education, with more educated mothers, and whose fathers carried out more traditionally feminine tasks in their childhood homes were generally more likely to have equitable views. And younger women in every country held more equitable views than their older counterparts. The result is that younger women in the region are yearning for more equality, but their male peers fail to share or support such aspirations."[53] The masculine role model in the family, be it the father, brothers, or cousins—remains a crucial factor of women's empowerment in the region. "Having fathers who encouraged daughters to take on non-traditional professions or to work outside the home, or who allowed daughters to choose their husbands, seems to contribute to the emergence of more empowered women. In some countries, among men, having more equitable and involved fathers or life circumstances that forced men to take on new household roles were the drivers of more equitable attitudes and practices."[54]

In most Arab cultures, a male member of the family acts as a guardian for women, and all the more for women who want to start their own business. The World Bank Gender Innovation Lab has found that male support networks and role models play a crucial role in encouraging female business owners to switch into higher-paying, male-dominated sectors.[55] In the ESCA École de Management's research on the place of women in Moroccan family businesses,[56] most of the thirty women interviewed recognize that they are expecting the male members of their family, fathers especially, to be guides and mentors for both operational and strategical decisions in the family business. Women particularly appreciate their moral and hands-on support at the beginning of the business transmission, when they took over from their father or brother or cousin. After a while, they appreciate making their own decisions for the business. In KSA, the law requires that women have a male guardian, "typically a father, brother or husband (a mahram). Girls and women are forbidden from traveling, conducting official business, or undergoing certain medical procedures without permission from their male guardian (Arabian Gazette 2013). In addition, women continue to encounter a Wakeel (legal male representative) requirement when starting their businesses, as the enforcement of its removal is not consistent. Secondly, there is a legal requirement for a 'Mudeer' (male manager) for a public-facing business. Despite its official repeal, many women are still required to appoint a male manager."[57] Saudi women entrepreneurs know that if they want to reach their professional goals, they need to partner financially with an investor, preferably a man from their family. The male partner helps "in sharing the business responsibility and in carrying on the business registration procedures at government departments."[58]

Besides social barriers, limited access to financial credit undermines women's entrepreneurship in the region. This access is often limited by restrictive laws that prevent women from opening a bank account or owning property. In MENA, only 38% of women have a bank account versus 57% of men.[59] Women entrepreneurs in the Arab world think that "on average, female-led startups receive 23% less money than male-run firms and are 30% less likely to have a positive exit according to the OECD."[60] As a result, women entrepreneurs, and even male entrepreneurs sometimes, have no choice but to ask for financial help from their families or friends. It is even worse when entrepreneurs start businesses in the social entrepreneurship field because "social enterprises exist in the space between traditional, grant-funded non-profits and profit-maximizing businesses. They may have access to the funding options of both, but without the clearly defined methods and access of either. Besides, many social entrepreneurs rely on funding from international donors and note the difficulty of procuring funds for their core operations and actions from these presenters. Because funding tends to focus on short-term project financing, the sector's ability to engage in long-term planning, develop self-sufficiency, and achieve larger impact is limited. Access to other sources of financing, such as repayable commercial loans from banks, remains a limited option for non-profit social enterprises. Social entrepreneurs that eventually become self-sustaining may never afford enough of a financial return to attract traditional backers or investors."[61] Consequently, getting credit is a huge challenge for entrepreneurs in the region. Despite the entrepreneurial dynamism in the Arab world, early-stage funding remains problematic for entrepreneurs except in the UAE, Jordan, Lebanon and, to a lesser extent, due to their respective economic and demographic weight, Saudi Arabia and Egypt. "There is a heavier emphasis on funding high-tech entrepreneurial ventures in Egypt and less interest in sectors such as manufacturing and agriculture. Similarly, financing in the region tends to focus on supporting technology firms, specifically in the areas of information and communications."[62] Another factor to consider is that the entrepreneur who starts a business is not sufficiently protected by countries' laws, whether a man or a woman. The United Nations underlines that, according to the Doing Business Index of the World Bank, "resolving insolvency is particularly critical for innovative startups and act as a strong deterrent: an indebted entrepreneur falling into an insolvency situation might simply end up in prison in most Arab countries. [...] Starting a business is good only in Oman, Morocco, and Mauritania and the regional leader, the United Arab Emirates; notable, there are also good levels of protection of minority investors in the United Arab Emirates and Saudi Arabia."[63]

It seems that even if there is a spirit of entrepreneurship and a real economic dynamism that drives new and innovative ideas of businesses in the Arab world, the culture of entrepreneurship is not yet fully ready.

In this context, women are all the more penalized. The United Nations proposed a list of recommendations to free female entrepreneurship in the region like "raise women's awareness about property and inheritance rights particularly in rural areas; provide incentives to growth-potential women-owned enterprises to move their business to the formal economy, such as tax exemptions, access to export markets, access to public procurement, access to better financial and non-financial services; sensitize women engaged in informal economy about the advantages of moving to the formal and introduce specific encouragement measures for formalization of women-owned enterprises; increase awareness of women employers about employment rights, labour laws, compliance requirements, and business registration through seminars in the urban and rural areas and developing online business registration portals to increase the number of business registrations and provide women entrepreneurs with training on their use; systematically tackle credit constraints that impede women in their attempts to start and grow a business; enhance access to markets, networks and technologies for different types of women entrepreneurs; support women's voices in policy dialogue and strengthen the mainstreaming of gender issues into policies and programs."[64]

The External Barriers are Only One Side of the Medal. On the Other Side and as a Consequence of a Long History of Restrictions, Some Women in the Arab World Also Face Internal Barriers

Due to the numerous restrictions and barriers they have had to face for decades, women seem to have less self-confidence and be more risk-averse in the Arab world than in other parts of the world. Again, the phenomenon depends on the countries and is particularly acute in KSA, where "more than half of women believe the biggest hindrance in their careers is the widespread belief that they do not have the right skills for the available job opportunities."[65] This lack of self-confidence is expressed through different signs like hesitancy in decision making, avoidance of commitment, intense fear of judgment and failure, or risk adversity. Even if more and more women are educated, and most of them benefit from a wide range of enabling qualities such as courage, determination, and will, they feel underqualified to start a business independently.

"While the women entrepreneurs display a lot of courage in following their chosen career path, they are often hesitant or averse to assuming tangible risks, such as leaving the security and social status of their government sector jobs or seeking external funding to support their businesses. The women entrepreneurs also suffer from a lack of self-reliance, self-sufficiency, and personal initiative. Restrictions imposed upon them at the societal level are often internalized to such an extent that they become complacent, if not complicit, in their lack of autonomy, with significant repercussions for their sense of self-esteem. [...] They also have a powerful fear of judgment and failure, which they must overcome if they are to succeed as entrepreneurs."[66] These internal barriers, particularly experienced by Saudi women, are a relatively unknown phenomenon but represent an obstacle significant enough to be underlined, as it holds women back from achieving their full potential.

Governments, Private Companies, and NGOs have Taken These Barriers into Account and are Starting to Create More Enabling Environments for Women Entrepreneurship

According to Price Waterhouse Coopers, "there is growing evidence in countries such as KSA, UAE, and Egypt that the gender-equality agenda is progressing, despite challenges including lack of support after a career break, deep-seated social norms, and gender stereotypes and bias."[67] Indeed, governments and NGOs have undertaken essential initiatives in the region in favor of women's empowerment because they understood that women could open new ways of development while respecting traditions and social norms. Tapping into the women's workforce is, among others, an opportunity to accelerate some Arab countries' industrial diversification away from oil and gas and to enter the digital era with confidence. According to the research "The power of parity" in Africa conducted by McKinsey, "beyond school, there is a pressing imperative to raise women's skills to equip them not only for the kind of jobs available in Africa's economies today but also for the jobs of the future as Africa increasingly digitizes and ultimately embraces automation technologies. Capability and skills training that have women in mind have been proven to enable them to thrive in the workplace. Given the large proportion of women in informal employment, it is critical that future skills programs are designed with this target group in mind."[68] This is also true for MENA countries where business training and soft skills training programs should be set up to make the most of women's economic power.

MENA countries and especially the GCC ones have already started to foster women entrepreneurship through operational and hands-on initiatives like setting up networking platforms to allow women to learn from each other; setting up women entrepreneurship funds to ease access to credit; enhance women's capabilities with skill training; offer formal mentorship and sponsorship programs to train and help women scaling up their businesses. For instance, the Saudi government has reserved 75% of its jobs for women, while in Oman, women entrepreneurs receive funding, education, and entrepreneurship training from the government. As for the UAE, the country offers worldwide connected platforms for women entrepreneurs to scale up their businesses. Some of the platforms, through local partnerships such as the International Trade Center's (ITC) SheTrades initiative, provide unique networks to connect to global markets, address trade barriers, and create worldwide opportunities. Through an interconnected ecosystem of tailored business solutions and knowledge-sharing, SheTrades supports and empowers female entrepreneurs to realize their fullest potential by connecting women buyers and suppliers across regions and offering training workshops on logistics concepts and best practices for global trade. In Lebanon, the IFC (International Finance Corporation) works with the private sector to expand access to capital and provide training for women entrepreneurs in areas like business management and leadership. Finally, in Morocco, credit services company Wafasalaf has implemented a formal sponsorship program linking women and senior individuals outside the organization.

To overcome the massive barriers that still hinder women entrepreneurship in the Arab world, governments, private companies, and NGOs are all together helping women with very concrete measures going from training programs to digital platforms and funding facilities. But the

Covid crisis, which struck the world in spring 2020, wiping out thousands of startups all over the world and in the Arab countries, has changed the paradigm in terms of women entrepreneurship. What are women entrepreneurs expecting for the post-Covid era? What are their dreams and aspirations?

The Covid Crisis has Brought New Forms of Female Leadership in the Arab World

Women have had increasing work and family responsibilities since the Covid crisis in 2020. According to the 2020 Arab Youth Survey "A voice for change", they "have been called upon to find work to bring additional income to their households and to take additional family responsibilities [...] More than half (54%) of young Arabs said women are more likely to look for a job and 67% said women are more likely to have family responsibilities". Since the pandemic, Arab women are particularly under pressure to keep up with their domestic responsibilities while looking for or keeping a job. In June 2020, the OECD issued a report stating that the Covid crisis will have significant repercussions for women of the MENA region, which "has the second-largest gender gap in unpaid care and domestic work worldwide. On average, women spend six times more on unpaid care and domestic work compared to men. [...] MENA women allocate 89% of their working day to unpaid care work, leaving them barely any time to work for pay, compared to 20% for their male counterparts."[69]

With unemployment rising since the pandemic, the regional job market is even more challenging for women, and women-led businesses have been especially stricken by the crisis. "Half of the women-led enterprises in the Euro-Mediterranean region have had to suspend all activity. The most vulnerable and marginalized populations—among which women—are always the most impacted. Due to the pandemic, women have had less access to financial capital, becoming sometimes impossible for them to rebuild their businesses."[70] Decision-makers in the region know that by putting women at the heart of their response to the pandemic, they will see a leap in progress. They know that it has never been so critical and urgent to invest in women and create a gender-equal business ecosystem. In Morocco, the AFEM[71] president, Leila Doukali highlighted that Moroccan women entrepreneurs have been particularly hit by the pandemic, their access to financial capital has dropped and many of them are currently on the verge of bankruptcy. The association launched the "Ensemble contre le Covid" platform to advice and inform Moroccan female entrepreneurs in times of crisis. In addition, the EBRD[72] also launched its online training platform in Morocco to help women entrepreneurs recover from the crisis and prepare the post-Covid era. Even young people consider that "supporting and reporting greater gender equality in access to education and the labor market"[73] is vital to overcome the unprecedented uncertainty brought by the Covid crisis.

On their side, women need, more than ever, mentoring and partnering with men and other successful businesswomen. They need feminine role models to inspire and guide them on an operational level. They also need to gather to be stronger together, leading to new forms of female leadership on a national and regional basis.

Women Need to Build Up More Women-Led Ecosystems

As a minority, women know that they are stronger when they unite. They need to create real ecosystems in which mentoring and partnering are key. More than ever, the Covid crisis has reinforced their need to be connected. Connected to other women but also their families. We've seen that families play a significant part in financing women-founded businesses. In today's uncertainty, they need to rely on the help and trust provided by the family to achieve their goal and success. "They realized the important role of their families in their businesses. They strategically involve them from the early stages through seeking advice and guidance from them. This family involvement strategy has made the family take part in the business providing support and care to ensure the success and growth of the business."[74]

They need to be united and create women-led ecosystems in which women hire other women and venture capitalists are women. It is commonly known that women venture capitalists are looking to invest as a priority in other women-owned businesses and that women-led companies hire more women. This is a virtuous circle. According to the World Bank, female-owned companies hire more women (25%) than their male counterparts (22%). Moreover, female-owned firms employ a higher percentage of women in managerial roles, helping them to climb up the ladder and break the glass ceiling. Finally, women-led businesses are hiring more workers in general. "In Jordan, Palestine, Saudi Arabia, and Egypt, firms run by women are growing their workforces at higher rates than those run by men."[75] Womena, an award-winning female-led investment group based in Dubai and co-founded by Elissa Freiha, facilitates tech companies' funding. At Womena, they believe that to have more women tech entrepreneurs, networks of women that support one another to grow and thrive, need to be built. They also believe that investing time, energy, money into female entrepreneurs will pay huge dividends. Its co-founder Elissa Freiha says: "women from the Arab World need to fight—the struggles they face in society, in their communities, and sometimes even their families, create an amazing resilience that makes these women incredible entrepreneurs. And if given the right platform, these women can become the business owners and leaders for the future of the region."[76]

To stay connected and act stronger together, women need to have support from their environment and culture. The media play a role in shaping mentalities and motivating women, especially in rural areas. For example, the NISAA Radio, founded by Maysoun Odeh Gangat in Palestine, empowers women's voices through debating, challenging traditional roles assigned to women, and presenting women as capable and assertive actors in society. NISAA, which means "women" in Arabic, has three radio frequencies across the Palestinian Territories and is listened by both women and men who actively participate in the conversation. NISAA empowers women by giving them a platform that entertains, informs, inspires and, most importantly, allows them to define their success, especially by helping one another, standing together, and never giving up even when all odds stand in their way. At last, women need physical places to gather and work in teams. Digital platforms already play this role, but physical spaces like co-working spaces must exist to offer women a chance to physically gather. "In most countries, there are now clusters of startups, brought together by co-working spaces like Astrolabs in Dubai or Cogite in Tunisia, which have connections to accelerators, incubators, and investors. Collaboration is common. Last month the Greek Campus, a hub for startups in downtown Cairo, hosted the Rise-Up summit, one of the largest gatherings of entrepreneurs in the region."[77]

Women Need to Act to Find Shared Innovation Solutions on a Regional Basis

Since the Covid crisis, women have realized that they need to find shared solutions for the Arab world. They already knew the importance of gathering nationally, but they need to act more broadly on a regional basis. They need to join forces regionally to empower themselves and make their voice heard even stronger. 2020 was the year of the Covid crisis but also the 25th anniversary of the Barcelona Process, which laid the foundations for the creation of the UFM (Union for Mediterranean), which acts at a regional level for women's empowerment in the Arab countries. In 2020, the UFM adopted a regional intergovernmental follow-up mechanism on gender balance to raise awareness on gender equality challenges, to monitor the progress made on women's rights, and to work collectively to accelerate women's full participation in the Arab region.

Also, regional initiatives in the Arab world are flourishing to empower women of the region. For example, the 30% Club, set up in UK in 2010, is now active in several countries with a GCC branch. It gathers chairs and CEOs taking action to increase gender diversity at board and senior management levels. Some of their key initiatives include "cross-company and cross-sector mentoring programs, offering women twelve months' experience on a major board to expand the pipeline of people with board experience, and partnering with leading business schools to offer scholarships to women for MBA and other Master's programs. There is also a place for presenting strong role models to inspire everyone."[78]

Similarly, CEED, which helps and grows communities of entrepreneurs in emerging countries, launched in the middle of the Covid crisis the CEED-Grow program Women's Edition, a women-entrepreneur focused capacity-building program in Morocco and Tunisia under the brand WE Inspire. "The overall objective of WE Inspire is to enhance the leadership, management and entrepreneurial skills of existing small and medium-sized businesses led by women, to allow them to create jobs and positively contribute to their nation. With CEED's cross border model, we committed to offering the opportunity to entrepreneurs from Tunisia and Morocco to network with like-minded entrepreneurs from the various countries to learn about different ways to overcome challenges while learning about various business opportunities internationally."[79] Gathering and acting at a regional level provides essential leverage for women, particularly in times of crisis. Indeed, the challenges are greater, and the unprecedented economic context has led many entrepreneurs to bankruptcy while others are fighting all the more to enter the workforce. The different regional initiatives, that women have put in place, show us that they realized the emergency to join forces and work inclusively beyond national barriers and gender considerations to build new solutions for the Arab region.

At last, in the longer run, we can expect that the Covid crisis could be an opportunity for governments to implement working condition reforms. In particular, they may regulate flexible working conditions since flexible work is gaining popularity all around the world, especially for women. The crisis could also be the opportunity to support the start-ups financially, and to open up more frankly the private sector to women. Indeed, the coming years will require both the public and private sectors to help women to recover from the impact of the pandemic.

Conclusion

The gender equality agenda is progressing in the Arab world. It is a crucial concern that Arab governments address for a few years with impactful political, legal, and social reforms and measures. Despite heavy social codes that still hinder women's empowerment in the region, populations are also shifting towards more equitable views, especially since the Covid crisis, which brought a global understanding that women represent inescapable social, economic, and political contributors to the development of Arab countries. They are a force for good for the whole region.

Even if women still struggle to enter the workforce in the Arab world and have to overcome massive and various challenges, more women start their businesses, break down gender barriers and push through the glass ceiling. These pioneers pave the way forward, become inspiring models for other Arab women and make them think that nothing is impossible in the Arab world. Specifically, the digital field into which women have dived opens up incredible opportunities for female entrepreneurs in the region who succeeded in making it a real tool for women's empowerment.

The Covid crisis brought unprecedented economic difficulties and hit women-led businesses in the region particularly. It has nevertheless surged the use of digital platforms, which will undoubtedly continue to empower women all the more with the economic difficulties. It has also been a catalyst for women who are leading in a more inclusive and borderless way. New forms of female leadership appear in which women have understood that this unprecedented crisis requires them to gather to be stronger, act more inclusively and on a larger scale, at a regional, even sometimes worldwide, level.

Notes

1. UN Women, 2017, *Understanding masculinities*, results from the international men and gender equality survey Middle East and North Africa: Egypt, Lebanon, Morocco and Palestine.
2. World Trade Press, OMAN, *Women in Culture, Business and Travel.*
3. Price Waterhouse Coopers, April 2019, *Women in Work Index, Insights from Middle East and North Africa.*
4. Benhassine N, and al., 2013, *Turning a shove into a nudge? A "labeled cash transfer" for education*, NBER working paper number 19227.
5. World Economic Forum, 2018, Article *Working Muslim women are a trillion-dollar market.*
6. Dr Vijaya, G.S., Dr Almasri R., 2016, *A study of women entrepreneurship in Saudi Arabia*, International Journal of Advanced Engineering, Management and Science, vol. 2, Issue 12.

7. International Finance Corporation (IFC), 2018, *Start-Ups in the Arab World: One Woman at a Time.*
8. World Economic Forum, 2018, Article *Working Muslim women are a trillion-dollar market.*
9. International Finance Corporation (IFC), 2018, *Start-Ups in the Arab World: One Woman at a Time.*
10. United Nations, Economic and Social Commission for Western Asia (ESCWA), 2019, *Innovation and Entrepreneurship: Opportunities and challenges for Arab youth and women.*
11. McKinsey, 2018, *Women entrepreneurship in GCC.*
12. Dr Vijaya, G.S., Dr Almasri R., 2016, *A study of women entrepreneurship in Saudi Arabia*, International Journal of Advanced Engineering, Management and Science, vol. 2, Issue 12.
13. https://data.worldbank.org/indicator/SL.TLF.CACT.FE.NE.ZS.
14. https://gulfnews.com/uae/government/big-boost-to-gender-parity-as-cabinet-passes-equal-pay-law-1.2203383.
15. United Nations, Economic and Social Commission for Western Asia (ESCWA), 2019, *Innovation and Entrepreneurship: Opportunities and challenges for Arab youth and women.*
16. 1380 men and 1402 women, aged 18 to 59, from five governorates across Egypt, were surveyed. Just under half of the respondents live in urban areas.
17. United Nations Development Programme (UNDP) and Regional Bureau for Arab States (RBAS), 2016, *Arab Human Development Report: Youth and the Prospects for Human Development in a Changing Reality.*
18. UN Women, 2017, *Understanding masculinities*, results from the international men and gender equality survey Middle East and North Africa: Egypt, Lebanon, Morocco and Palestine.
19. https://data.worldbank.org/indicator/SL.TLF.CACT.FE.NE.ZS.
20. https://gulfnews.com/uae/government/big-boost-to-gender-parity-as-cabinet-passes-equal-pay-law-1.2203383.
21. United Nations, Economic and Social Commission for Western Asia (ESCWA), 2019, *Innovation and Entrepreneurship: Opportunities and challenges for Arab youth and women.*
22. ILO stat database, August 2018, https://www.ilo.int/ilostat.
23. The Arab Youth Survey, 2020, *A voice for change.*

24. United Nations, Economic and Social Commission for Western Asia (ESCWA), 2019, *Innovation and Entrepreneurship: Opportunities and challenges for Arab youth and women.*
25. Nieva F.O., 2015, *Social women entrepreneurship in the Kingdom of Saudi Arabia*, Journal of Global Entrepreneurship Research.
26. Salama H., 2020, *Women entrepreneurship in MENA: An analysis*, EcoMena.
27. The Arab Youth Survey, 2020, *A voice for change.*
28. McKinsey, 2018, *Women entrepreneurship in GCC.*
29. World Bank Enterprise Survey data available at http://www.enterprisesurveys.org/data/exploretopics/gender.
30. Gulfnews, Condamine J.F., 2020, *Middle East women entrepreneurs will get their dues.*
31. UNESCWA, compiled for ILO, 2016.
32. The World Bank Group, 2018, *The Arab World competitiveness report*, p. 75.
33. World Trade Press, OMAN, *Women in Culture, Business and Travel.*
34. Analysis done by Thami Ghorfi and Dr. Amine Mounir from ESCA École de Management, on a panel of 20 listed and family-owned Moroccan companies.
35. IPSOS "She Speaks", 2016, *10 things you need to know about women in MENA.*
36. International Finance Corporation (IFC), 2018, *Start-Ups in the Arab World: One Woman at a Time.*
37. https://whenwomenwinpodcast.com/purpose-execution-and-building-a-successful-business-ghizlan-guenez/.
38. Dr Vijaya, G.S., Dr Almasri, R., 2016, *A study of women entrepreneurship in Saudi Arabia*, International Journal of Advanced Engineering, Management and Science, vol. 2, Issue 12.
39. United Nations, Economic and Social Commission for Western Asia (ESCWA), 2019, *Innovation and Entrepreneurship: Opportunities and challenges for Arab youth and women.*
40. Lincoln University New Zealand, Fallatah, H., 2012, Thesis *Women Entrepreneurs in Saudi Arabia: Investigating strategies used by successful Saudi women entrepreneurs.*
41. Tharawat Magazine, William B. Gartner and Matthew Allen, 2020, *Entrepreneurship across the world is family entrepreneurship.*

42. Ghorfi, T., and Jurd de Girancourt, D., 2020, *Femmes au cœur des entreprises familiales, secrets de réussite*, La Croisée des Chemins.
43. Lincoln University New Zealand, Fallatah H., 2012, Thesis *Women Entrepreneurs in Saudi Arabia: Investigating strategies used by successful Saudi women entrepreneurs.*
44. United Nations, Economic and Social Commission for Western Asia (ESCWA), 2019, *Innovation and Entrepreneurship: Opportunities and challenges for Arab youth and women.*
45. Review of Economic and Political Science, Amr Seda, Mamdouh Ismail, 2019, *Challenges facing social entrepreneurship: The implication for government policy in Egypt.*
46. Nieva, F.O., 2015, *Social women entrepreneurship in the Kingdom of Saudi Arabia*, Journal of Global Entrepreneurship Research.
47. Review of Economic and Political Science, Amr Seda, Mamdouh Ismail, 2019, *Challenges facing social entrepreneurship: The implication for government policy in Egypt.*
48. Halabi, S. and others, 2017, *Social Enterprise development in the Middle East and North Africa, A qualitative analysis of Lebanon, Jordan, Egypt and Palestine.*
49. World Economic Forum, 2018, *Working Muslim women are a trillion-dollar market.*
50. World Economic Forum, 2017, *These start-ups are changing the Arab world.*
51. United Nations, department of economic and social affairs, 2010, *Achieving gender equality, women's empowerment and strengthening development cooperation*, dialogues at the economic and social council.
52. Nieva, F.O., 2015, *Social women entrepreneurship in the Kingdom of Saudi Arabia*, Journal of Global Entrepreneurship Research.
53. UN Women, 2017, *Understanding masculinities*, results from the international men and gender equality survey Middle East and North Africa: Egypt, Lebanon, Morocco and Palestine.
54. UN Women, 2017, *Understanding masculinities*, results from the international men and gender equality survey Middle East and North Africa: Egypt, Lebanon, Morocco and Palestine.
55. World Bank, 2019, Goldstein, M., Gonzalez Martinez, P., and Papineni, S., *Tackling the global profitarchy—Gender and the choice of business sector.*
56. Ghorfi, T., and Jurd de Girancourt, D., 2020, *Femmes au cœur des entreprises familiales, secrets de réussite*, La Croisée des Chemins.

57. Nieva, F.O., 2015, *Social women entrepreneurship in the Kingdom of Saudi Arabia*, Journal of Global Entrepreneurship Research.
58. Lincoln University New Zealand, Fallatah, H., 2012, Thesis *Women Entrepreneurs in Saudi Arabia: Investigating strategies used by successful Saudi women entrepreneurs.*
59. OECD, 2020, *Covid-19 crisis in the MENA region: Impact on gender equality and policy responses* report.
60. International Finance Corporation (IFC), 2018, *Start-Ups in the Arab World: One Woman at a Time.*
61. Nieva, F.O., 2015, *Social women entrepreneurship in the Kingdom of Saudi Arabia*, Journal of Global Entrepreneurship Research.
62. United Nations, Economic and Social Commission for Western Asia (ESCWA), 2019, *Innovation and Entrepreneurship: Opportunities and challenges for Arab youth and women.*
63. United Nations, Economic and Social Commission for Western Asia (ESCWA), 2019, *Innovation and Entrepreneurship: Opportunities and challenges for Arab youth and women.*
64. United Nations, Economic and Social Commission for Western Asia (ESCWA), 2019, *Innovation and Entrepreneurship: Opportunities and challenges for Arab youth and women.*
65. Price Waterhouse Coopers, 2019, *Women in Work Index, Insights from Middle East and North Africa.*
66. Lavelle, K., and Al Sheikh, H., 2013, *Giving voice to women entrepreneurs in Saudi Arabia*, Women's Entrepreneurship Initiative in collaboration with Ashridge Business School, Gill Coleman.
67. Price Waterhouse Coopers, 2019, *Women in Work Index, Insights from Middle East and North Africa.*
68. McKinsey Global Institute, 2019, *The power of parity: Advancing women's equality in Africa.*
69. OECD, 2020, *Covid-19 crisis in the MENA region: Impact on gender equality and policy responses* report.
70. https://ufmsecretariat.org/women-industry-innovation-building-women-global-challenges/.
71. Association des Femmes Chefs d'Entreprises du Maroc.
72. European Bank for reconstruction and development.
73. The Arab Youth Survey, 2020, *A voice for change.*
74. Lincoln University New Zealand, Fallatah, H., 2012, Thesis *Women Entrepreneurs in Saudi Arabia: Investigating strategies used by successful Saudi women entrepreneurs.*

75. World Economic Forum, Ommundsen, K., Kteily, K., 2018, *How women are transforming the Arab world's startup scene* report.
76. International Finance Corporation (IFC), 2018, *Start-ups in the Arab world. One woman at a time.*
77. The Economist, 2017, *Set them free. Startups in the Arab world.*
78. Price Waterhouse Coopers, 2019, *Women in Work Index, Insights from Middle East and North Africa.*
79. https://ufmsecretariat.org/ceed-supporting-women-entrepreneurs-covid/.

References

Benhassine, N., et al. (2013). Turning a Shove into a Nudge? A "Labeled Cash Transfer" for Education. *NBER Working Paper No. 19227.*

Ghorfi, T., & Jurd de Girancourt, D. (2020). *Femmes au cœur des entreprises familiales, secrets de réussite.* La Croisée des Chemins, Casablanca, Morocco.

Halabi, S., et al. (2017). *Social Enterprise Development in the Middle East and North Africa: A Qualitative Analysis of Lebanon, Jordan, Egypt and Palestine.*

International Finance Corporation (IFC). (2018). *Start-Ups in the Arab World: One Woman at a Time.* Report.

IPSOS "She Speaks". (2016). *10 Things You Need to Know about Women in MENA.*

Lavelle, K., & Al Sheikh, H. (2013). *Giving Voice to Women Entrepreneurs in Saudi Arabia.* Women's Entrepreneurship Initiative in collaboration with Ashridge Business School, Gill Coleman.

Lincoln University New Zealand, & Fallatah, H. (2012). *Women Entrepreneurs in Saudi Arabia: Investigating Strategies Used by Successful Saudi Women Entrepreneurs.* Thesis.

McKinsey. (2018). *Women Entrepreneurship in GCC.*

McKinsey Global Institute. (2019). *The Power of Parity, Advancing Women's Equality in Africa.*

Nieva, F. O. (2015). Social Women Entrepreneurship in the Kingdom of Saudi Arabia. *Journal of Global Entrepreneurship Research, 5*, 11.

OECD. (2020). *Covid-19 Crisis in the MENA Region: Impact on Gender Equality and Policy Responses.* Report.

Price Waterhouse Coopers. (2019, April). *Women in Work Index, Insights from Middle East and North Africa.*

Review of Economic and Political Science, Amr Seda, Mamdouh Ismail. (2019). *Challenges Facing Social Entrepreneurship: The Implication for Government Policy in Egypt.*

Salama, H. (2020). *Women Entrepreneurship in MENA: An Analysis*. EcoMENA.

The Arab Youth Survey. (2020). *A Voice for Change.*

The World Bank Group. (2018). *The Arab World Competitiveness Report*, p. 75.

United Nations, Department of Economic and Social Affairs. (2010). *Achieving Gender Equality, Women's Empowerment and Strengthening Development Cooperation*. Dialogues at the Economic and Social Council.

United Nations Development Programme (UNDP) and Regional Bureau for Arab States (RBAS). (2016). *Arab Human Development Report: Youth and the Prospects for Human Development in a Changing Reality.*

United Nations, Economic and Social Commission for Western Asia (ESCWA). (2019). *Innovation and Entrepreneurship: Opportunities and Challenges for Arab Youth and Women.*

United Nations Women. (2017). Understanding Masculinities, Results from the International Men and Gender Equality Survey Middle East and North Africa: Egypt, Lebanon, Morocco and Palestine.

Vijaya, G. S., & Almasri, R. (2016). A Study of Women Entrepreneurship in Saudi Arabia. *International Journal of Advanced Engineering, Management and Science, 2*(12).

World Bank. (2019). Goldstein, M., Gonzalez Martinez, P., & Papineni, S. *Tackling the Global Profitarchy—Gender and the Choice of Business Sector.*

World Economic Forum. (2017). *These Start-ups are Changing the Arab World.*

World Economic Forum. (2018). *Working Muslim Women are a Trillion-Dollar Market.*

World Economic Forum, Ommundsen, K., & Kteily, K. (2018). *How Women are Transforming the Arab World's Startup Scene*. Report.

World Trade Press. OMAN. *Women in Culture, Business and Travel.*

Articles

Gulfnews, & Condamine, J. F. (2020). *Middle East Women Entrepreneurs Will Get their Dues.*

Tharawat Magazine, Gartner, W. B., & Allen, M. (2020). *Entrepreneurship across the World is Family Entrepreneurship.*

The Economist. (2017). *Set Them Free. Startups in the Arab World.*

6

Entrepreneurship and Education: Between Trendy and Usefulness

Thami Ghorfi and Imad-eddine Hatimi

Introduction

Entrepreneurship is certainly one of the oldest economic activities. However, as a theory, it had not been introduced until the turn of the twentieth century with Schumpeter (1934, p. 74) who defined entrepreneurship as "The carrying out of a new combination we call 'enterprise', the individuals whose function is to carry them out we call 'entrepreneurs.'" Since then, many researchers have tried to better understand the concept of entrepreneurship and identified educational practices and methodologies that could strengthen the entrepreneurial skills of university graduates. To do so, these researchers have leveraged several disciplines, namely educational sciences, psychology, and social sciences (Béchard & Grégoire, 2005).

According to Sagie and Elizur (1999), entrepreneurship education is a multidimensional process that relies on cognitive, affective, and conative

T. Ghorfi (✉) • I.-e. Hatimi
ESCA École de Management, Casablanca, Morocco
e-mail: tghorfi@esca.ma

N. Azoury, T. Hafsi (eds.), *Entrepreneurship and Social Entrepreneurship in the MENA Region*, https://doi.org/10.1007/978-3-030-88447-5_6

(doing) aspects, whose aim is to promote and prepare entrepreneurial behavior among students and individuals, in general. This implies not only developing the students' willingness to be entrepreneurs but also their ability to undertake such journey (Peterman & Kennedy, 2003). Its role is also to develop the self-confidence of students and their desire to succeed by themselves (sense of autonomy). The first entrepreneurship courses have been offered, in the United States of America at the University of Michigan[1] in 1926 and in Japan, thanks to the efforts of Professor Emeritus Shigeru Fuji in 1938. Since then, entrepreneurship education has grown and more particularly with the boom of technological start-ups and the disruption of traditional markets by a large number of entrepreneurs. According to Seymour (2001), more than 1500 universities have offered entrepreneurship programs in the United States compared to 16 in 1970. In Europe, entrepreneurship education has become an important topic for all member countries; a third of them have even developed national entrepreneurship education strategies. According to European Commission (2011), all member countries have launched programs where entrepreneurship education is an integral part.

In this chapter, we will, first of all, introduce the theoretical fundamentals of entrepreneurship education. Secondly, we will focus on the development of this activity in the Arab world. We will conclude this chapter by looking at the key role that entrepreneurship education can play through two important growth drivers, namely youth and women's entrepreneurship, and the firms' competitiveness, especially family businesses.

Entrepreneurship Education: What & Why?

One of the first questions that researchers have addressed is whether or not the entrepreneurship mindset can be developed by means of education. Related to that, Kuratko (2005) argues that entrepreneurship education is crucial for the development of entrepreneurs in a given context. While Ronstadt (1987) confirms this statement, he further explains that the key question is about identifying the right approach to achieve an effective entrepreneurship education, the content to be taught, and learning activities to leverage. Porter (1994) and Garavan and O'Cinneide (1994) distinguish between entrepreneurship education and management education. The first type emphasizes the development of entrepreneurial mindsets while the second focuses more on mastering business knowledge and practice. In management education, Business Schools have certainly succeeded in identifying the knowledge to be taught and educational approaches to develop the necessary business skills. However, more efforts should be deployed to build learning journeys that allow the development of entrepreneurial attitudes.

Entrepreneurship education is based on the principles of Planned Behavior theory (Ajzen & Fishbein, 2000), which states that it is possible to predict human behavior and the choices of individuals through their intentions towards the desired situation. Such intentions depend on positive attitudes towards the desired behavior, the social pressures encouraging it, and the freedom of action that individuals enjoy while undertaking it. AlHarbi et al. (2018) have found a positive correlation that links the entrepreneurial intentions of Saudi students to their favorable attitudes towards self-employment, the social norms that encourage it, and the ease of achieving it. Entrepreneurship education, then, could be considered as an effective way to develop entrepreneurial intention in students.

In this perspective, three approaches have been used (O'Connor, 2013). The first one that is frequently practiced in higher education is *Teaching about Entrepreneurship*, which introduces students to entrepreneurship by sharing theoretical content. The second, *Teaching for Entrepreneurship*, goes further by equipping learners with key knowledge and skills for entrepreneurship through a dedicated and focused course. The third approach, *Teaching through Entrepreneurship*, develops students' entrepreneurial skills through an experiential approach. This last approach is the most appropriate since it invites students to learn in real situations and achieve entrepreneurial initiatives that would transform opportunities into positive impacts (economic, social, etc.).

Technically, entrepreneurship education should enable the development of three types of skills: Opportunity Identification, Resources Mobilization, and Business Model Execution (Department of Business Innovation and Skills of the UK, 2015). The European Commission (EC) Joint Research Center identifies, for each type of skills, their

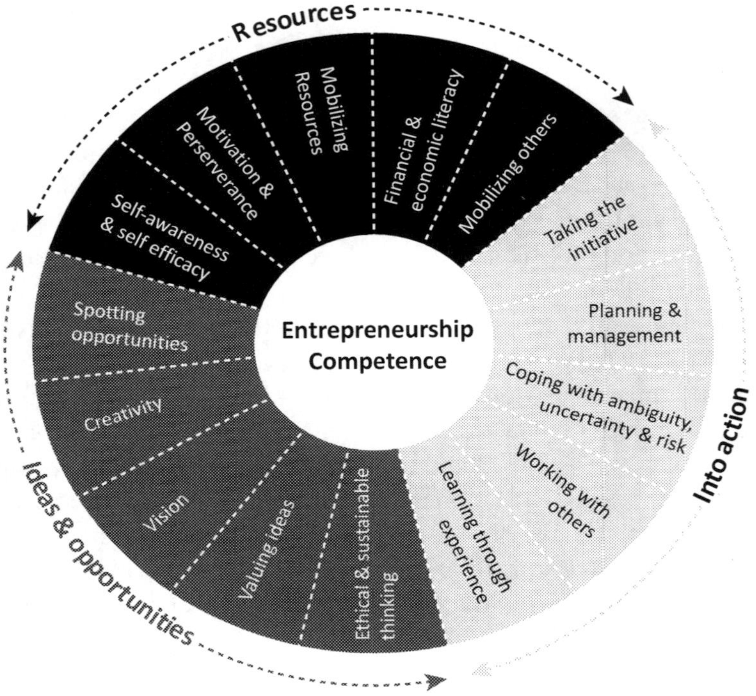

Fig. 6.1 Types of entrepreneurial skills. (Source: adapted from Bacigalupo (2016))

underlined soft skills (see Fig. 6.1) (Bacigalupo et al., 2016). In this perspective, entrepreneurship education should be based on a teaching approach that allows young people to develop from primary to higher education, a mindset equipped with creativity, autonomy, perseverance, risk taking, self-confidence, and so on. It differs from Entrepreneurship Training which is more appropriate for entrepreneurs who have already launched their startups and are aiming at supporting them as a continuing education (Valerio et al., 2014).

According to previous research, specific content, methods, and learning environment must be built to prepare entrepreneurs. El-Gohary and Eid (2013) highlight the impact of course content, teaching activities, and the study environment. El-Gohary et al. (2012) argue that it is important to increase the attractiveness of the learning experience and updating the Know How provided in entrepreneurship programs. In addition, according to Valerio et al. (2014), the incorporation of creative activities into curricula contributes to the development of entrepreneurial spirit. Also, it is essential to provide a learning environment that allows students to have a real experience through prototyping and the realization of small-scale projects. We can note, in this case, the examples of initiatives like the x-lab and Maker Innovation Center in China, Me & My City and InnoOmnia in Finland which promote the development of entrepreneurial skills by combining work and learning in a collaborative space that allows interaction with other entrepreneurs (Greene et al., 2016).

In terms of academic content, entrepreneurship education involves three teaching axes: (1) management knowledge, (2) personal development, and (3) entrepreneurship techniques. According to Gottleib and Ross (1997), its objective is to develop three competencies, namely (a) Analysis and identification of business opportunities, (b) Planning and allocation of resources and (c) Methodologies needed to create and manage a firm. Valerio et al. (2014) explain that entrepreneurship education generally includes content that aims to develop personal traits (self-confidence, leadership, creativity, motivation, resilience, etc.), to raise individuals' awareness about the specific nature of entrepreneurial activities and finally to equip them with business knowledge and techniques (accounting, marketing, finance, etc.). Souitaris et al. (2007) identify four blocks that a program structure should have, teaching, business planning workshops, practice activities, and provision of entrepreneurship-dedicated resources within universities.

In terms of methods, previous studies highlight the importance of using a different approach from the one traditionally used in the teaching of management disciplines. Entrepreneurship education should be more based on project-based pedagogy, collaboration, multi-disciplinarity, experiential learning, problem solving, work on real situations, and so on. Hynes (1996) argues that it is essential to mobilize teaching methods that emphasize both the development of personal skills and entrepreneurial motivation. Gibb (2002) argues that the learning environment for the development of entrepreneurial attitudes is also different. Jones and English (2004) confirm this statement by explaining that the learning environment must allow experiential learning, problem solving, project execution, and creativity activities. In this regard, Baptista and Naia (2015) refer to learning methods such as case studies, group discussions, simulations, company visits, internships, student–student interactions, and meetings with entrepreneurs. This teaching approach allows learners to discover, solve problems, and interact with entrepreneurs in real-life situations. El Ghoul and Amrouni (2017) argue that from a methodological point of view, the competency-based approach seems appropriate for teaching entrepreneurship. They explain that it is based on a pedagogical approach which is mostly oriented towards action and behavior.

Concerning the faculty to assign for entrepreneurship education, it is recommended to rely on a multidisciplinary staff with field experience, involving a group of teachers and practitioners, according to a Babson study.[2] Teachers provide the necessary knowledge for the development of entrepreneurial abilities and act as coaches to facilitate learning, while practitioners, emanating from different backgrounds, serve as role models whose respective experiences inspire young entrepreneurs. However, the recruitment and training of teachers involved in such programs is essential though. They are required to master the concepts and techniques necessary to develop a sense of entrepreneurship. Furthermore, they need to have a positive attitude towards entrepreneurship as the promotion and development of the learners' confidence are highly recommended.

Entrepreneurship Education in the Arab World

In the Arab world, a 2011 World Economic Forum survey has showed that less than 10% of Arab universities offered entrepreneurship courses, less than 4% had set up entrepreneurship centers, and less than 1% had a course dedicated to entrepreneurship. This report concluded that Arab universities were not doing enough to support the entrepreneurship efforts of their respective countries, and that most university graduates lack the entrepreneurial skills and mindset. In fact, a UNESCO study (2013) reveals several weaknesses in the education system in Arab countries, especially when it comes to developing entrepreneurial skills. First, teachers lack the field experience and the mindset necessary to promote entrepreneurship. Second, the programs are designed in a standardized way, do not take into account the context's specificities, and do not target those with the highest entrepreneurial potential. Third, universities still lack connectivity with the corporate world. Fourth, entrepreneurship training programs in the Arab world are seen more as academic pathways whose performance is still measured more by the number of degrees awarded than by the impact generated in terms of developing entrepreneurial attitudes and the number of businesses created. According to El Ghoul and Amrouni (2017), the pedagogies used do not allow the development of creativity and the sense of initiative. Existing programs focus only on entrepreneurship through social projects.

Most recently, the situation has changed given the role of entrepreneurship for Arab countries as a driver for job creation. Today, entrepreneurship education in the region takes many forms as elsewhere in the world by:

1. Promoting business games and simulations to enable entrepreneurship skills through practice activities,
2. Using business cases to develop critical thinking skills,
3. Organizing competitions and Hackathons,
4. Hosting workshops dedicated to entrepreneurship,
5. Encouraging meetings and conferences with entrepreneurs to share experiences and inspire students,
6. Teaching management outside Business Schools in different fields (Engineering, Medical Studies, Human Sciences, Law, etc.),
7. Setting up incubators to welcome, advise and support startups and help them achieving a financial and management autonomy,
8. Creating accelerators, in order to quickly develop valuable entrepreneurial ideas and ensure their "fit to market".

In Arab countries, there are all types of programs: degrees, executive education, a university course, a summer program, a workshop, a mentoring session, and so on. For example, the United Arab Emirates University offers an entrepreneurship minor in its Bachelor program. This minor is generally dedicated to students who come from tracks other than Business whose objective is to introduce the field of entrepreneurship to students. This would allow them to discover the necessary techniques to create a business or lead intrapreneurship project in an organization as an employee. The Holy Spirit University of Kaslik (USEK) does the same by offering a minor in entrepreneurship which aims at preparing students to launch start-ups. It has established the Asher Center for Innovation and Entrepreneurship to support the entire university community in exploring ideas for innovations to create products or services, or even businesses to serve the development of Lebanon. The American University of Beirut also offers many activities around entrepreneurship, both in its Business School (the Suliman S. Olayan School of Business) and its School of Engineering and Architecture (Maroun Semaan Faculty of Engineering and Architecture). Its *Entrepreneurship Initiative* offers comprehensive programs ranging from basic entrepreneurship training to coaching through an accelerator, and numerous events aimed at developing networks of entrepreneurial students. At the American University in Cairo, the minor devoted to entrepreneurship offers an entrepreneurial perspective of the business world and provides the necessary knowledge in finance and business law to create and manage a startup. This minor also allows students to start from an idea and achieve a study that allows them to make the decision about their entrepreneurship future. In this perspective, the AUC Venture Lab's mission supports students with projects in different stages of the entrepreneurship journey by providing them with various mentoring and acceleration services. ESCA École de Management, in Morocco, has developed a master's degree program called "*Entrepreneurship and International Development*", which aims to prepare both entrepreneurs or intrapreneurs. The international dimension allows these students to define and seize opportunities in a globalized market. Its incubator, named ESCubator, hosts students with entrepreneurial initiatives and prepares them to join one of Casablanca's accelerators, and to capture the value of open ecosystems, available in their environment. Qatar University also grants the opportunity to all students to take entrepreneurship courses and offers a dedicated path that leads to a specialized minor in entrepreneurship. In Tunisia, most universities offer a cross-interdisciplinary module on entrepreneurship.

Such importance given to entrepreneurship education is due to the contribution it makes to the socio-economic development of countries, by generating more wealth through innovation and job creation, as well as the development of SMEs (Dana, 2001). Actually, three types of positive impact can be identified: (1) favoring economic growth, job creation, and competitiveness; (2) strengthening student motivation and (3) promoting social advancement and people empowerment. From the social perspective, according to the Arab Region Outcome Statement (UNESCO, 2018), entrepreneurship education is considered as a key dimension of the United Nations essential life and civic skills matrix. It appears in the so-called instrumental skills block (Learning to Do).

Youth and Women Entrepreneurship in Arab Countries

Young people and women present a segment of the population whose potential and entrepreneurial spirit must be exploited. According to the Arab Youth Survey (2020), 23% of young people would prefer entrepreneurship or working in their family business. 40% of young Arabs intend to start a business (55% in the Gulf countries and 44% in North Africa compared to 22% in the Levant countries). Also, it is argued that young people take more risk and show more creativity and innovation.

The Global University Entrepreneurial Spirit Student's Survey—GUESSS is carried out in different countries around the world. Herein, we will use its findings to analyze some Arab countries. In 2016, according to the GUESSS—Morocco report,[3] 6% of the responding students have the intention to initiate a business-creation process once they have finished their university degree. Working in companies as an employee certainly remains the general intention for more than 85% of the responding students but there are 38% who think of entrepreneurship after a horizon of five years after their studies. This being said, these young Moroccans perceive, according to the same report, that their society does not sufficiently value innovators and reward performance.

In Saudi Arabia (KSA), entrepreneurship has, since 2016, become an important driver in the Saudi Arabia Vision 2030. The promotion of entrepreneurship is one of the five pillars to support the creation and development of SMEs in order to diversify and strengthen the Saudi economy. To do so, Saudi Arabia has created a dedicated agency, called Monsha'at,[4] to support entrepreneurship and ease the capital access to Small and Medium-sized Enterprises. The GUESSS—KSA report,[5] carried out in 2018–2019, shows that 5.67% of the students interviewed intended to start a business at the end of their studies. 36.44% intend to create a business within five years after their studies. This report also shows that higher education studies has helped students develop the needed entrepreneurship knowledge. In fact, students strongly agreed with the survey item "*my course enhances my ability to identify an opportunity*" (18.4%).

In the United Arab Emirates (UAE), the 2019 GUESSS report[6] shows that among the students surveyed, only 5% intend to become entrepreneurs at the end of their studies, and 41% say they consider entrepreneurship five years after completing their studies. Students at UAE recognize the need for practical experience before starting their own business. However, this report stated: "*Even though the university context plays an important role in developing entrepreneurial intentions, the UAE university system has not tailored specific paths to develop entrepreneurial behavior*".

It is worth noting that entrepreneurship education is particularly important for young people given the unemployment challenges that Arab countries face, especially if we take into account that this segment represents a large part of the population, one that is the most impacted by social disparities. According to the UNDP (2019), young people represent 27% of the population of Arab countries but only 29% of the labor force compared to 42% globally. Young people in the Arab world face a very difficult context when it comes to entering the professional world. The unemployment rate among young people is estimated to be at 23% in 2020 compared to 13.7% globally (ILO, 2020). Such a situation is more problematic in the case of young women where the unemployment rate has reached the level of 42.1% in 2020.

Alongside this, there is the need for development and social advancement that young people express in Arab countries, and which they are seeking to satisfy by all means. In 2011, young people were largely behind the fall of several regimes in Arab countries during the Arab Spring. In 2020, 42% of young people in Arab countries said they had considered immigrating to another country and this choice is unfortunately irreversible for 40% of them, according to the Arab Youth Survey (2020). The main reasons of this decision are mainly linked to the economic conditions and the corruption problems their countries face. Thus, entrepreneurship education would help to give young people a positive perception about their future, attenuate the feeling of social injustice that young people have (27%), and compensate for the lack of quality jobs (29%). This would also help to reduce the anger of young people towards their respective governments which pushes them to support protests in their countries. According to the Arab Youth Survey, a large majority of young people supported the protests taking place during 2019, in Algeria (89%), Iraq (89%), Lebanon (82%) and Sudan (88%).

However, youth entrepreneurship faces major challenges. According to YBI (2013), youth entrepreneurship depends on the economic development of the country, the business opportunities it offers and the degree of urbanization. In addition, according to a survey by the African Development Bank, the lack of professional experience, funds, and social networks are factors that do not favor the identification of entrepreneurial opportunities from young people (Brixiová et al., 2014), especially that they must also deal with a significant debt. According to YBI (2013), 35% of young Arabs say they have personal debts in 2020 compared to 15% in 2015, because of their student and car loans in 46% of cases. Finally, youth entrepreneurship faces difficult access to capital (YBI, 2013).

This being said, it is argued that such challenges would be more easily met in the case of young entrepreneurs who have pursued studies and training in entrepreneurship. In fact, the longer the training is and the higher the quality is, the better is the performance of young entrepreneurs (Montrose, 2016). This is very important if we take into account that the main problem, in the case of young entrepreneurs, is related to their lack of planning and logical reasoning skills and that students in the region are confident in the ability of their universities to prepare them to start an entrepreneurship journey (YBI, 2016).

Also, entrepreneurship education has proven to have a greater impact on young people than on adults. According to Cho and Honorati (2013), the benefits in terms of job creation and business performance, generated by entrepreneurship education, are greater among young populations than others. Nevertheless, such an impact remains moderated by the availability of financing solutions. The evaluation of the *Transforming Lives Through Entrepreneurship* in Kenya program has showed that launching a start-up and generating an income were more observed in the case of young entrepreneurs who received a loan (Lewins, 2014). Put differently, entrepreneurship education among young people, alongside the access to a capital, would have a greater impact on promoting entrepreneurship among young people (Blattman & Ralston, 2015). According to YBI (2011), financial institutions (including banks) are more encouraged to lend to young entrepreneurs who have followed an entrepreneurship training program, considering them less risky and more capable to succeed in their initiatives.

For women entrepreneurs, the stakes are higher because, in addition to political and economic constraints, there are cultural barriers. This explains the poor performance of women entrepreneurial initiatives in the context of Arab countries. The percentage of women entrepreneurs who have suspended their activities in the region is the highest one, after Sub-Saharan Africa (GEM, 2019). According to the Global Entrepreneurship Monitor (2019), women entrepreneurship is almost half that of men in Arab countries because of the lack of gender equity. Entrepreneurship has generally been associated with strong men, able to endure the entrepreneurship adversity and to succeed alone against all (Hytti, 2005).

Such a situation is of course reinforced in the context of Arab countries because of the social inequalities that women have to face. According to the Arab Youth Survey (2020), 35% of young women believe that men have more professional opportunities than them. Indeed, the region has the largest gap according to the Global Gender Index (WEF, 2020). 17 out of the 33 countries belonging to the bottom of the ranking are Arab countries. Unfortunately, the situation is not improving and causes gender disparities in terms of participation in the economy and in politics. Women represent only 21% of the workforce in the Arab world while they make up around 48% of the total population according to World Bank data.[7] This is the lowest rate compared to other regions of the world. Only 17.8% of parliamentary seats are held by women in Arab countries.[7] Also, only 29% of leadership positions in organizations are held by women and only 23% of companies have a woman among the shareholders in the MENA region (Fig. 6.2). In Arab countries, this rate varies between 7% in Yemen and 48% in Tunisia.

In view of that, entrepreneurship education can play an important role in promoting women entrepreneurship. In fact, 59% of Arab women consider that education is a lever that can promote access to leadership positions in companies (AWLO, 2011).[8] On the one hand, it is argued that a large part of women would hesitate to launch a start-up because of their lack of entrepreneurial skills (Terjesen & Lloyd, 2015). On the other hand, unlike men, women would find it difficult to grow their start-ups and reach an advanced level of development due to their need of entrepreneurship training (Brookings Institute, 2013). In addition to this, we must also note that the type of entrepreneurship differs between women and men because of inequalities in terms of training and social status in developing countries. Women entrepreneurship is often found in the service and retail sectors, and very little in technology sectors where the level of engineering is higher (OECD, 2017). It is also characterized by the informal aspect and mainly motivated by the necessity and lacks innovation because of the differences in terms of the educational level (Aghion et al., 2009). Women's educational level affects their ability as well to identify opportunities (Jamali, 2009) and their propensity to

World
34%
East Asia & Pacific
47%
Europe & Central Asia
33%
Latin America & Caribbean
50%
Middle East & North Africa
23%
South Asia
18%
Sub-Saharan Africa
29%

Fig. 6.2 Share of enterprises with a woman in the ownership structure (%). (https://blogs.worldbank.org/opendata/women-entrepreneurs-needed-stat)

explore international markets (OECD, 2017). Finally, in Arab countries, girls are often forced to drop studies for economic and/or cultural reasons. These arguments demonstrate the important need for entrepreneurship education in the case of women to support their social advancement (UNESCO, 2014).

Actually, by not promoting women entrepreneurship as needed, most of Arab countries are unfortunately not leveraging one of the most important drivers for economic growth and social development. Entrepreneurship education in Arab countries must absolutely not ignore the significant potential for value creation from women entrepreneurs. It should also allow start-ups and SMEs to benefit from gender diversity, synergy, and collective effort which can be a source of innovation and creativity. Indeed, it is proven that the success of entrepreneurial initiatives is the result of a collective effort, in most cases (Klotz et al., 2014). Also, it is argued that developing countries would benefit from women's education more than developed countries in terms of economic growth and poverty reduction (Hanushek & Woessmann, 2007). Therefore, developing entrepreneurship education in universities in the Arab world would help strengthen the notion of "equal opportunities" in Arab societies. To do this, entrepreneurship education must take the gender dimension into account by offering modules or programs that are specific to women entrepreneurship. For instance, the Goldman Sachs 10,000 Women program has been designed specifically for this type of entrepreneurship and deployed in the region with support from AUB in Lebanon and AUC in Egypt.

Entrepreneurship Education as a Pillar for Competitiveness

Entrepreneurship education is also a way to strengthen the firms' competitiveness. According to The Arab World Competitiveness Report (2020), the competitiveness of the Arab companies is still weak in most cases due, in particular, to their poor performance in terms of innovation and business complexity. Thus, the recruitment of students who have pursued entrepreneurship education can allow organizations to renew themselves. As intrapreneurs, these recruited profiles are able to identify development opportunities, to generate growth and maintain the companies' competitive advantage. They are able to show leadership, creativity, and initiative to carry out innovation and/or transformational change despite the associated risks. In fact, intrapreneurs play an essential role nowadays in companies, especially those dealing with a fierce competition in their markets due to the globalization of markets, the convergence of sectors, and technological dynamism. More precisely, market changes are frequent and rapid, and by consequence, companies need to consequently adapt. To do this, organizations must have a good number of intrapreneurs who are ambitious, innovative, and courageous, and who can lead business transformation journeys on a regular basis. By doing so, they can align their strategies and practices with the emerging requirements of their industries and meet the increasingly high expectations of their clients (Fig. 6.3). Such a dimension should be reinforced in the Arab countries, compared to the countries of Europe and North America, according to the GEM survey (2019).

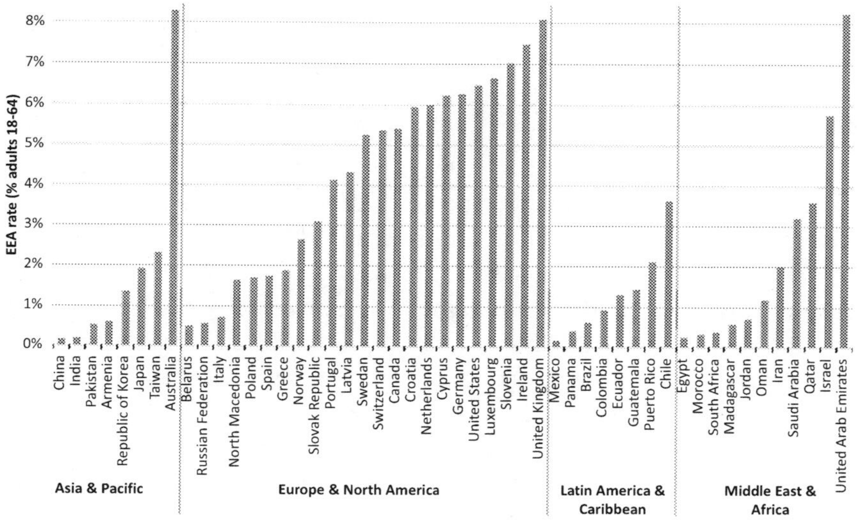

Fig. 6.3 Entrepreneurial employee activity. (Source: GEM, 2019)

Entrepreneurship education would also contribute to the competitiveness of Arab countries by promoting the success of family businesses. This category of firms largely contributes to the GDP of Arab countries by ensuring the needed economic development and job creation (Ghorfi, 2017). In the Middle East, family businesses represent over 90% of Middle-Eastern companies, generate over 60% of GDP, and employ 80% of the workforce (PWC, 2016).[9] Actually, entrepreneurship education can help family businesses meet several challenges that family businesses widely face in Arab countries (Ghorfi, 2017), and that we can state as follows:

- The involvement/commitment of the next generations in the management of the family businesses.
- The preparation of leadership succession.
- The improvement of governance structures.
- The reinforcement of HR management (family members and external skills).
- The development of growth and internationalization strategies.
- The strengthening of the innovation and entrepreneurial spirit.

According to Babson's study,[10] successful family business activities are very diversified. Also, family businesses that invest in the most value-creating activities are better prepared to survive market disruptions. Finally, family businesses that encourage their members to explore new ventures are the most sustainable. In other words, family businesses with an entrepreneurial culture are capable of growing and sustaining themselves. Such arguments are more important in the case of Arab countries. A 2019 PWC study has found that in the Middle East, 63% of family businesses expressed their willingness to strengthen their innovation activities but, at the same time, 66% of them expressed the need for well-skilled people. More precisely, these companies are requested to renew their business models and develop a culture of innovation (PWC, 2019). According to the same survey, the leaders of these companies from the Middle-East region indicated that their priority is to attract the best talent (94% of cases) and to be more innovative (81%).

Thus, entrepreneurship education is crucial in supporting family business development activities. It prepares the upcoming generation of family entrepreneurs by equipping them with the entrepreneurial skills necessary to guarantee successful transition from one generation to another. Entrepreneurship education can also help in building an entrepreneurial culture within family businesses, by fostering the integration of younger generations who are often in search of innovation and change. According to Kansikas and Laakkonen (2009), students do not see family entrepreneurship as an opportunity. They certainly perceive it as a major economic player actively contributing to the development of their countries. However, they consider the family enterprise as being a structure, which has existed for a long time and therefore, difficult to renew or host an entrepreneurial activity. The students also consider that family businesses are usually embedded by the values of the founding members with a paternalistic culture and a centralized decision-making process.

According to Pistrui et al. (2000), entrepreneurial intent is one of the main factors that drives students to become a manager/owner of a family business. In order to promote family entrepreneurship among students, Kansikas and Laakkonen (2009) recommend that entrepreneurship education should:

- Develop specific programs for family entrepreneurship by mobilizing relevant academic content and best practices in the management of family businesses.
- Foster the interaction of researchers to produce up-to-date knowledge on family businesses.
- Promote interactions with the local professional world to adapt teaching content on family businesses according to the economic and social characteristics.
- Invite mentors from family businesses to promote and develop the field of family entrepreneurship, together with academics and practitioners.
- Build international collaborations between universities to strengthen the educational offer on family entrepreneurship and enrich it through comparative studies.

By doing so, entrepreneurship education would not only provide entrepreneurs or intrapreneurs to existing family businesses but also encourage young students to start businesses with other members of their families. Wang and Wong (2004) argue that the family plays an important role, in particular by encouraging/supporting the entrepreneurial initiatives of their members or by embarking them in the journey (parents as entrepreneurs). 75%[11] of entrepreneurs claim that family members were part of their projects when they started. Indeed, many family businesses have understood the importance of entrepreneurship education for their succession plan and sent their members to good universities to pursue general management or specialized studies alongside an entrepreneurship training.[12] Actually, it is more appropriate to speak about entrepreneurial families than entrepreneurial family businesses, since families with an entrepreneurial spirit are often invested in more than one business. However, such entrepreneurial initiatives must rely on a rational approach, based on well-articulated business plans and projects whose return on investment is demonstrated.

In this perspective, the governance of family businesses will play a key role (Ghorfi, 2017). Students who see themselves as future entrepreneurs are often motivated by disruptive projects. They see new opportunities and their aspirations are different from the family business founders. Then, the challenge is to support them in setting up modes of governance and promoting diversification while limiting risks. By doing so, these entrepreneurs of the new era will contribute to the enrichment of family assets through the creation of start-ups or the development of new projects. Family businesses should also favor the participation of women and leverage it as an entrepreneurship force. Women are certainly facing many obstacles to reach leadership positions in family businesses. However, according to Ghorfi and Jurd de Girancourt (2021), those who succeed play a key role in family business development and resilience by setting new leadership modes and a strong corporate culture based on innovation, diversity, and equity.

Entrepreneurship Education and the Business Environment

From the arguments presented earlier in this chapter, it is clear that entrepreneurship education offers several advantages. Integrating entrepreneurship education within higher education institutions will promote:

1. The reduction of business failure, thanks to innovative and well-skilled graduates,
2. Strengthening businesses by linking them to networks of entrepreneurs and allowing them to discover best practices from successful stories,
3. The integration of technologies within new companies, thanks to the interaction between entrepreneurs and researchers within universities,
4. A better impact in terms of job creation and economic development.
5. The social advancement of young and women population.

However, it appears that entrepreneurship education is necessary but not sufficient. According to Dyer (1994), entrepreneurship depends on three types of factors. The first type is based on individual traits. According to previous research, personal characteristics concern creativity (Kuratko, 2004; Burke et al., 2002), degree of risk acceptance, gender and age (Asamani & Mensah, 2013), motivation (Verheul et al., 2005), self-confidence (Varghese & Hassan, 2012), and professional background (Kristiansen & Indarti, 2004). The second type of factors relies on social relationships/norms that enhance the entrepreneurial behavior of individuals. In fact, social and cultural dimensions are also underlined as contributing to entrepreneurship (Ismail et al., 2012). Finally, economic factors are also important, synonymous with growth opportunities (Tucker & Selcuk, 2009). In other words, personal characteristics are important in promoting entrepreneurship, but the surrounding social and economic conditions are more so.

Actually, it is not enough to equip entrepreneurs with the will and the ability to start a business or launch a new project. The environment should be favorable to entrepreneurial initiatives. Indeed, the political, social, and economic context is important since it provides entrepreneurs with the necessary regulations, funding and cultural support for their initiatives (Mason & Brown, 2014; Auerswald, 2015). This is critical for young and women entrepreneurs who often lack resources and experience and who have to deal with hostile environments, cultural barriers, and obstacles to markets and capital access (Fatoki & Chindoga, 2011).

According to the Global Entrepreneurship Monitor (2019), entrepreneurial activity in the MENA region remains limited in terms of the percentage of the participating population. In fact, it should be noted that in the MENA region there is a relatively high percentage of entrepreneurial intentions but few of them are materialized through a startup, compared to other regions of the world. To resolve this issue, Arab countries should intensify their efforts to promote entrepreneurship among the population both as a job creation and also as economic growth driver and among companies as a source of competitiveness. In this regard, Arab universities should multiply conferences and seminars, build expert groups, and create awards for entrepreneurial initiatives. By doing so, they will promote not only the understanding of entrepreneurial skills but also the buy-in from different interest groups (parents, students, governments, businesses, etc.). Universities should also support potential entrepreneurs by enriching their educational offer for lifelong learning. In addition, they must foster experiential learning in their pedagogies by allowing students to go through real entrepreneurial situations. In this perspective, universities should interact more with the professional world and more particularly, with entrepreneurs.

Indeed, it appears that Arab countries need to review their educational systems by integrating relevant and structured content, interactive and experiential methods (internships, projects, simulations, etc.) as well as extracurricular activities in order to promote entrepreneurial behavior among students and equip them with the techniques needed to successfully launch their businesses. They must also provide training for teachers and entrepreneurship coaches. Such efforts should, according to ESCWA (2019), be made from primary school to vocational training, including higher education. In addition, entrepreneurship education should be supported by training activities for entrepreneurs as well. The involvement of entrepreneurs in programs is also recommended. For instance, we can mention the Injaz Al Arab program[13] which has succeeded in preparing young people for entrepreneurship by mobilizing the community of established entrepreneurs who support young people and serve as a role model. Finally, Arab universities must also allow their students to interact with their international peers through joint classroom, group projects, competitions, or events. ENACTUS, an international organization with a strong presence in the Arab world, illustrates the way in which students are mobilized to resolve societal issues through entrepreneurial initiatives while benefiting from the international network.

Governance bodies of higher education in Arab countries should allow universities more flexibility in terms of programs structure, content, and methods. They must put in place incentive policies to encourage and reward universities that develop entrepreneurship training. National authorities can also structure the efforts of all actors under the umbrella of a national entrepreneurship education strategy with specific and committed agencies and interest groups. They must also encourage entrepreneurial initiatives of academic institutions. Indeed, a university or business school with an entrepreneurial spirit would be more likely to develop entrepreneurs. In this regard, we refer to the example of the National Center for Entrepreneurship in Education (National Center for Entrepreneurship in Education[14]) which supports universities in their entrepreneurship strategies and offers programs for the development of the entrepreneurial spirit among their leadership team.

Thus, it is clear that we cannot have an impactful entrepreneurship education without improving the business environment for entrepreneurs. The report on the new development model from the Economic, Social and Environmental Council of the Kingdom of Morocco, states that entrepreneurship could be a key source of social advancement and inclusion but only if the government strongly improves the business environment for entrepreneurship and investment. This report noted that "*Releasing energies also means releasing economic initiative and entrepreneurship, and allowing talents to express themselves, to develop their creativity and to realize their potential*". This implies the definition of clear economic rules to favor value creation as well as the establishment of a strong support mechanism for entrepreneurs.

These institutional efforts are essential to make entrepreneurship and its incubation within universities a real source of opportunities in the future. Otherwise, young people will go to entrepreneurship by necessity given the lack of employment opportunities offered by the public service or the private sector in various Arab countries. Indeed, it should also be noted that youth and women entrepreneurship should have great aspirations and capture a higher value. In the developing Arab countries, a significant part of young people undertake entrepreneurship by default and not necessarily by seizing an opportunity for differentiation. Necessity motivations are behind around 30% of entrepreneurial initiatives in the MENA region, compared to 20% in Europe and Central Asia and 9% in North America (GEM, 2019). Actually, young people undertake entrepreneurial activities that are easy to access, technically and financially, and, by consequence, oversaturated, which explains the weak sustainability of their initiatives (OECD, 2017). For Kew et al. (2015), such a trend may change among young people with a high level of education.

Likewise, Arab countries should support Research and Development (R&D) in order to improve the quality of entrepreneurship and increase the value it creates through more initiatives in the business services and technology sectors. In fact, there is a strong correlation between the level of investment in Research and Development in a country and the creation of valuable businesses. In the MENA region, the average investment in R&D was 0.9% in 2012 with low numbers for Arab countries (0.1% of GDP in Kuwait, 0.49% of GDP in the Emirates, 0.68% of GDP in Tunisia, 0.51% of GDP in Egypt and 0.71% of GDP in Morocco). The IRES[15] study on "Scientific Research and Innovation in the Arab World" of July 2019 highlighted this collective failure in the region, especially when we look at the intensity of R&D compared to the size of the population. This situation explains the low number of patents in the various Arab countries between 2013 and 2017, according to the World Intellectual Property Organization.[16] It is also linked to the development of start-ups in the region. The MAGNiTT report,[17] which lists 10,000 start-ups in the MENA region, announced a record investment in 2020, which exceeds $ 1 billion for 496 deals in total. The average investment is 2.1 million USD.

According to Fig. 6.4, the United Arab Emirates takes the most important share by capturing 26% of deals. It is the country that offers the best environment for young entrepreneurs and innovative entrepreneurs. Abu Dhabi accelerators provide infrastructure according to international standards with services that also include medical coverage for entrepreneurs and their families for a period of two years. This obviously shows the reasons for the success of the UAE and the disparities that exist in the Arab world with regard to the business environment. The three innovation hubs in the Arab world defined by MAGNiTT 2021 are therefore the UAE, Egypt, and the KSA. They alone capture 68% of deals in 2021. Most of the Arab countries need to deploy more efforts to promote start-ups through a positive business context and supportive financial programs. It is also worth noting that these capital transactions have shown

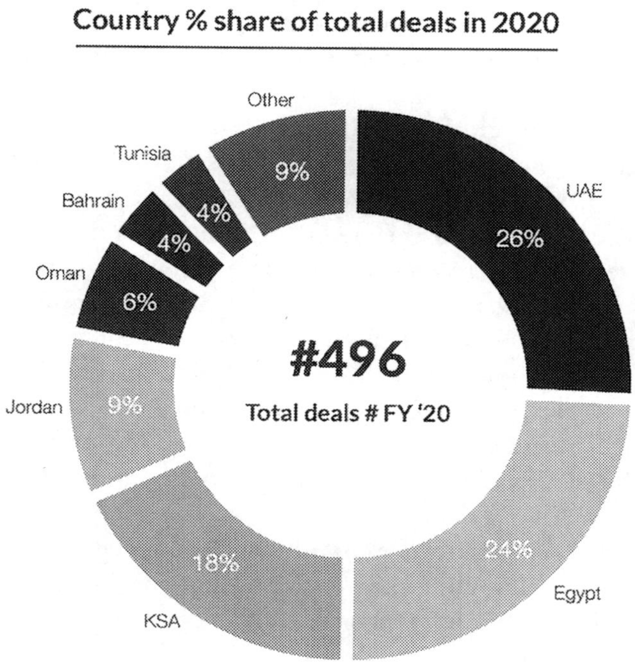

Fig. 6.4 Country's percentage share of total deals in 2020. (Source: MagniTT (2021))

that the sectors that have attracted most of the deals are electronic commerce with 162 million USD, food & beverage with 122 million USD and health with 72 million USD. Unfortunately, the Covid pandemic has mobilized part of these investments to help solve urgent economic and social problems the Arab states are facing in the short term.

Finally, Arab countries must also provide the necessary financing solutions to benefit from their efforts in entrepreneurship education. Their authorities must, on the one hand, multiply and strengthen programs to support entrepreneurship projects. In this perspective, several years ago, Morocco has launched funding programs for start-ups such as *Intelak*, initially launched for technology startups with high growth potential. This financial program has allowed companies to cover up to 90% of their post-creation expenses (salaries, rents, support, etc.) with a reimbursement plan at zero rate, after five years. Other financial programs have also been created to encourage banks to finance projects coming from young and women entrepreneurs. More precisely, Morocco has launched an entrepreneurship support program with more than $ 6 million to guarantee, for banks, the loans granted to entrepreneurs through the *Damane Intelak* and Start-TPE (All Small Businesses) programs. In this perspective, the *Caisse Centrale de Garantie*[18] (CCG), a public financial agency, plays an important role by sharing the risk with financial institutions, up to 89% of the credit. In addition to this program, the CCG has set up the *Damane Capital Risque* option to guarantee contributions from venture capitalists. It has also developed programs called *Innov Idea* and *Innov Start*, which benefit innovative companies with patents and new technologies in Morocco, respectively. Finally, the CCG also offers so-called *Innov Risk* and *Innov Dev* programs to support startups having succeeded in raising funds from investors but requesting a cash flow for development and marketing purposes during the launch or the growth phases.

Thus, the Arab countries must ultimately integrate the subject of entrepreneurship education into their various public policies as an essential approach to develop young and women entrepreneurial spirit. Entrepreneurship is highly needed not only to boost jobs in different sectors but also to solve societal and economic issues. States which will seize this solution as a strategic approach need to create coherent ecosystems which include financing, taxation, regional development plans, access to public projects, support for incubators universities, and accelerators. Such an environment will help stimulate a type of innovative entrepreneurship to solve the problems of Arab societies. These new entrepreneurs will thus contribute to major subjects such as access to education, improvement of healthcare services, the production of value-added products, and even the advancement of democracy.

Notes

1. https://www.entrepreneur.com/article/237387.
2. https://entrepreneurship.babson.edu/family-entrepreneurship-family-business/.
3. http://guesssurvey.org/resources/nat_2016/GUESSS_Report_2016_Morocco_e.pdf.
4. https://www.monshaat.gov.sa/en/about.
5. http://guesssurvey.org/resources/nat_2018/GUESSS_Report_2018_SaudiArabia.pdf.
6. http://guesssurvey.org/resources/nat_2018/GUESSS_Report_2018_UAE.pdf.
7. https://data.worldbank.org/region/arab-world.
8. Arab Women Leadership Outlook.
9. Price Waterhouse Coopers.
10. https://entrepreneurship.babson.edu/family-entrepreneurship-family-business/.
11. https://entrepreneurship.babson.edu/family-entrepreneurship-family-business/.
12. https://www.tharawat-magazine.com/sustain/entrepreneurship-educate-generation/.
13. https://www.injazalarab.org/.
14. https://ncee.org.uk/about-us/.
15. Institut Royal d'Études Stratégiques (Royaume du Maroc) www.ires.ma.
16. "La Recherche Scientifique et l'Innovation dans le monde Arabe" IRES Juillet 2019, page 28.
17. MAGNiTT 2021 Emerging Venture Markets report.
18. https://www.ccg.ma/.

References

Aghion, P., Boustan, L., Hoxby, C., & Vandenbussche, J. (2009). The Causal Impact of Education on Economic Growth: Evidence from the United States. *Brookings Papers on Economic Activity*. https://www.brookings.edu/wp-content/uploads/2016/07/2009_spring_bpea_aghion_etal.pdf

Ajzen, I., & Fishbein, M. (2000). Attitudes and the Attitude-Behavior Relation: Reasoned and Automatic Processes. *European Review of Social Psychology, 11*(1), 1–33.

Alharbi, J., Almahdi, H., & Mosbah, A. (2018). The Impact of Entrepreneurship Education Programs (EEPs) on the Entrepreneurial Attitudes Among Higher Education Students. *International Journal of Management, Economics and Social Sciences, 7*(3), 245–271.

Arab Youth Survey. (2020). *A Voice for Change*. A White Paper on the findings of the 12th Annual ASDA'A BCW Arab Youth Survey 2020. https://www.arabyouthsurvey.com/whitepaper.html

Asamani, L., & Mensah, A. O. (2013). Entrepreneurial Inclination Among Ghanaian University Students: The Case of University of Cape Coast, Ghana. *European Journal of Business and Management, 5*(19), 113–125.

Auerswald, P. E. (2015). Enabling Entrepreneurial Ecosystems: Insights from Ecology to Inform Effective Entrepreneurship Policy. In *Kauffman Foundation Research Series on City, Metro, and Regional Entrepreneurship*. School of Policy, Government, and International Affairs, George Mason University.

AWLO. (2011). *Arab Women Leadership Outlook 2009–2011* (1st ed.). Dubai Women Establishment. https://www.pwc.com/gx/en/women-at-pwc/assets/arab-women-leadership-outlook.pdf

Bacigalupo, M., Kampylis, P., Punie, Y., & Van den Brande, G. (2016). *EntreComp: The Entrepreneurship Competence Framework*. Publication Office of the European Union, EUR 27939 EN. https://doi.org/10.2791/593884

Baptista, R., & Naia, A. (2015). Entrepreneurship Education: A Selective Examination of the Literature. *Foundations and Trends in Entrepreneurship, 11*(5), 337–426.

Béchard, J. P., & Grégoire, D. (2005). Entrepreneurship Education Research Revisited: The Case of Higher Education. *Academy of Management Learning & Education, 4*(1), 22–43.

Blattman, C., & Ralston, L. (2015). *Generating Employment in Poor and Fragile States: Evidence from Labor Market and Entrepreneurship Programs*. World Bank. https://ssrn.com/abstract=2622220

Brixiová, Z., Ncube, M., & Bicaba, Z. (2014). *Skills and Youth Entrepreneurship in Africa: Analysis with Evidence from Swaziland*. Working Paper 204. African Development Bank.

Brookings Institute. (2013, September). *Women Entrepreneurship and the Opportunity to Promote Development and Business*. Policy Brief. http://www.brookings.edu/~/media/research/files/reports/2013/09/private-sector-global-poverty-blum-roundtable/2013-bbr-women-entrepreneurship.pdf

Burke, A. E., Fitzroy, F. R., & Nolan, M. A. (2002). Self-Employment Wealth and Job Creation: The Roles of Gender, Non-pecuniary Motivation and Entrepreneurial Ability. *Small Business Economics, 19*(3), 255–270.

Cho, Y., & Honorati, M. (2013). *Entrepreneurship Programs in Developing Countries: A Meta Regression Analysis*. Policy Research Working Paper 6402. World Bank.

Dana, L. P. (2001). The education and training of entrepreneurs in Asia. *Education and Training, 43*, 405–415.

Dyer, W. G., Jr. (1994). Towards a Theory of Entrepreneurial Careers. *Entrepreneurship Theory and Practice, 19*(2), 7–21.

El Ghoul, A., & Amrouni, H. (2017, November 17). *L'enseignement de l'Entrepreneuriat en Tunisie: Université versus hors Université: Vers la mise en place de l'Approche par Compétence*. BEMM 2017: International Conference on Business, Economics, Marketing & Management Research (BEMM-2017), Sousse, Tunisia.

El-Gohary, H., & Eid, R. (2013). Leadership Teaching Impact on Tourism Students' Attitudes and Perceptions Toward Leadership in Developing Economies: The Case of Egypt. *Journal of Hospitality & Tourism Education, 25*(4), 180–192.

El-Gohary, H., O'Leary, S., & Radway, P. (2012). Investigating the Impact of Entrepreneurship Online Teaching on Science and Technology Degrees on Students attitudes in Developing Economies: The case of Egypt. *International Journal of Online Marketing, 2*(1), 29–45.

ESCWA. (2019). *Innovation and Entrepreneurship: Opportunities and Challenges for Arab Youth and Women*. United Nations. https://www.unescwa.org/sites/www.unescwa.org/files/page_attachments/innovation-entrepreneurship-women-youth-arab_region-en_0.pdf

European Commission. (2011). *Entrepreneurship Education: Enabling Teachers as a Critical Success Factor*. A Report on Teacher Education and Training to Prepare Teachers for the Challenge of Entrepreneurship Education. Final Report, Bruxelles.

Fatoki, O., & Chindoga, L. (2011). An Investigation Into the Obstacles to Youth Entrepreneurship in South Africa. *International Business Research, 4*(2), 161–169. https://doi.org/10.5539/ibr.v4n2p161

Garavan, T. N., & O'Cinneide, B. (1994). Entrepreneurship Education and Training Programmes: A Review and Evaluation Part 1. *Journal of European Industrial Training, 18*, 3–12. https://doi.org/10.1108/03090599410068024

Ghorfi, T. (2017). *Entreprises Familiales: Des paradoxes aux opportunités* (p. 328). Editions La Croisée des chemins.

Ghorfi, T., & Jurd de Girancourt, D. (2021). *Femmes au cœur des entreprises familiales* (p. 224). Editions La Croisée des chemins.

Gibb, A. (2002). In Pursuit of a New 'Enterprise' and 'Entrepreneurship' Paradigm for Learning: Creative Destruction, New Values, New Ways of Doing Things and New Combinations of Knowledge. *International Journal of Management Reviews, 4*(3), 233–269.

Global Entrepreneurship Monitor. (2019). *2019/2020 Global Report*. https://www.gemconsortium.org/report/gem-2019-2020-global-report

Gottleib, E., & Ross, J. A. (1997). Made Not Born: HBS Courses and Entrepreneurial Management. *Harvard Business School Bulletin, 73*, 41–45.

Greene, P. G., Brush, C. G., Eisenman, E. J., Neck, H., & Perkins, S. (2016). *Entrepreneurship Education: A Global Consideration from Practice to Policy Around the World*. https://www.wise-qatar.org/app/uploads/2019/04/appli-babson_2016-03-03_0.pdf.

Hanushek, E. A., & Woessmann, L. (2007). *The Role of Education Quality for Economic Growth*. Policy Research Working Paper; No. 4122. World Bank. License: CC BY 3.0 IGO. https://openknowledge.worldbank.org/handle/10986/7154

Hynes, B. (1996). Entrepreneurship Education and Training: Introducing Entrepreneurship Into Non-Business Disciplines. *Journal of European Industrial Training, 20*(8), 10–17.

Hytti, U. (2005). New Meanings for Entrepreneurs: From Risk-Taking Heroes to Safe-Seeking Professionals. *Journal of Organizational Change Management, 18*, 594–611.

ILO. (2020). *Global Employment Trends for Youth 2020: Arab States*. https://www.ilo.org/wcmsp5/groups/public/%2D%2D-dgreports/%2D%2D-dcomm/documents/briefingnote/wcms_737672.pdf

Ismail, K., Ahmad, A. R., Gadar, K., & Yunus, N. K. Y. (2012). Stimulating Factors on Women Entrepreneurial Intention. *Business Management Dynamics, 2*(6), 20–28.

Jamali, D. (2009). Constraints and Opportunities Facing Women Entrepreneurs in Developing Countries: A Relational Perspective. *Gender in Management, 24*(4), 232–233.

Jones, C., & English, J. (2004). A Contemporary Approach to Entrepreneurship Education. *Education + Training, 46*(8/9), 416–423.

Kansikas, J., & Laakkonen, A. (2009). Students' Perceptions of Family Entrepreneurship—A Study on Family Business Academic Education. *International Management, 14*(1), 55–65.

Kew, J., Namatovu, R., Aderinto, R., & Chigunta, F. (2015). *Africa's Young Entrepreneurs: Unlocking the Potential for a Brighter Future*. IDRC (International Development Research Centre) and GEM.

Klotz, A. C., Hmieleski, K. M., Bradley, B. H., & Busenitz, L. W. (2014). New Venture Teams A Review of the Literature and Roadmap for Future Research. *Journal of Management, 40*, 226–255.

Kristiansen, S., & Indarti, N. (2004). Entrepreneurial Intention Among Indonesian and Norwegian Students. *Journal of Enterprising Culture, 12*(01), 55–78.

Kuratko, D. F. (2004). *Entrepreneurship Education* in the 21st Century: From Legitimization to Leadership. *Proceedings of the U.S. Association for Small Business & Entrepreneurship, 29*, 45–60.

Kuratko, D. F. (2005). The Emergence of Entrepreneurship Education: Development, Trends, and Challenges. *Entrepreneurship Theory and Practice, 29*, 577–597.

Lewins, R. (2014). *Transforming Lives Through Entrepreneurship in Kenya: Final Evaluation Report*. Kenya Youth Business Trust and YBI (Youth Business International).

MagniTT. (2021). https://magnitt.com/research/2021-mena-venture-investment-report-50736

Mason, C., & Brown, R. (2014). *Entrepreneurial Ecosystems and Growth Oriented Entrepreneurship*. Background paper for OECD LEED Programme and Dutch Ministry of Economic Affairs Workshop on Entrepreneurial Ecosystems and Growth-Oriented Entrepreneurship, The Hague, Netherlands, November 7, 2013. Final Version: January 2014.

Montrose. (2016). *External Evaluation of YDP and NUYEP Programs: Final Evaluation Report*. Department for International Development, Government of United Kingdom. http://iati.dfid.gov.uk/iati_documents/5707277.pdf

O'Connor, A. (2013). A Conceptual Framework for Entrepreneurship Education Policy: Meeting Government and Economic Purposes. *Journal of Business Venturing, 28*, 546–563.

OECD. (2017). *Unlocking the Potential of Youth Entrepreneurship in Developing Countries: From Subsistence to Performance* (Development Centre Studies). OECD Publishing. https://doi.org/10.1787/9789264277830-en

Peterman, N. E., & Kennedy, J. (2003). Enterprise Education: Influencing Students' Perceptions of Entrepreneurship. *Entrepreneurship: Theory & Practice, 28*, 129–144.

Pistrui, D., Welch, H. P., Wintermantel, O., Liao, J., & Pohl, H. J. (2000). Entrepreneurial Orientation and Family Forces in the New Germany: Similarities and Differences Between East and West German Entrepreneurs. *Family Business Review, XIII*(3), 251–264.

Porter, L. (1994). The Relation of Entrepreneurship Education to Business Education. *Simulation and Gaming, 25*(3), 416–419.

Price Waterhouse Coopers. (2016). Middle East Family Business Survey 2016. Online Report. http://www.pwc.com/m1/en/publications/family-business-survey.html

Price Waterhouse Coopers. (2019). Future-Proofing Middle East Family Businesses: Achieving Sustainable Growth During Disruptive Times. *PWC Middle East Family Business Survey 2019*. https://www.pwc.com/m1/en/publications/documents/family-business-survey-2019.pdf

Ronstadt, R. (1987). The Educated Entrepreneurs: A New Era of Entrepreneurial Education Is Beginning. *American Journal of Small Business, 11*(4), 37–53.

Sagie, A., & Elizur, D. (1999). Achievement Motive and Entrepreneurial Orientation: A Structural Analysis. *Journal of Organisational Behavior, 20*, 375–387.

Schumpeter, J. A. (1934). *The Theory of Economic Development*. Harvard University.

Seymour, N. (2001). *Entrepreneurship Education in American Community Colleges and Universities*. ERIC Clearinghouse for Junior Colleges (ED463784).

Souitaris, V., Zerbinati, S., & Al-Laham, A. (2007). Do Entrepreneurship Programs Raise Entrepreneurial Intentions of Science and Engineering Students? The Effect of Learning, Inspiration and Resources. *Journal of Business Venturing, 22*(4), 566–591.

Terjesen, S., & Lloyd, A. (2015). *The 2015 Female Entrepreneurship Index (FEI): Analyzing the Conditions that Foster High-Potential Female Entrepreneurship in 77 Countries*. Global Entrepreneurship and Development Institute.

Tucker, D., & Selcuk, S. S. (2009). Which Factors Affect Entrepreneurial Intention of University Students? *Journal of European Industrial Training, 33*(2), 142–159.

UNDP. (2019). Youth in the Arab Region. *Youth Newsletter 2019.* https://www.arabdevelopmentportal.com/sites/default/files/publication/booklet_final_upload.pdf

UNESCO. (2013). *Entrepreneurship Education in Arab States.* A Joint Project Between UNESCO and StratREAL Foundation, UK. Final Evaluation Report. https://unevoc.unesco.org/fileadmin/user_upload/docs/EPE_Final_Evaluation_Report__EN_.pdf

UNESCO. (2014). *Girls' and Women's Right to Education: Overview of the Measures Supporting the Right to Education for Girls and Women.* Reported by the Member States. https://unesdoc.unesco.org/ark:/48223/pf0000227859

UNESCO. (2018). *Arab Region Outcome Statement Towards Inclusive and Equitable Quality Learning Opportunities for All.* https://unesdoc.unesco.org/ark:/48223/pf0000266236.locale=en

Valerio, A., Parton, B., & Robb, A. (2014). *Entrepreneurship Education and Training Programs Around the World: Dimensions for Success.* World Bank. https://doi.org/10.1596/978-1-4648-0202-7

Varghese, T., & Hassan, A. (2012). Youth's Entrepreneurial Attitudes in Oman. *World Journal of Social Sciences, 2* (7). November 2012 Issue. 302–325.

Verheul, I., Uhlaner, L., & Thurik, R. (2005). Business Accomplishments, Gender and Entrepreneurial Self-Age. *Journal of Business Venturing, 20*, 483–518.

Wang, C. K., & Wong, P.-K. (2004). Entrepreneurial Interest of University Students in Singapore. *Technovation, 24*(2), 163–172.

WEF. (2020). *Global Gender Gap Report 2020.* http://www3.weforum.org/docs/WEF_GGGR_2020.pdf

YBI. (2011). *Global Youth Entrepreneurship Survey: How Non-financial Support Is Valued by Young People Starting and Growing a Business.* https://www.youth-business.org/wp-content/uploads/2012/08/YouthEntrepreneurshipSurvey2011.pdf

YBI. (2013). *Global Youth Entrepreneurship Summit: Business as Unusual. Report.* https://youtheconomicopportunities.org/sites/default/files/uploads/resource/YBI-Global-Summit-Report.pdf

YBI (Youth Business International), Ernst & Young. (2016). *Supporting Young Entrepreneurs: What Works? An Evidence and Learning Review from the YBI Network.* https://www.youthbusiness.org/wp-content/uploads/2016/12/YBI-Learning-Review-web-version.pdf

7

Strategies for Managing Institutional Pressures in a Turbulent and Dynamic Institutional Context

Sofiane Baba, Taïeb Hafsi, and Omar Hemissi

Introduction

Middle Eastern and North African countries are generally characterized by relatively intense and persistent institutional instability. This is particularly Algeria's case, which has experienced an unstable institutional and political situation since its hard-earned independence in 1962. Undertaking entrepreneurial endeavors in this type of context is naturally arduous. So much so that private entrepreneurship is barely taking off

S. Baba (✉)
Université de Sherbrooke, Sherbrooke, QC, Canada
e-mail: sofiane.baba@usherbrooke.ca

T. Hafsi
HEC Montréal, Montreal, QC, Canada
e-mail: taieb.2.hafsi@hec.ca

O. Hemissi
École Supérieure de Commerce d'Alger, Koléa, Algeria
e-mail: o_hemissi@esc-alger.dz

N. Azoury, T. Hafsi (eds.), *Entrepreneurship and Social Entrepreneurship in the MENA Region*, https://doi.org/10.1007/978-3-030-88447-5_7

and suffers greatly from this institutional instability. Institutional pressures, taking the form of contradictory prescriptions, are a regular feature of the institutional environment (Amrouni, 2019). This issue has been at the core of many research studies over the last few decades (Baba et al., 2021). Organizations' strategic responses to institutional pressures are an integral component of institutional theory (Micelotta et al., 2017; Quirke, 2013; Ramus et al., 2017). Institutional pressures can be defined as the set of demands, expectations, and requirements explicitly or implicitly formulated by various institutional actors to induce other actors to conform to specific rules, practices, norms, values, and beliefs.

Mainly motivated by the observation that organizations tend to adopt positions of retaliation or resistance rather than conforming to institutional pressures as posited by classic institutional theorists, the literature on this topic has undergone significant development. Overall, these studies have enriched our understanding of the origins of institutional pressures, the various strategies adopted by organizations, and the antecedents and outcomes of these strategies (Oliver, 1991; Suchman, 1995; Tian et al., 2009; Wijethilake et al., 2017). Nevertheless, entrepreneurs' strategic behavior when facing public authorities' institutional pressures has not received the attention required. Mainly fuelled by Western examples and phenomena, the extant research has mostly studied stable institutional environments, where actors' behaviors are relatively predictable and framed by well-established legal anchors. However, other—more turbulent and dynamic—institutional contexts, such as those in North African countries, can enhance our knowledge about how private entrepreneurs perceive, understand, make sense of, and respond to institutional pressures emanating from state structures. In this vein, the North African context is institutionally emergent insofar as the rules and regulations are still unclear and primarily informal, and the environment is both dynamic and turbulent. As a result, institutional pressures on companies are more substantial (Tian et al., 2009).

Thus, North Africa appears to be a suitable field to study the management of institutional pressures in an unstable and dynamic context (George et al., 2016). More generally, the African continent has been increasingly marked by significant social, economic, and political transformations over the past five decades (Kolk & Rivera-Santos, 2018).

These transformations have had a considerable impact on the way institutional and business actors interact, and at the same time, generate areas of uncertainty, tribulation, and contestation, revealing the extent of institutional complexity (Greenwood et al., 2011). Cultural and institutional patterns inherited from the colonization period amplify institutional complexity issues as actors work to find new arrangements consistent with emerging national values, cultures and norms (George et al., 2016). Moreover, the progressive liberalization of African economies, driven by critical socioeconomic needs, generates added tension between the historically centralizing administrative logic and the logic of private sector's entrepreneurial efficiency. This is calling for a redefinition of the traditional relationship between public authorities and private entrepreneurs.

Algeria, our empirical context, illustrates well these broader African institutional and organizational realities (McDougall, 2017). The emergence of the private sector in Algeria has been characterized since the 1980s by a substantial change in the relationship between private firms and the state (Hemissi & Hafsi, 2017; Martinez & Boserup, 2016). Since its independence in 1962, Algeria has adopted a socialist regime where the state is at the same time regulator, investor, entrepreneur, and producer of goods and services. However, successive socioeconomic crises have led to the gradual involvement of private initiatives to compensate for the increasingly wide gaps between the needs of the population and the public's means and capacities to deliver economic prosperity (Hafsi, 2012). The gradual liberalization of the market and the increasing role of the private sector have generated major conflicts between public authorities and private entrepreneurs, especially since the 1990s. Increasing complexity and disputes, which have reached their peak in the early 2000s, have intensified again since the 2010s, with significant institutional pressures on entrepreneurs. Difficult access to industrial land, blackmail and corruption, punishing licensing and authorization systems, and media controversies, characterize the state–private entrepreneurs relationships.

With this background in mind, this chapter focuses on a simple yet intriguing and overlooked research question: *how do private entrepreneurs make sense of and strategically respond to institutional pressures in a turbulent and complex institutional environment?* To sketch some answers to this question, we study the strategic responses of four Algerian entrepreneurs using a qualitative methodological approach.

Theoretical Background: From Institutional Complexity to Institutional Pressures

Pioneering work in institutional theory emphasizes the homogeneity of organizational forms, structures, and behaviors (D'Aunno et al., 1991; Deephouse, 1996). Institutional pressures that actors face lead them to conform to increase their legitimacy, a critical condition for access to resources and survival (DiMaggio & Powell, 1983; Elsbach & Sutton, 1992; Suchman, 1995). The continuous quest for legitimacy is the basis of institutional isomorphism, defined as "a constraining process that forces a unit of a population to resemble other units facing the same set of environmental conditions" (DiMaggio & Powell, 1983: 149). In contrast to the institutionalist tradition, Oliver (1991) argued that organizations could respond more strategically to institutional pressures and somewhat depart from outright conformism.

In her theoretical article, Oliver (1991) identifies five strategies that actors can adopt to respond to institutional pressures: acceptance, compromise, avoidance, confrontation, and manipulation. She predicted the use of these strategies based on organizational and contextual backgrounds. Isomorphic behavior is stimulated by the need to improve actors' socioeconomic situation, or their dependence on the source of institutional pressures. It may also be a logical response to contradictory or inconsistent institutional pressures, their conflict with the actor's objectives. It can also be affected by the binding or non-binding, voluntary or coercive nature of the pressures, and the degree of uncertainty and interdependence that characterizes the institutional field (Oliver, 1991: 160).

Empirical research has tested and contextualized Oliver's hypotheses (see Tian et al., 2009). The literature has also focused on contradictory pressures in the context of institutional complexity (Seo & Creed, 2002). Institutional complexity, we said, can result from conflicting or ambiguous institutional demands. The literature suggests that institutional complexity exposes actors to conflicting institutional demands and requirements (Greenwood et al., 2011; Raaijmakers et al., 2014), blurring the trajectories by which organizations can reasonably respond and maintain legitimacy (Kostova & Zaheer, 1999; Pache & Santos, 2010).

Nevertheless, despite its quantitative and qualitative development, the literature on strategic responses to institutional pressures remains partial for four main reasons. First, actors' strategic behaviors are assumed to be *de facto* reactive. Organizational intentions and strategies to influence the source of institutional pressures are overlooked. At least anecdotal evidence shows that firms may go beyond the survival strategies evoked to actively manage institutional pressures, influencing their source or changing their nature. A relational approach, based on the way actors manage their relationships with the sources of pressure, is thus a promising avenue.

Second, the literature considers that dependence on the source of institutional pressures mainly favors acceptance and compromise strategies. We know that when institutional pressures are characterized by force and coercion, the target seems to have no choice but to comply (Lawrence et al., 2001). However, actors' responses to coercive institutional pressure (such as those from public authorities) are poorly documented (Raaijmakers et al., 2014). Even though actors' dependence on institutional pressure sources is a determinant of strategic responses, this aspect received little attention in the literature, even when the actors' dependence is very strong.

Third, in the study of strategies used by actors to respond to institutional pressures, the importance of actors' interpretations of the pressures imposed upon them remains marginalized (Raaijmakers et al., 2014). Yet, the literature shows that institutional actors interpret, analyze and make sense of institutional pressures (Dhalla & Oliver, 2013; Oliver, 1991), which greatly influences their motivations and management strategies. For example, Berrone et al. (2010: 82) suggest that family firms tend to respond to institutional pressures to preserve their social-emotional wealth.

Finally, the fourth limitation is empirical. Despite a few exceptions (He et al., 2007; Tilcsik, 2017), the literature on institutional pressures have mainly examined Western cases with relatively stable, predictable, and mature institutional contexts (Greenwood & Suddaby, 2006). In contrast, emerging institutional contexts, such as the African context, have been little studied and this is true for management in general (George et al., 2016; Kolk & Rivera-Santos, 2018). This biases our understanding of strategic responses to institutional pressures to the extent that institutional fields are the predominant source of pressures for institutional compliance (Zietsma et al., 2017). The nature and extent of institutional pressures depend significantly on the institutional context in which they take shape. However, emerging institutional contexts are rather unstable, unpredictable, and turbulent (Lawrence et al., 2002; Maguire & Hardy, 2009). In the case of Africa, the state and in general state-related actors are dominant in institutional dynamics. Thus, the study of emerging institutional contexts is likely to generate new insights and can enrich our understanding of how organizational actors interpret and respond to institutional pressures.

Taken together, these theoretical considerations lead us to focus more on how entrepreneurs manage institutional pressures from the state in a volatile and complex institutional context. In this chapter, we conceptualize institutional pressures from the perspective of institutional complexity (Ramus et al., 2017; Smets & Jarzabkowski, 2013), understood as a situation of conflict and opposition between several institutional logics. Institutional logics represent "the socially constructed, historical patterns of material practices, assumptions, values, beliefs, and rules by which individuals produce and reproduce their material subsistence, organize time and space, and provide meaning to their social reality" (Thornton & Ocasio, 1999: 804). We thus recognize an administrative logic, adopted by public authorities, and a more entrepreneurial logic, to which private entrepreneurs adhere. When these logics come into confrontation, they can generate revealing behavior, strategies, and practices. This chapter intends to reveal these and contribute to the understanding of both state and firm practices in complex institutional settings.

Methods

Research Design

To investigate the strategies used by Algerian entrepreneurs for managing institutional pressures in a turbulent environment, we made three specific methodological choices. First, we adopted a qualitative approach because of its usefulness in exploratory research. It allows researchers to explore, analyze, and understand the motivations, perceptions, and strategies deployed by social actors to propose theories (Patton, 2002). Second, our study is process-based, focusing on "how and why things emerge, develop, grow, or terminate over time" (Langley et al., 2013: 1). Finally, four revealing case studies were selected in our multi-case study (Yin, 2003). They describe four Algerian SMEs chosen from a panel of family businesses. In particular, we focused on the behavior of the entrepreneurs leading these firms. Considering the data's sensitive nature, we anonymized these firms in relation to their strategic behavior toward the state. In what follows, we shall talk about Lion, Fennec, Chameleon, and Duck.

Data Sources

We collected primary and secondary data for the four organizations studied to ensure data triangulation and our research quality. The data was progressively collected between 2007 and 2018. The primary data is based on 60 semi-structured interviews conducted with executive teams, including the founding presidents, the chief executive officers, and board members. Semi-structured interviews were also conducted with senior Algerian state officials, including heads of regulatory agencies and senior officials in ministries directly involved in economic and business activities. Concerning secondary data, numerous press articles were sorted and analyzed from Algeria's leading electronic media.[1] In sum, our immersion in the organizational contexts studied started in 2007 and was going on while writing this chapter. This has provided a unique and in-depth perspective on the issues studied.

Data Analysis

The collected data were analyzed in an abductive manner (Patton, 2002) by comparing the preliminary results from our data with strategies and tactics discussed in the literature on an ongoing and iterative basis. This continuing and iterative process between our data and the literature allowed us to propose an interpretive framework that gives structure and meaning to our data. This framework is based on two particular factors related to strategies for managing institutional pressures: the degree of proximity of the organization/entrepreneur with the state (complicity or adversity) and the strategic posture (or strategic modes) of the organization/entrepreneur towards institutions (preserving the status quo to increase acceptance or reforming institutions through institutional work).

Analysis: Strategies for Managing Institutional Pressures in State-Business Relations in Algeria

The complexity of the Algerian institutional context, we said, translates into survival issues for entrepreneurs and SMEs. In this vein, they must continuously develop strategic approaches to avoid or mitigate institutional pressures. The analysis section presents these approaches by distinguishing (a) the actors' motivations, (b) their approach, and (c) the outcomes. Our empirical analysis of the four entrepreneurs allows us to distinguish two strategies, each of which appears under two strategic modes. First, there is a proactive strategy, aiming to reform institutions to reduce institutional pressures. The proactive strategy thus focuses on entrepreneurs' actions directing to influence the sources of pressures. Here, two modes are identified depending on the entrepreneurs' proximity with the sources of pressures: proactive collaboration or confrontation. The second strategy is more passive, which is reflected in the nature of the relationship that entrepreneurs have with public authorities. The two related modes are collaborative avoidance (strategic discretion to develop their activities in the shadows) or collaborative compliance (assimilation into the system to mitigate the effect of these pressures and

Table 7.1 Summary of the four strategies for managing institutional pressures by Algerian entrepreneurs

Case	Strategies	Postures or strategic modes	Intentions	Relationship with the source of the pressures
Lion	Proactive strategy	Confrontation	Reforming institutions to reduce institutional pressures	Distance
Chameleon		Proactive cooperation		Proximity
Fennec	Passive strategy	Collaborative avoidance	Gain acceptance to reduce institutional pressures	Distance
Duck		Collaborative compliance		Proximity

preserve their social status). This section presents the cases in the following sequence: Lion and Chameleon (proactive strategy), then Fennec and Duck (passive strategy). Table 7.1 below summarizes the strategies and postures adopted by the Algerian firms studied. Moreover, Table 7.2 summarizes the analysis of the four cases and provides empirical illustrations (Table 7.2).

The Lion Case: The Strategy of Confrontation for External Change

Lion is one of the largest private Algerian companies. Active in several industries, it has been officially operating in Algeria for just over two decades. Its founder was the owner of other companies previously. Lion used to operate mainly in the food industry before becoming a conglomerate that operates worldwide. Its situation is the archetype of the opposition of an entrepreneurial logic to bureaucratic and administrative logics. As a symbol of the still nascent freedom of enterprise in a traditionally socialist country where economic statism is taken for granted, Lion is naturally the target of significant institutional pressures and harassment, ranging from barriers erected for access to resources and means, to recurrent blockages of its projects, to confrontations with high-ranking officials through the media. In this context, the company has adopted a

Table 7.2 Summary of the analysis of the four cases and empirical illustrations

Strategies and cases	Motivations	Postures and actions
Lion *Proactive response strategy* Chameleon	• Reducing institutional pressures • Changing institutions from the outside • Getting the authorities to reform the institutions	• Open confrontation with public authorities • Denunciation and uncovering of institutional dysfunctions
	• Avoid institutional pressures • Changing institutions from within • Fostering greater openness of institutions to the business world	• Economic and institutional collaboration with public authorities • Attempt to reconcile the entrepreneurial and administrative logics
Fennec *Passive response strategy* Duck	• Reconciling the entrepreneurial logic of efficiency with the values and traditions of the community • Reducing institutional pressures by being discreet and conformist	• Maintaining harmonious and positive relations with local authorities • Gradual distancing from the public sector by moving away from segments dependent on public procurement
	• To perpetuate the activities of the firm • Acceptance by the authorities to alleviate institutional pressures	• Maintaining a collaborative relationship with public authorities • Positioning as strategic partners of the state, particularly in sectors that are not very coveted.

Results	Empirical illustrations
• Limits the influence of institutional pressures due to strong media coverage of the firm and its difficulties with the state • Increased legitimacy in the eyes of segments of the national population	• Many of *Lion's* projects are stalled, either by the backlog of imported equipment at customs or by obstacles encountered in industrial land granting. • The number of jobs created and the social actions undertaken for the benefit of both the public and university associations of civil society have strengthened *Lion's* position and led public authorities to exercise caution.
• Significant reduction in institutional pressures • Increased legitimacy in the eyes of local actors and public authorities, but eroding legitimacy in the eyes of the population more critical of the state	• *Chameleon* is a major player in the bodies playing the role of intermediary between the business world and public authorities. • The state involves its partner in many actions while granting it advantages and facilities, which brings it closer to public authorities but calls into question its proximity and notoriety with the population.
• Maintain respectful relationships with the authorities to reduce institutional pressures • Internal conflicts related to the reconciliation between corporate efficiency and community values	• Heavily dependent on public contracts to develop its activities, *Fennec* had to reconcile its values and the acceptance of the conditions imposed by the state and its institutions. • A major and progressive change is being made in its business model to move away from institutional pressures by leaning towards the retail market.
• Mitigation of institutional pressures through discretion and deployment in low-profile activities. • Reinforcing its position through the exclusivity granted by public authorities and the diversification of services in adaptation to remote geographic areas.	• Acting from the outset as a cohort to support the state's strategic partners by providing them with various services and benefits, *Duck* has found a place where it is sheltered from pressure. • *Duck* has legitimized his role as a collaborator and has succeeded in alleviating institutional pressures, meeting the expectations, and adapting to partners' needs in a disadvantaged region.

strategy of confrontation by questioning the legitimacy of the mechanisms put in place by state institutions and demonstrating their dysfunction and responsibility for the failures of the global economic and even social configuration.

Motivations

Analysis of *Lion*'s strategic behavior shows two main interrelated motivations. First, the executives continue to grow their businesses, expand their market share, and contribute to local development through job creation. Second, *Lion aims to* change the logic of public authority action toward economic operators.

Protect the Organization from Blockages

Lion is a fast-growing company. Leader in Algeria in several fields of activity, it is going international with strategic investments in Africa and Europe. However, several of its development projects—recognized as avant-garde and useful for the country's development—are blocked. Blockages generally take three forms: investment authorizations that are not granted, draconian administrative hassle to authorize any new investment projects in Algeria and abroad, punitive customs procedures for the importation of needed equipment. Some projects have been blocked since 2006, even though—according to feasibility studies—they promise to reduce food dependency in some areas. Recently, an advanced technological innovation project has been stalled for more than a year due to a dispute over imported machinery valuation. These deliberate actions are clearly a response to *Lion*'s confrontational approach.

Radically Transform Institutions

In their media statements and at professional forums and academic gatherings, *Lion*'s leaders cite weakened and dysfunctional state institutions as the reason for the country's socioeconomic underdevelopment. These dysfunctions are said to be the source of administrative and bureaucratic slippages that could destroy the company. This media strategy aims to expose public actions' contradictions and their inconsistency with legislation governing economic development. By their motivations and procedures, *Lion*'s actions are determinedly in line with the strategic management of institutional pressures.

Approach

In terms of the strategic management of institutional pressures, *Lion's* action is based on three main pillars: continuously displaying its critical stance toward the decisions and pressures of the public authorities, uncovering their inconsistencies and dysfunctions, and strengthening as much as possible its position as an active economic operator and job creator.

Critical Position Towards the Decisions of the Public Authorities

Lion adopts an approach of confrontation with the Algerian public authorities through the media, social networks, and public speaking. Between 2010 and 2019, the company strengthened its media presence. This has enabled it to maintain a counter-pressure in the face of the authority's behavior. *Lion*'s media efforts are focused on two elements: (1) highlighting its place in the market and its desire to develop its activities and (2) questioning the institutional pressures as detrimental to Algeria's economic development.

Revealing Public Institutions' Inconsistencies and Dysfunctions

The company has a transparency strategy, where all the details of projects, blockages, and government actions contrary to the law are disclosed. This allows the company to denounce decisions and actions openly and factually by public authorities that run counter to public policies' economic objectives. In this context, the founder left the most important Algerian employers' organization, deemed too close to the Algerian authorities, thus publicly displaying his distance from the state's representatives and symbols.

Reinforcement of the Position as an Economic Actor

Through the speeches of its senior leaders, recurring press releases and public statements, *Lion* does not fail to highlight its contributions to the socioeconomic development of the country, displaying the results of its investments, the direct and indirect jobs created and those in perspective, as well as its social responsibility. *Lion*'s CEO often states: "for every dinar we earn, we pay 60% in taxes, we reinvest 39% and only 1% is shared among shareholders." Thus, *Lion* exerts a counter pressure likely to work in his favor against public authorities' pressure.

Outcomes

Lion's approach in dealing with the state leads to three interesting outcomes. First, it strengthened popular legitimacy. In a turbulent sociopolitical context, notably marked by a major popular protest against the state, *Lion*'s confrontation strategy has enabled the company to increase its legitimacy and popular support. The expression of popular support has even taken the form of marches and demonstrations in support of the company against the bureaucratic hassles its investments face, particularly in the region where *Lion*'s investments are mainly concentrated. Second, *Lion*'s approach led to the creation of a balance in the relationship with the state. In particular, Lion's confrontational approach has enabled him to develop considerable resilience, which has led some public institutions' representatives to avoid confrontation with the population. Therefore, this approach has enabled him to be visible enough to encourage public authorities to be cautious about institutional pressure. Indeed, as a key player in the country's economic scene, Lion's social media approach allows it to transform its popular legitimacy into a mechanism for maintaining a certain balance. Finally, the company's approach did not entirely eliminate institutional pressures as they persist. Despite its means of retaliation, the company continues to face institutional pressure and large-scale blockages. Both local authorities and customs services block several projects under legally questionable conditions. Legal and media imbroglios regularly occur, thus delaying the realization of the announced projects.

Chameleon's Case: The Strategy of Proactive Collaboration and Change Through Compliance and Proximity

Chameleon has a large market share in two agri-food sectors. The company is a leader in processing agricultural products and one of the main producers of mass consumption products. Its strategy is centered on controlling the value chain starting from the agricultural upstream and concentrating its activities in a region specialized in producing its agricultural supplies. Given its size and its influence on the local environment, *Chameleon* is subject to institutional pressures of various kinds, particularly in terms of the conditions for developing its activities and obtaining administrative authorizations for the import of raw materials and production equipment. Several of its projects have been blocked for often unclear reasons. The company adopts a strategy based on close relations with all state structures, both local and central, and collaboration and direct involvement in public–private ventures. This strategy reveals the will to change the behavior of institutional actors. *Chameleon* has turned its proximity and collaboration strategy with public authorities into a proactive approach to lead and accompany them in a change conducive to entrepreneurial freedom.

Motivations

The proximity strategy adopted by *Chameleon* highlights three main motivations: to bring the public authorities to change their attitude towards entrepreneurs, to develop its negotiation skills by getting involved in the logic of the public authorities, and to develop its business through better relationships with state decision-making actors.

Impulse a new "State-Business" Relational Logic Through Concession

Chameleon began its business journey with a sizeable concession, accepting to forgo the land allocated to it for the construction of the plant, to the benefit of another operator, who had close relationships with political actors. It was then unknown and powerless. The newly obtained land was located in an isolated area, far from roads and with limited infrastructure. Besides, the new lot was listed as a protected agricultural site and required special construction authorizations. *Chameleon* also had to agree to sign an agreement with a shaky public packaging company on the brink of bankruptcy to make an exclusive supplier. With this cooperative attitude, *Chameleon* attempted to create links with local and territorial authorities and bring them to maintain co-development relations that would benefit both the company and the state.

Replace the State as an Actor-Partner

Chameleon favors relationships based on collaboration, involvement, and active participation in economic development to show its willingness to be a loyal partner. The company positioned itself as a promoter of modern agriculture, providing assistance and support to farmers, helping them to grow essential supplies for *Chameleon*'s processing plants. Later, public authorities asked *Chameleon's* CEO to partner with a public company in difficulty through a public–private project. *Chameleon* was granted full control and exclusive responsibility for the management of the new mixed company.

Growing Sheltered from Pressure

Motivated by its desire for growth and expansion, and strengthened by its leadership position in a segment where its dependence on public authorities is relatively low, *Chameleon* developed a strategy of proximity to mitigate the impact of political pressures on businesses in general. The company worked with the population, local elected officials, and public authority representatives to open up the region and create an entrepreneurial spirit, thereby building a solid, unified front to counter institutional pressures.

Approach

The company built closer ties with public authorities, seeing this as a winning strategy to reduce pressure and change institutions from within.

Involvement and Collaboration in Socioeconomic Life

Chameleon's strategy includes associating itself with public sector agencies, including some in charge of developing sensitive sectors of Algerian agriculture. Partnership actions with public sector companies ensure the required proximity and reduce institutional pressures. Dozens of small companies have sprung up around *Chameleon*'s factories to take charge of transport, logistics, packaging, and various services. The company's plants have become training and employment centers for the region's future engineers and technicians.

Proximity to the Community and the Authorities

This posture is reflected in the deployment of significant means for collaboration and involvement as well as strong social and community commitment. It is also focused on meeting the local population's needs, through recruitment, internships for students and apprentices, financial aid for needy families, and work to improve the local living environment.

Chameleon has also invested in state bodies to develop agriculture and collaborate with public authorities around common challenges. In this way, it positions itself as a partner of the state in search of solutions to food insecurity.

Promotion of an Image of Progress and Development

Quality, performance, and social commitment are the keywords of *Chameleon*'s institutional communication. Fulfilling the role of promoter and facilitator of entrepreneurship, financing educational, community, and even sports activities helped develop a positive image of *Chameleon*, deserving a favorable relationship with the state. Financial aid to the poor, management and maintenance of local cemeteries, help to public vocational training centers, and local school laureates' encouragement have reinforced this image. The company spares no effort to involve the public authorities in its successes to share the credit.

Outcomes

Chameleon's approach to dealing with institutional pressures have generated two main outcomes. First is a noticeable reduction of institutional pressures. To establish its strategy, *Chameleon* has gradually asserted itself as a public authorities partner in the regional economic development. It collaborates and is involved in the structures responsible for policy implementation. It stands out for its resilience and its ability to adapt to the vagaries of public decision-making. In three decades, it has built a solid and diversified industrial company while working to impel a change in the state's perception of entrepreneurs' role in economic development. Second, another unexpected outcome was the ambivalent impact on the firm's legitimacy. In fact, *Chameleon*'s proximity and collaboration have earned it a favorable attitude from public authorities. It benefits from advantages and support to develop its activities. The populations and local elected officials, in particular, have become fervent defenders of *Chameleon* with higher state authorities. However, some parties see this proximity as a strategy to benefit from undue facilities and privileges, affecting its community legitimacy. Unlike *Lion*, who enjoys growing legitimacy among the population for its confrontational approach, *Chameleon* is seen with ambivalence by the population for its proximity to a state which is losing legitimacy.

The Fennec Case: The Ambiguous Strategy of Avoidance-Collaboration

Fennec is a leading family-owned company in the extrusion manufacturing of pipes and profiles for PVC (polyvinyl chloride) and polyethylene carpentry. The company's strengths lie in its expertise in the production of products widely used for the distribution of drinking water and pressurized gas according to international standards. The two significant markets targeted by the company, water and gas, are mainly related to public contracts awarded through competitive tendering. The main clients are housing construction companies, state-owned energy distribution companies and municipalities for road works. These products and services are distributed throughout the country and, on a small scale, in some African countries. Over the last five years, the growth has been significant. *Fennec* is regularly called upon to collaborate with public authorities in the context of large public contracts. In a country where corruption is endemic, pressures to be involved are substantial. *Fennec* is the property of a family with strong religious values, incompatible with corrupt practices. So, the company adopts a strategy of distance and discretion to guard against institutional pressures and remain faithful to the Muslim ethical values that form the foundation of its corporate culture.

Motivations

Two main motivations related to institutional pressures are related to administrative blockages and corruption. On the one hand, *Fennec* wishes to maintain the organization's ethical principles by reducing institutional pressures. According to the managerial team, this justifies a distance from public authorities, even though they are highly dependent on them for public infrastructure and procurement contracts. On the other hand, the firm also wishes to sustain its activities, thus conceding certain compromises while ignoring the tendency of some members to reject those compromises for moral reasons. This state-of-affairs generates tensions within the organization.

Maintain the Ethical Principles of the Organization

The culture of the firm's founder is based on ethics, with strong religious roots. However, in these circles heavily affected by endemic corruption, *Fennec* faces a dilemma: on the one hand, to develop their business, they must work without reluctance with state agencies. On the other hand, to preserve their ethical virtues, they are forced to distance themselves from the state. Family members are divided on the behavior to be favored. Tensions with the authorities then lead to internal tensions at the level of corporate governance.

Reduce Institutional Pressures and Sustain the Activities of the Organization

Fennec is aware of its vulnerability to institutional pressures, given the importance of public procurement to its business model. The company remains dependent on public contracts and is working to earn them by developing quality delivery capacity and maintaining relationships with decision-makers. Dominated by a philosophy of ethical behavior that imposes distances from state decision-makers, but at the same time subject to extra-contractual requirements that are often at the limit of business ethics, the company is reactive and protective of resisting pressures.

Approach

For the management of institutional pressures, *Fennec's* behavior is rather passive. Three types of action are used: proximity to local decision-makers; discretion in one's affairs; and strategic reorientation. The latter appears to be the most obvious behavior.

Proximity with Local Decision-Makers

The company's executives adopt traditional behaviors of maintaining informal relationships with representatives of local and territorial authorities. The latter show kindness to the managers during meetings to which they are invited. They also involve them in the professional meetings they organize, making relationships natural and contacts frequent.

Discretion

The company executives are part of a pious and conservative family, which respects Islam's great precepts, with special attention to maintaining a respectable and benevolent relationship with the community, but without ostentation. Modest behavior in everyday life accentuates this discreet character. This modesty is illustrated in the nature of the relationship between executives and their staff and the entire community. This is particularly evident on religious holidays, where family members modestly show their perfect integration into the community while maintaining total discretion, which testifies the importance of the family's religious referents.

Strategic Reorientation

Fennec defines itself as a company dedicated to the quality of its services and operational efficiency on the one hand, and to social responsibility on the other. Its relationship with the state is ambiguous. They are both friendly and rigorous. Fennec focuses primarily on managing economic imperatives when carrying out its public projects, ignoring or diminishing extra-contractual requests from public authority representatives. This explains the firm's strategic reorientation to gradually move away from public procurement, a source of existential tension, and towards the consumer market.

Outcomes

The legitimacy and respect that the company enjoys among public authorities, employees, and civil society reinforce its approach of discretion and distant collaboration with public authorities. It is thus able to considerably reduce institutional pressures while reconciling the logic of efficiency and ethics. There main outcomes are noted.

First, the legitimacy and respect by the community and the authorities are important outcomes. *Fennec* imposes respect through its general behavior rather than through the systematic promotion of its image. The authorities perceive the founder as "a moral pillar." Philanthropic actions reinforce this image (complementary school, help for the sick, donations to community and religious associations), and the executives' religious values. Second, Fennec's approach led to a reduction of institutional pressures. Particularly thanks to its posture of strategic discretion and a rather distant relationship with public authorities, *Fennec* has been able to weather the institutional pressures that emerge from an environment conducive to corruption and unethical behavior. While these pressures have not really disappeared, the company is proactive in maintaining a harmonious balance between economic imperatives, public authority expectations, and the organization's moral pillars. Third and last, difficulties in reconciling ethics and efficiency are unexpected outcomes related to *Fennec*'s approach. Debates in the family on how to remain ethical are frequent. They are never resolved by a principle but by a search for compromise, which is a source of real internal tensions. The company's executives regularly question themselves on how to reconcile economic objectives with the organization's moral principles. Institutional pressures related to corruption are at the very heart of the tension between economic efficiency and ethics.

The Duck Case: A Strategy of Responsive Collaboration

Duck is a company providing various services that initially targeted a little known and therefore little coveted market. It operates mainly in isolated areas located in the country's south to benefit other companies whose profession requires continuous work and employees' permanent presence. However, the areas covered by the company are known for the administrative, security and regulatory requirements imposed by local authorities, given the sensitive nature of these territories for the country's energetic independence. To circumvent these requirements, the company has established contractual relationships with multinational companies operating in the region to benefit from their protection, maintaining exclusivity in providing services and thus justifying the investments made to meet all requests. The multinational partners are all foreign companies operating in Algeria under state contracts.

Motivations

Duck's strategies for responding to pressure are mainly motivated by the desire to evolve close to the sources of pressure to understand them better and develop its business by strengthening the partnership relationship with key actors in the region. The will of *Duck* is not so much to change institutions, but to be accepted in order to perpetuate its activities.

Evolve Near Sources of Pressure

The company's leaders support the idea that the best way to respond to institutional pressures is to be close to the sources of those pressures. In a desert region where operators are scarce, *Duck* has gradually made its way first by providing office supplies, beverages and other miscellaneous services, then providing ground and air transport and building and managing living bases for partner companies' benefit. In the absence of state means and infrastructure, the territorial authorities looked at *Duck* as a useful source of solutions needed to induce involvement and investment by foreign companies.

Work in Groups to Better Manage the Pressures

The partnership strategy has been the spearhead of *Duck*'s efforts to adapt to foreign companies' expectations and needs in the region. *Duck* invested in logistics and related activities because they were needed by client companies, sometimes at their request. In doing so, it has become an important partner and player, acquiring strength that protects it considerably from institutional pressures.

Approach

Duck's approach to dealing with institutional pressures is a passive one based on proximity to increase acceptance. It revolves around two behaviors.

The Partnership with State Partners

Collaboration with foreign companies was a key strategic action deployed by *Duck,* which, aware of its vulnerability by being alone, has strengthened its position through exclusive contracts with foreign companies. The latter, linked by strategic partnerships with the state, handled sensitive relationships with state officials. Therefore, *Duck* was naturally part of a powerful front that could keep public authorities at arm's length. Its activities in the heart of a key sector for the country are thus perceived as important, favoring a more conciliatory approach on the part of the public authorities.

Rapprochement and Collaboration with the State

To ensure close relationships with the state, the company's executives have approached the territorial authorities to request all the necessary authorizations, brandishing the contracts signed with foreign companies as a guarantee of integration in these areas and as a means of proving the usefulness, even necessity, of their presence and business. Since they do not have the means to provide such services and facilities in deprived areas, local authorities have facilitated the company's integration as a service provider, making it easier for foreign companies to operate in this isolated region.

Outcomes

All in all, Duck's approach is conducive to two primary outcomes. First, its collaboration with the state leads to mitigated institutional pressures. *Duck*'s response strategies to institutional pressures have focused primarily on proximity to public authorities, through companies that are already partners. This has facilitated its acceptance and preserved it from the effects of pressures that are exerted on similar operators. *Duck*'s presence is considered beneficial by local authorities, due to their inability to ensure the regular delivery of all products and services needed by important foreign partners. *Duck* therefore compensates for this absence and acts as an intermediary between the state and its partners, thereby gaining support from both parties. The second outcome is related to the strengthening of *Duck*'s position through exclusivity and diversification. Being the best supplier of basic services to several companies in a strategic area for the state, but where competition is low, has ensured a market with a high potential for diversification, given the growing needs of companies established in the region. The company has gradually established itself as a preferred supplier of services, ranging from ordinary supplies to private aircraft leasing and the management of living bases.

Discussion and Contributions

This chapter examined how Algerian entrepreneurs strategically deal with institutional pressures in a context marked by volatility and complexity. We began our analysis by suggesting that our current understanding of the management of institutional pressures has been developed primarily in Western contexts that are relatively stable, predictable, and institutionally mature (Greenwood & Suddaby, 2006). Therefore, this research is intended to contribute to the important research on institutional pressures in emerging countries where high institutional volatility is to be expected. Our analysis focused on the manifestation of this phenomenon in an African country characterized by a turbulent and dynamic institutional context with a substantial impact on the relationship between private companies and the state.

Through the study of four Algerian entrepreneurs and firms, we identified four strategies through which these organizations manage institutional pressures: confrontation, proactive cooperation, collaborative avoidance, and collaborative compliance. As shown in Fig. 7.1, these

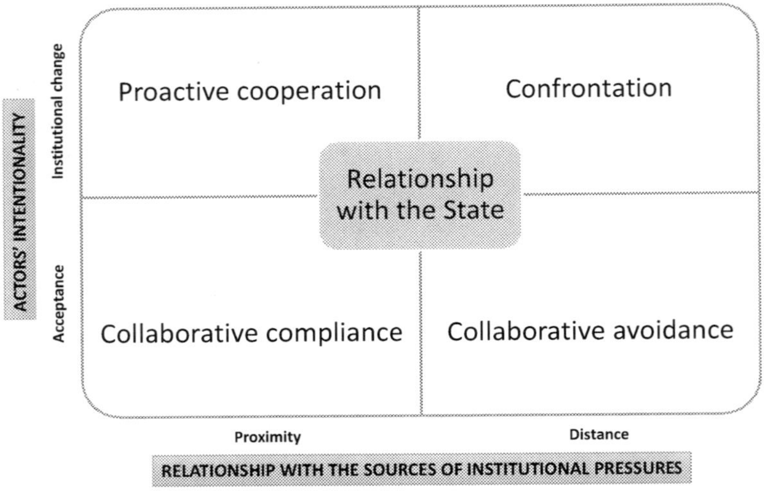

Fig. 7.1 Summary of the analytical framework for the four relational strategies for managing institutional pressures

strategies are clearly differentiated at two levels. On the one hand, some entrepreneurs wish to manage institutional pressures by changing institutions, either from within or from outside (proactive strategy). On the other hand, some entrepreneurs wish to manage institutional pressures by being close to or distancing themselves from public authorities, to accept and mitigate institutional pressures (reactive strategy). Core to this proposed framework are two important variables for understanding the strategies for managing institutional pressures deployed by actors in a situation of strong dependence: intentionality and the relationship maintained with the source of the institutional pressures.

All in all, our chapter does not challenge the strategies developed in the literature around Oliver's (1991) pioneering contribution. Although taken together, the strategies studied allow us to enrich theoretically and empirically the literature on managing institutional pressures at three levels. First, our main contribution lies in the relational theorization of institutional pressures. While the literature assumes that organizations are *de facto* in a reactive approach of survival, our chapter rather suggests that entrepreneurs develop strategies and intentions to survive in complex institutional environments and at times can work at changing the very nature of institutions and sources of pressure. Thus, we have highlighted four strategies that reveal these intentions and how they allow some organizations to be in a rather proactive posture towards the source of institutional pressures. This relational approach, based on the way entrepreneurs manage their relationships with sources of pressure, allows us to understand better strategic responses to institutional pressures in contexts where organizational actors are highly dependent on sources of institutional pressure. This relational approach, which is sensitive to the actors' intention and proximity, allows us to illustrate the possible existence of two different strategies that share the same intention, highlighting the contingent nature of managing institutional pressures. For example, *Chameleon* and *Duck* collaborate with the source of institutional pressures, but their intentions are different. Moreover, while the literature inspired by Oliver's (1991) model predicts that dependence on the source of institutional pressures mainly favors acceptance and compromise strategies (Lawrence et al., 2001), we show on the contrary that firms adopt different postures, even in the presence of strong dependence and coercive risk. This suggests that understanding their intentions and motivations is essential to understanding the trajectory of strategic responses to institutional pressures beyond actors' strategies.

Second, our article also contributes to the literature on managing institutional pressures by uncovering the collateral effects of organizations' strategies to respond to institutional pressures. By going beyond the strictly relational framework between the company and the source of institutional pressures, we have shown that companies' strategic choices influence their legitimacy with many stakeholders, including part of civil society. In a turbulent socio-political context where the state's legitimacy is at the heart of debates, confrontation is possible because it can strengthen the organization's reputation and legitimacy. At the same time, proximity to the state tends to influence reputation and legitimacy negatively. In the case of the confrontation strategy, Lion's popular support has even allowed them to create a balance in the range of institutional pressures that can be exerted. Indeed, numerous social mobilizations of support have led public authorities to become aware that their behavior is scrutinized and observed by various stakeholders. A balance is then imposed by the arrival of a third actor in the equation: civil society. As far as the strategy of proactive collaboration is concerned, it has generated a double effect in terms of legitimacy for *Chameleon*: on the one hand, the local population and the authorities have reinforced this legitimacy, but on the other hand, he has experienced a certain erosion among the other actors who are more critical of close relations with state representatives, whose legitimacy is questioned. For *Fennec*, the firm's ambiguous collaboration and avoidance strategy leads it to manage daily the tension linked to the balance between collaboration with public authorities for economic survival and avoidance for coherence with the organization's and family's morals and Islamic values. This collateral effect internal to the organization is vital since it calls into question its very values. In a more general way, the research track of collateral consequences, which has not been the subject of research to our knowledge, is an interesting one to consider understanding better the direct and indirect impacts of institutional pressure management strategies.

Conclusion

The argument developed in this chapter can be seen as bold because it does not strictly explain the proximity between private entrepreneurs and public authorities strictly from a practical and opportunistic perspective. According to traditional reading, *Chameleon* would be a company close to the public authorities mostly to monopolize the country's wealth through unhealthy political relations. This is too simplistic in our eyes in a turbulent and dynamic institutional context, where decision-making related to organizational survival is a matter of instinct. Our examples provide a more nuanced theory of how companies may be threading to build workable lifelines in unusual situations. The cases presented here suggest more research into these lightly understood dynamics. Beyond the four cases presented in this chapter, the authors have studied and analyzed more than 30 Algerian firms in recent years. These companies are all family-owned, and most of them are in positions of leadership or sustained growth. They are mainly present in the food processing industry sectors, construction and public works, mechanical industry, and services. Two of them are centenarians, three are more than 50 years old, and others are less than 30 years old. Their behavior reflects well the theory developed here. Yet, more research is needed to shed light on complementary dynamics to better understand economic development and private entrepreneurship in a volatile institutional context such as Algeria's (Baba et al., 2020).

Note

1. We consulted the following newspapers: El Watan, Maghreb Émergent, Économie 360 and TSA.

References

Amrouni, M. 2019. Classement doing business: l'algérie toujours à le traîne. *Algérie 360*.

Baba, S., Hafsi, T., & Hemissi, O. (2020). Construire son entreprise et la société: quatre cas algériens. In S. Frimousse (Ed.), Africa Positive Impact: Agir pour un meilleur impact sociétal (pp. 59–71). France: Éditions EMS.

Baba, S., Hemissi, O., & Hafsi, T. (2021). National Identity and Organizational Identity in Algeria: Interactions and Influences. *Management, 24*(2), 66–85. https://doi.org/10.37725/mgmt.v24.7809

Berrone, P., Cruz, C., Gomez-Mejia, L. R., & Larraza-Kintana, M. (2010). Socioemotional Wealth and Corporate Responses to Institutional Pressures: Do Family-Controlled Firms Pollute Less? *Administrative Science Quarterly, 55*(1), 82–113.

D'Aunno, T., Sutton, R. I., & Price, R. H. (1991). Isomorphism and External Support in Conflicting Institutional Environments: A Study of Drug Abuse Treatment Units. *The Academy of Management Journal, 34*(3), 636–661.

Deephouse, D. L. (1996). Does Isomorphism Legitimate? *Academy of Management Journal, 39*, 1024–1039.

Dhalla, R., & Oliver, C. (2013). Industry Identity in an Oligopolistic Market and Firms' Responses to Institutional Pressures. *Organization Studies, 34*(12), 1803–1834.

DiMaggio, P. J., & Powell, W. W. (1983). The Iron Cage Revisited: Institutional Isomorphism and Collective Rationality in Organizational Fields. *American Sociological Review, 48*(2), 147–160.

Elsbach, K. D., & Sutton, R. I. (1992). Acquiring Organizational Legitimacy through Illegitimate Actions: A Marriage of Institutional and Impression Management Theories. *Academy of Management Journal, 35*(4), 699–738.

George, G., Corbishley, C., Khayesi, J. N., Haas, M. R., & Tihanyi, L. (2016). Bringing Africa In: Promising Directions for Management Research. *Academy of Management Journal, 59*(2), 377–393.

Greenwood, R., Raynard, M., Kodeih, F., Micelotta, E. R., & Lounsbury, M. (2011). Institutional Complexity and Organizational Responses. *The Academy of Management Annals, 5*(1), 317–371.

Greenwood, R., & Suddaby, R. (2006). Institutional Entrepreneurship in Mature Fields: The Big Five Accounting Firms. *Academy of Management Journal, 49*, 27–48.

Hafsi, T. (2012). *Issad Rebrab: commencer petit, voir grand et aller vite.* Éditions Casbah.
He, Y., Tian, Z., & Chen, Y. (2007). Performance Implications of Nonmarket Strategy in China. *Asia Pacific Journal of Management, 24*(2), 151–169.
Hemissi, O., & Hafsi, T. (2017). *Amor Benamor, une réussite algérienne.* Éditions Casbah.
Kolk, A., & Rivera-Santos, M. (2018). The State of Research on Africa in Business and Management: Insights From a Systematic Review of Key International Journals. *Business & Society, 57*(3), 415–436.
Kostova, T., & Zaheer, S. (1999). Organizational Legitimacy Under Conditions of Complexity: The Case of the Multinational Enterprise. *Academy of Management Review, 24*, 64–81.
Langley, A., Smallman, C., Tsoukas, H., & Ven, A. H. V. d. (2013). Process Studies of Change in Organization and Management: Unveiling Temporality, Activity, and Flow. *Academy of Management Journal, 56*(1), 1–13.
Lawrence, T. B., Hardy, C., & Phillips, N. (2002). Institutional Effects of Interorganizational Collaboration: The Emergence of Proto-Institutions. *Academy of Management Journal, 45*(1), 281–290.
Lawrence, T. B., Winn, M. I., & Jennings, P. D. (2001). The Temporal Dynamics of Institutionalization. *Academy of Management Review, 26*(4), 624–644.
Maguire, S., & Hardy, C. (2009). Discourse and Deinstitutionalization: The Decline of DDT. *Academy of Management Journal, 52*(1), 148–178.
Martinez, L., & Boserup, R. A. (2016). *Algeria Modern: From Opacity to Complexity*. Oxford University Press.
McDougall, J. (2017). *A History of Algeria*. Cambridge University Press.
Micelotta, E., Lounsbury, M., & Greenwood, R. (2017). Pathways of Institutional Change: An Integrative Review and Research Agenda. *Journal of Management, 43*(6), 1885–1910.
Oliver, C. (1991). Strategic Responses to Institutional Processes. *Academy of Management Review, 16*(1), 145–179.
Pache, A.-C., & Santos, F. (2010). When Words Collide: The Internal Dynamics of Organizational Responses to Conflicting Institutional Demands. *Academy of Management Journal, 35*(3), 455–476.
Patton, M. Q. (2002). *Qualitative Research and Evaluation Methods* (3rd ed.). Sage Publications.
Quirke, L. (2013). Rogue Resistance: Sidestepping Isomorphic Pressures in a Patchy Institutional Field. *Organization Studies, 34*(11), 1675–1699.

Raaijmakers, A. G. M., Vermeulen, P. A. M., Meeus, M. T. H., & Zietsma, C. (2014). I Need Time! Exploring Pathways to Compliance under Institutional Complexity. *Academy of Management Journal, 58*(1), 85–110.

Ramus, T., Vaccaro, A., & Brusoni, S. (2017). Institutional Complexity in Turbulent Times: Formalization, Collaboration, and the Emergence of Blended Logics. *Academy of Management Journal, 60*(4), 1253–1284.

Seo, M.-G., & Creed, W. E. D. (2002). Institutional Contradictions, Praxis, and Institutional Change: A Dialectical Perspective. *Academy of Management Review, 27*(2), 222–247.

Smets, M., & Jarzabkowski, P. (2013). Reconstructing Institutional Complexity in Practice: A Relational Model of Institutional Work and Complexity. *Human Relations, 66*, 1279–1309.

Suchman, M. C. (1995). Managing Legitimacy: Strategic and Institutional Approaches. *The Academy of Management Review, 20*(3), 571–610.

Thornton, P., & Ocasio, W. (1999). Institutional Logics and the Historical Contingency of Power in Organizations: Executive Succession in the Higher Education Publishing Industry, 1958–1990. *American Journal of Sociology, 105*(3), 801–843.

Tian, Z., Hafsi, T., & Wu, W. (2009). Institutional Determinism and Political Strategies: An Empirical Investigation. *Business & Society, 48*(3), 284–325.

Tilcsik, A. (2017). From Ritual to Reality: Demography, Ideology, and Decoupling in a Post-Communist Government Agency. *Academy of Management Journal, 53*(6), 1474–1498.

Wijethilake, C., Munir, R., & Appuhami, R. (2017). Strategic Responses to Institutional Pressures for Sustainability: The Role of Management Control Systems. *Accounting, Auditing & Accountability Journal, 30*(8), 1677–1710.

Yin, R. K. (2003). *Case Study Research: Design and Methods*. Sage Publications.

Zietsma, C., Groenewegen, P., Logue, D. M., & Hinings, C. R. B. (2017). Field or Fields? Building the Scaffolding for Cumulation of Research on Institutional Fields. *Academy of Management Annals, 11*(1), 391–450.

8

The Cultural Side of Entrepreneurship in the Middle East: Religion, Gender and Family

Marwan Azouri and Lindos Daou

Introduction

Culture in the Middle East presents a very important aspect of people's social lives as it is integrated into every aspect of personal and professional relationships among people. The cultures within the region are based on traditional norms, practices and behaviors that have been passed on from one generation to another. In the region, culture acts as an invisible guiding hand for people in their private as well as in their professional lives.

M. Azouri (✉) • L. Daou
Notre Dame University—Louaize, Zouk Mosbeh, Lebanon
e-mail: mazouri@ndu.edu.lb; ldaou@ndu.edu.lb

N. Azoury, T. Hafsi (eds.), *Entrepreneurship and Social Entrepreneurship in the MENA Region*, https://doi.org/10.1007/978-3-030-88447-5_8

The Influence of Middle Eastern Culture in Business

Culture in the Middle East is a major component of every business fabric due to the reason that people have a high tendency to involve their societal norms, traditions and practices in their business. The organizational cultures in family-owned businesses and in small businesses arise out of the business practices which are mainly derived from the national culture. Thus, organizational culture is those practices which exists in companies and derive out of the national culture.

Culture as a Descriptive Term

The cultures within societies are both felt and lived. People like to tell never-ending stories about their culture, to describe it in words and actions, and they are very familiar with it as it is integrated into their daily practices and behaviors. Thus, the society's culture is transmitted to children by their parents at home, and then taught to the children at school. Later on, it is shaped by the society we live in including friends, coworkers and fellow members in various organizations.

Regional Subcultures

There is quite a difference between culture and subculture, as the latter is defined for a distinct cultural group that exists as an identifiable segment within a larger, more complex society. Major subcultural categories include nationality, religion, geographic location, race, gender, age, occupation and social class. All these categories can divide the major culture into smaller groups who belong to, or who can identify with, the various categories in the region. The major subcultures are based on religion and nationality, as people strongly identify themselves with these categories, and entrepreneurs consider them as major segmentation variables for the market.

The Hofstede Framework for Assessing National Cultures

In the context of national cultures, in the 1970s Geert Hofstede (2001) developed a framework that he used to understand the differences in culture across countries and to discern the ways that business is carried out across different cultures. He focused his research on forty countries at first and later extended it to include fifty countries in total. The analysis led to identify, in total, six dimensions of national culture that can be summarized as the following:

- *Power Distance*: The extent to which people accept and expect that the power is distributed unequally. A lower score on this dimension identifies that people question authority and attempt to distribute power.
- *Individualism vs Collectivism*: This dimension of collectivism explains to what degree the community is based upon mutual help and support to others, and people are in these societies are integrated within groups. In contrast, individualistic cultures have loose ties with groups and are related only by their core/direct family members.
- *Uncertainty Avoidance*: The extent to which people tolerate ambiguity and unexpected events. Cultures who rank high on this dimension prefer routine and abiding by the status quo.
- *Masculinity vs Femininity*: Masculinity refers to achievement, heroism, assertiveness and material rewards, while femininity is more oriented toward caring for the weak, nurturing roles and quality of life.
- *Long-Term Orientation vs Short-Term Orientation*: This is the dimension which associates connection with past traditions with current and future actions/challenges.
- *Indulgence vs Restraint*: This refers to the degree of freedom that gives people the chance to fulfill human desires.

Characteristics of Middle Eastern Cultures

According to Geert Hofstede's framework for assessing national cultures, Middle Eastern societies are known to be collectivist societies that value societal norms. People are concerned for and look after their own family's interests, and tend to think as a group rather than having each person focussing on their own personal aims. Furthermore, Middle Easterners maintain a high power distance, whereby a great deal of respect is given to the elderly and especially to religious and political leaders. Middle Easterners rank low on uncertainty avoidance and are short-term oriented where traditions play an important role in the society. Furthermore, they are masculine societies which are very paternalistic and that is highly reflected within organizations. Lastly, these societies contain a dimension of restraint due to an abundance of norms and taboos that significantly restrain individual behavior.

The Perception of Gender in Entrepreneurship

In entrepreneurship job creation, innovation, growth and branding are important elements. In addition to these, gender plays a major role in shaping entrepreneurship. In previous decades men were considered as the catalyst of entrepreneurship. They had more powerful entrepreneurial intentions than women according to De Bruin et al. (2007).

Perception has always been linked to the way people see or analyze a concept, behavior, brand or a product according to their own understanding while using multiple senses. Moreover, perception has played a major role in the growth of businesses and their survival in highly competitive environments.

Entrepreneurial Intentions

Personal attraction, subjective norm and perceived behavioral control are the main characteristics of any behavioral intentions for individuals. These characteristics are used to analyze and examine the intentions of all entrepreneurial actions (Díaz-García & Jiménez-Moreno, 2010; Ajzen, 1991).

We can witness three types of barriers: lack of support, lack of competency and fear of failure, as well as behavioral intentions (Wagner, 2007). Moreover, behavioral intentions will be our focus in understanding the perception buildup between gender and entrepreneurship.

Barriers to Entrepreneurship

Values related to culture will always play a part in shaping the societal role of gender and its stereotypes in the business working environment for both women and men.

It's good to know that gender stereotypes are not only perceived as descriptive but also as prescriptive. Being descriptive means to study and understand the differences in how men and women are and prescriptive means to study and understand the norms that are suitable in a way or another on how women and men should behave in business (Heilman, 2001).

Traditionally, entrepreneurship has been male-oriented and male-dominant. This is why individuals' choices and incentives for pursuing certain careers might thus be shaped by widely held societal attitudes about gender roles. The above-mentioned perceived value of entrepreneurship may have caused women to be more hesitant and more unlikely to be willing to venture into entrepreneurship roles due to seeing themselves as unsuitable for entrepreneurial activities. These factors lead to a focus on two of the three types of barriers: the fear of failure and lack of competency.

Gender perception and gender differences were noted mainly in the study "Fear of failure"; many other studies have shown that women are more impacted by the fear of failure than men. This has been linked with women's perception of failing due to their lack of competency. This also shows that women are more likely to analyze the situation from a helicopter point of view, rather than from the intentional point of view of "yes, let's do this business, let's take the risk ..." Various studies have also shown that women are less self-assured in leading a business due to previous perceptions they have built up that regard women as poor entrepreneurs. All the above factors play an important role in the improvement in gender equality between women and men, and for ways of changing those negative perceptions and poor images.

Women as Perceived in Media and Advertising

Mass media and advertising are highly controversial topics nowadays. As one of the multiple factors influencing culture, behavior and lifestyles, mass media has played an enormous role in transmitting those social values. It has been demonstrated for decades that women, and more precisely women's bodies are used in advertising to attract and create a better and more appealing image of a product. Advertising is the number one catalyst in terms of stereotyping women. Advertising has always delivered images and perceptions portraying women as unimportant, as not achieving great things, as being always dependent on men, as lacking competency, and always ending in failure whenever they are not surrounded or backed by men.

Such images were delivered to all four corners of the world due to globalization and the ease of access to mass media and social media. Globalization has shifted regional markets into global non-bounded markets. We now have a worldwide market. As we know, advertising is a viable way of delivering a message. Featuring women in advertising has been the key to success in terms of delivering the message and creating a positive attractiveness to the product or the brand. This image has assisted in the lowering of women's image in business, which also leads to a gap in terms of seeing women as successful entrepreneurs.

Often, advertisements that use women in a central role have mislead customers due to misleading information, or no congruence of the product with the advertisement. Moreover, sometimes advertisers use women in an advertisement while knowing that the use of women is not even the main target of the product, or that women are not even the target consumers.

Let's take the example of "Even angels will fall" by Axe/Lynx. In this advertisement we can see angels falling from the sky as soon as the main character (played by a man) uses the deodorant. It goes without saying that all angels are more than attractive with their perfect bodies, skin and shape. This ad has created a lot of controversy and has been banned in several countries, South Africa and some MENA (Middle East and North African) regions due to the fact that the ad is breaking many taboos (religious, sexual, erotic, etc.).

Featuring women in mass media and advertising has been linked with:

- The stereotyping of women (mothers, wives, sexual models, bait);
- Objectification of women (women are viewed as sexual objects);
- Artificiality;
- Manipulative (buying decision);
- Unrealistic (stripping women of their identities).

As we all know, we are bombarded on a daily basis by advertising from TV advertisements, magazines, social media and social networks, billboards, etc. We are constantly exposed to more than 2000 ads on a daily basis (depending on the country), and this plays a major role both in shaping society and in shaping our behavior toward women. It goes without saying that advertising has played a large part in forming our ways of thinking about and imagining women. More precisely, it has played a negative role in the perception of women in business, particularly as entrepreneurs.

The Working Woman Segment

While many studies have focussed on the enhancement of women's equality, empowerment and social inclusion, in recent years we have witnessed a spike in women entrepreneurs. That spike is due to multiple factors: women opening up to business, women standing up for their rights and more precisely the abolition of virtual boundaries between countries due to the rise of social media. It was shown in a recent OECD study on the role of gender that women are increasingly making a significant contribution to the world economy and to its growth, as well as in poverty reduction in both developing countries and high-income countries, which demonstrate that the fear of failure and lack of competency were pure perceptions and not a reality.

Numbers do not lie, and in the year 2020 we can see that the number of female entrepreneurs in the world have become more significant (Fig. 8.1).

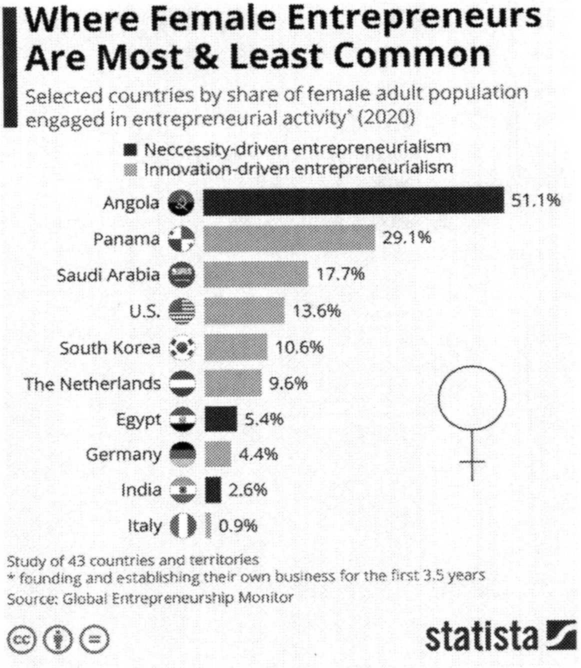

Fig. 8.1 Countries where female entrepreneurs are the most and least common. (Source: Katharina Buchholz, Statista 2021)

The Importance of Family Businesses

According to several articles and research, family business are flourishing in the Middle East and are one of the most important factors in term of economic revenue for Middle Eastern countries. We know that more than 60% of the Middle Eastern companies are family-owned businesses. Those business contribute approximatively 60–70% of country GDP. In the Middle East, family-owned business are crucial in terms of the prosperity and growth of any country. It's good to add that family-owned businesses are part of Middle Eastern culture and reflect the true essence of family entrepreneurship.

It's also important to mention collectivism regarding family-owned business. Family-owned businesses work and are managed in collective ways rather than in an individual way. Everyone will benefit from the success of the business.

A major drawback in family-owned businesses is that change is quite impossible, even in shifting environments. This impossibility is due to the resistance to change applied by the company's owner. Another drawback is in the advancement in terms of job position and responsibilities. Family disputes can also play a major role in the company's achievements and success. Family pressure applied in the recruitment process can lead to recruiting the wrong person. One last major drawback is the lack of organizational structure and culture, because it depends solely on the family culture and the family hierarchy.

The Role of Religion in Business

Religion has usually been considered as a taboo subject in term of research or study for business. Religion is a social force that has affected ways of managing business and for social behavior. "Corporate Social Responsibility" and ethics are highly related to religion. Religion has always played the role of catalyst in business via religious institutions, especially in the Middle East.

Religion has also been a force of regulation due to its role as a cultural force that affects business both directly and indirectly. Religion is also part of the daily role and routine that any company or business plays in society. Such roles are shaped by religion even if only indirectly. Having to label "Halal" on meat products is one major example of how religion plays a role in our daily business tasks.

But sometimes religion has also played a dark role in business when organizations and companies use the excuse of religion to legitimate their actions and defend them under the flag of religion. Sometimes governmental bodies use verses from biblical books to cover certain actions or regulations.

What need to be retained from the impact of religion on business is that it's an important catalyst that shapes social forces and aids in better management when and only when it's used in the correct way. Sometimes religion is used as a business shield to cover certain unethical decisions taken by organizations, or to cover certain actions that lead to a "better" economic outcome.

References

Ajzen, I. (1991). The Theory of Planned Behavior. *Organizational Behavior and Human Decision Processes, 50*(2), 179–211.

De Bruin, A., Brush, C. G., & Welter, F. (2007). Advancing a Framework for Coherent Research on Women's Entrepreneurship. *Entrepreneurship Theory and Practice, 31*(3), 323–339.

Díaz-García, M., & Jiménez-Moreno, J. (2010). Entrepreneurial Intentions: The Role of Gender. *International Entrepreneurship and Management Journal, 6*, 261–283.

Heilman, M. E. (2001). Description and Prescription: How Gender Stereotypes Prevent Women's Ascent Up the Organizational Ladder. *Journal of Social Issues, 57*, 657–674.

Hofstede, G. (2001). *Culture's Consequences: Comparing Values, Behaviors and Institutions across Nations* (2nd ed.). Sage Publications.

https://www.statista.com/chart/19254/female-adult-population-engaged-in-entrepreneurial-activity-per-country/

Kirkman, B. L., Lowe, K. B., & Gibson, C. B. (2006). A Quarter Century of Culture's Consequences: A Review of Empirical Research Incorporating Hofstede's Cultural Values Framework. *Journal of International Business Studies, 37*, 285–320.

Wagner, J. (2007). What Difference a Y Makes—Female and Male Nascent Entrepreneurs in Germany. *Small Business Economics, 28*, 1–21.

9

Social Entrepreneurship and Job Creation in the Lebanese Market

Diala Kozaily

Introduction

Different research papers have viewed a significant number of varied definitions of social entrepreneurship (Zahra et al., 2009) judged by practice rather than by theory (Mair & Marti, 2006). Typically, social entrepreneurship is defined as entrepreneurship with a social mission, and is often considered as the combination of two concepts: entrepreneurship and social mission. Dees has defined social entrepreneurship as a "change agent" within the social sector (Dees, 1998). A more realistic approach considers that social entrepreneurship is the earning of financial revenues in the pursuit of social impact through a well-defined structure (Kruse, 2019). Haugh offers another view: the synchronization of financial, societal and environmental missions by enterprise structures (Haugh, 2007). Social entrepreneurship rests on a "continuum" (Munro & Belanger, 2017) and depends on the domain of study, which makes its definition

D. Kozaily (✉)
Holy Spirit University of Kaslik (USEK), Jounieh, Lebanon
e-mail: diala.y.kozaily@net.usek.edu.lb

N. Azoury, T. Hafsi (eds.), *Entrepreneurship and Social Entrepreneurship in the MENA Region*, https://doi.org/10.1007/978-3-030-88447-5_9

inexact and disunited. Adding to what has been elaborated, the increase in social enterprise activity has intensified interest in social entrepreneurship on three different levels. First, academicians, scholars and researchers add value to the theoretical part. Second, policymakers and law experts work on the enhancement of law and government regulations that support social entrepreneurship. Third, practitioners and social entrepreneurs contribute through their activities and experiences in the field (Munro & Belanger, 2017).

In the Arab world, entrepreneurship and social entrepreneurship have formed a very important role in the economy. According to the Arabnet/Dubai SME (Small- and Medium-Sized Enterprises) report, in the Arab market between 2012 and 2017 the number of active investors increased by a compound annual rate of 31%. In fact, the number rises from 51 active entrepreneurs in 2012 to 195 in 2017. The increase shows a busy time for startups, since between 2015 and 2016 40 new funds were created. Also, between 2017 and May 2018 30 new funds were created from which 33% of the funding institutions were UAE based and 25% are in Lebanon. Also, in 11 different Arab countries from 2013 to 2017 the number of accelerators studied increased by 16% (ZAWYA, 2018).

In their book *The World Guide to CSR: A Country-by-Country Analysis of Corporate Sustainability and Responsibility*, in the chapter dedicated to the Middle East the writer highlighted that the Arab world is becoming an "international hubs of commerce and industry," adding that the Middle East is becoming a "major player in today's global business market" (Nick & Wayne, 2017).

Anass Boumediene, one of the founders of Dubai-based eyewa.com, told Zawya in a private interview that entrepreneurial development still lacks government support as in Europe, the US, etc.

European and US governments foster entrepreneurial initiatives through different approaches which have easy, simple and accessible legal frameworks, financial support funds and ecosystem-developing substructures (Zawya, 2018).

A higher level of entrepreneurial activity is related to higher growth and job creation as mentioned in the Arab Competitive Report released in August 2018 (World Economic Forum, 2018). Employment creation is a top priority for the MENA (Middle East and North African) region. The region suffers from a long-term high unemployment rate (Anthony et al., 2011).

Social Entrepreneurship: Stipulation and Particularities

Social entrepreneurship is a subject that contains its own specific particularities and dilemmas. Researchers, scholars and practitioners have not come to an agreement on one single definition to explain social entrepreneurship, which would add interest to research and provide researchers with the capacity to continuously add value to the subject. A social entrepreneurship definition remains subject to the discipline and background by which we choose to examine the subject. To establish the disciplines of our study we choose to do it in the following section by diagnosing the particularities of social entrepreneurship. We focus on the characteristics of entrepreneurship and the paradoxical combination between entrepreneurship and the social identity of the social enterprise. Also, we search for an understanding of social entrepreneurship particularities by comparing the concept to other models such as NGOs, CSR (Corporate Social Responsibility) activities and commercial entrepreneurship.

Entrepreneurship: What It Is and Is Not

Do all new businesses initiatives fall within the entrepreneurial discipline? In order to answer this question it is imperative to elaborate on the definition of entrepreneurship.

Commonly, entrepreneurship is basically known as starting a business. However, the concept of entrepreneurship is far richer than this simple description.

Entrepreneurship might appear as a new concept, but it is only new as a terminology since it has a profound history in the life of different institutions. "It means different things to different people" (Dees, 1998).

When asked "what is entrepreneurship?" Coase and Wang in "*Coase on Entrepreneurship*" (Terjesen & Wang, 2013) highlight the novelty contained in the entrepreneurship model, where innovations could concern the market, the product, the marketing and trading process and the manufacturing operations. They added to these factors the importance of risk-taking. It is well known in the world of entrepreneurship that success is not always within reach. In fact, the ratio of failure is nine out of ten for entrepreneurship initiatives. Although this might be true, the influence of a successful entrepreneurship initiative influences the entire economic sector.

Nevertheless, not all enterprise or ideas are entrepreneurial. Entrepreneurship concerns different parts in the process. For example, the individual is an entrepreneur when they are ready to act, and have the mindset to find a gap in the market and bear the risk by acting toward covering it. Added to that, innovation might be essential to determine if the idea is entrepreneurial or not. When talking of entrepreneurship, the process and/or the result are novel. Then entrepreneurship can be linked to the potential scalability. To define an enterprise as entrepreneurship it should present a potential scalability. Being able to benefit from the same idea in different countries making profit and/or solving a social problem is entrepreneurial.

In this paper, we take time to discuss innovation, scalability and other aspects of entrepreneurship in order to link them specifically to social entrepreneurship, which is the aim of the study.

Social Entrepreneurship: Paradoxical Conceptualization

The social and entrepreneurial areas of life are not compatible. Thus it is a paradox to combine the two different missions: social and financial.

Indeed, social entrepreneurship aims to balance two missions. One mission is to accomplish social improvements in societal, educational, environmental and health areas; while another aim concerns the achievement of financial profit (Munro & Belanger, 2017). Social entrepreneurship is a "hybrid organization" (Teasdale, 2012). In other words, the aim of an entrepreneurial company is to make financial income from social entrepreneurship initiative(s).

Social entrepreneurship has conflicting institutional logics. It is subject to criticism because of its unlikeliness for dual, different or opposing missions (Mair et al., 2015). For example, when a decision needs to be made on giving preference to one mission or another—which mission should take the lead? In other words, it is not possible to equally assume two missions. For a business to be successful it should have a very clear and well-defined mission, being either financial or providing benefit to the stakeholders; in other words, aiming to make maximum profit—or social solutions to help the community.

According to different researchers, practitioners and specialists, the success of entrepreneurial experience shows that the concept of social enterprise is not only plausible but of great potential. It influences the economic sector by pointing resources to social gaps not only as problems but also as great potential for economic development. Adding to that, social entrepreneurship creates new industries and validates innovative business models (Santos, 2012).

Furthermore, the dual mission of social entrepreneurship gives an added-value compared to the commercial entrepreneurship, such as: easier resources availability, a wide network circle and varied market accessibility (Davies et al., 2019).

Correspondingly, the alignment achieved between social and economic value is identified as a "value-creating synerg[y]." The achievement of one value, either the economical or the social value, may support the achievement of the second value. That's what dictates the sustainability and success of social entrepreneurship businesses (Lozano et al., 2006).

Social Entrepreneurship Particularities: Neither Charitable nor Philanthropic

In this section we compare and contrast different types of activities and initiatives aiming to highlight some particularities of the social entrepreneurship concept. We do this in Table 9.1.

Table 9.1 Comparison between NGOs, CSR activity, financial entrepreneurship and social entrepreneurship

	NGO	CSR activity	Financial entrepreneurship	Social entrepreneurship
Dominant mission	Pure social: giving the society	Financial with social para-activities (donations, community work, stakeholders wellbeing, etc.)	Pure financial: making the maximum profit for the stockholders could include CSR activities	Mix between social and financial: making a financial income while solving a social problem neglected or sometimes even created by the government
Financial activities	Not frequent sometimes to collect some funds	No financial return Invest the financial income of the commercial regular activity	Main objective	One of the objectives
Social activities	Only	Different than main commercial activities for the image of the company for tax exemption purpose Philanthropic matter	Not necessary present or as a CSR initiative	Main objective: make the life of the population belter
Financial income	Grants government funds, private donations, etc.	Regular income invested in CSR activities	Sell/lease of products and/or services	Sell/lease of products and/or services
Dominant logic of spirit	Benevolence	Control business management with a philanthropic approach	Control business management	Empowerment (Santos, 2012)
Human capital	Employees and volunteers	Employees	Employees	Employees and volunteers

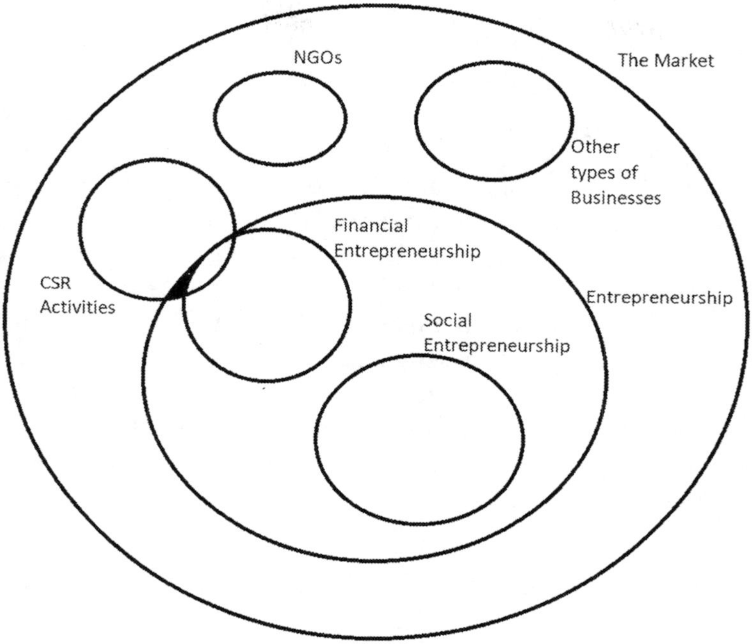

Fig. 9.1 In the market: social entrepreneurship, financial entrepreneurship, CSR activities, NGOs, etc.

Figure 9.1 shows the overlaps between the different initiatives already discussed earlier in this section.

The Social Entrepreneur: Pillar of Social Entrepreneurship

Social entrepreneurship meets the stakeholder theory developed by Freeman in 1984. In fact, according to Freeman, the firm has the responsibility to creates value for all stakeholders, to the stockholders as well as to the firm's environment. By analogy, social entrepreneurship serves both for the benefit of society and also the social entrepreneur. For instance the decision-making process, particularly in social entrepreneurship, affects the internal and external stakeholders and vice versa. Indeed, the internal and external stakeholders affect the decision-making process. In detail, the social entrepreneur is an important internal stakeholder force, primarily associated with the social entrepreneurship idea. In fact, the entrepreneur is equipped with the "entrepreneurial skills" to find and exploit opportunities to create a solution regardless of resources and assets accessibility (Lozano et al., 2006). The social entrepreneur is shown to have a direct influence on the firm's size through the strategic decision-making undertaken during the different stages of the firm's life-cycle.

We will study the social entrepreneur according to three determinants. We start with the social entrepreneur's educational level and training. Next we discuss the social entrepreneur's previous experience and family history. To finish, we deliberate on the social entrepreneur's financial support. We do so in order to study the influence of the social entrepreneur on the social enterprise size, and its capability for creating jobs in the market (Rey-Marti et al., 2016).

The Social Entrepreneur's Educational Qualifications and Training

Professional and general training and academic education provide the individual, in this case the social entrepreneur, with the necessary knowledge and skills to effectively and efficiently manage the company. Thus, the company would be able to grow and also create more job opportunities. Research has shown that companies managed by individuals with a certain educational level perform better than other companies managed by individuals without any educational diploma. So social entrepreneurs having the necessary understanding of general business knowledge and/or specific industrial knowledge should make better planning and strategic decisions, develop and grow the company and influence stakeholders in a positive way. In other words, with accurate and necessary knowledge the company would better serve its society, benefit its stockholders, and offer employment to its environment.

According to Becker, human capital theory explores the importance of investing in schooling. It highlights that investing in an individual's education and training is likewise a business investment in assets. Different type of education (formal, informal, general or specific to entrepreneurship, etc.) predicts success from finding, exploring and growing opportunities.

Notably, education and training in the context of entrepreneurship covers different types of knowledge at different stages. For example, entrepreneurial awareness leads the individual to pursue a career in entrepreneurship instead of employment. It promotes an entrepreneurial mindset. Studies show a positive relation between entrepreneurial education and the abilities, intentions and outcomes of human capital (Bae et al., 2014).

Added to this, educational fulfillment includes both general education and also business knowledge acquired through courses at undergraduate or graduate levels of business administration in universities or business schools. A formal education in business knowledge is expected to affect the efficiency of new ventures through affecting the skills and motivation of entrepreneurs and/or social entrepreneurs (Soriano & Castrogiovanni, 2012).

Furthermore, educational attainment also includes industry-specific education. It concerns in-depth education within a certain sector, product/service or industry. Accordingly, it is a formal education pursued in specialized institutions with specific programs and professional courses. Specific education fulfillment enhances the ability of the entrepreneur to effectively identify opportunities, market potential, customer needs, etc. Moreover, specialized knowledge works on the capabilities of the entrepreneur to acquire and use resources professionally; so the cost of the firm operations are reduced and its performance is improved (Soriano & Castrogiovanni, 2012).

Last but not least, innovation having a significant presence and influence in entrepreneurship and social entrepreneurship highlights the need for continuous education and training to protect and increase the firm's market shares. We will take time to discuss innovation later in the chapter.

To conclude, a social entrepreneur's training and educational attainment affect the social enterprise management. Consequently, it affects the potential of innovation, scalability and growth of the business. As a result, the social entrepreneur's education and/or training affects the enterprise's ability for creating employment in general and in its environment in particular.

However, education and training are not the only influences on social enterprises. Their size can be influenced by the social entrepreneur's previous professional experience, and the experience gained while growing up in a family with an entrepreneurial history.

The Social Entrepreneur's Previous Experience and Family History

In practice, management and governance are not only the result of education and training but also the fruits of previous experience in either professional in previous job positions. Added to that is the experience gained from growing up in a family with entrepreneurial history which gives the (social) entrepreneur, whether consciously and/or unconsciously, a background in (social) entrepreneurship. Professional experience includes either previous experience at a managerial level or in the same industry as the current social enterprise. The decision-making process is enhanced when it's also combined with personal understandings based on previous familiarity.

Furthermore, an entrepreneurial family history provides individuals with indirect training that helps the entrepreneur to make better strategic management decisions, and in consequence to work more efficiently.

An entrepreneur with a family background in entrepreneurship and/or previous experience in an entrepreneurial industry or managerial position makes less mistakes and take less time to succeed. The entrepreneurship initiative and development is more likely to achieve its goals. Through effective and efficient management, the enterprise masters the entrepreneurship or social entrepreneurship field and the specific business and gains a significant place in the competition and large market shares (Rey-Marti et al., 2016).

The effective performance of the (social) entrepreneur generates high productivity in the (social) enterprise. Arising from this, the need for hiring might increase. Thus, new job opportunities are available in the market. Entrepreneurs with entrepreneurial family histories have a higher probability for success than those entrepreneurs with different family backgrounds. Family support gets translated into providing advice and guidance leading to better and faster solutions to a higher number of difficulties encountered, and to make the least possible mistakes (Soriano & Castrogiovanni, 2012).

In addition to education and previous experience, financial support has a major influence on the success of an enterprise, and in consequence to its capacity for job creation.

The Social Entrepreneur's Financial Support

It is no secret that one of the most challenging parts of enterprise management is its financials. The inflow and outflow of financial resources influences the productivity and efficiency of the company, its potential to compete in the market, its capacity for grow, its strategic plan, etc.; therefore, in particular the social entrepreneur's financial support will influence the capacity of the company for creating job opportunities. According to value-based decision-making, the development of social entrepreneurship is not only subject to finance but also to ethics (Davies et al., 2019). In this section we take the time to discuss the finances of the social entrepreneur.

The social mission of the social entrepreneur is parallel to the duties of the government. The social entrepreneur sees an opportunity that either the government is not meeting its responsibility for, or the effort made is insufficient to meet the demands of the population. In both cases, social entrepreneurs are participating in ensuring citizens' rights. Added to the social mission, job creation is an additional benefit that social enterprises offer to the community, and in consequence taking charge of another governmental role. Governments have an interest in supporting social enterprises, expressed through direct financial injections or special tax exemptions. Nevertheless, the legal form of social enterprise is still a major question in the literature and in the practical world.

Nowadays, the significance and need for social enterprise is on the increase, but unfortunately government support has tended to decrease and social enterprises are constrained to find different financial resources.

Social finance is a new category of financing which began years ago, giving access to social enterprises to finance their work (Nicholls et al., 2015). In addition, donations and subsidies that believe in the enterprises' mission also finance social enterprises. Some entrepreneurs benefit from Social Enterprise Foundations, Social Business Angels and Eco Angels as mentioned in the study submitted by Davies et al. (2019). They also highlight the importance of alignment between the social mission and the financial mission of the enterprise, as the leveraging of the social mission mobilizes funds.

We aim to study the effect of the three determinants previously mentioned: the educational level, experience, and family background and financial support of the social entrepreneur—on the capacity of the social enterprise to create new opportunities for the market. These three determinants defining the scope of study will be considered in relation to the success of the social enterprise, implying job creation in the market.

Social Enterprise: The Idea Taking Form

The social entrepreneur's idea is transformed into a plan. It takes a legal form to start the operation process and market its product or service. To elaborate on the subject of the social enterprise, we choose to discuss the following topics. First, talking about entrepreneurship is talking about innovation. Second, scalability is an essential ingredient of the social enterprise. Third, a social enterprise, in general, is the realization of the social entrepreneur's idea. When the idea turns into a plan and the plan is executed, the idea takes the form of a social enterprise involving a team which is formed by individuals from different backgrounds, collaborating and joining forces in order to give life to the initial social idea. At this stage, the social entrepreneur attracts a team who share responsibilities, management, benefits and credits and gives the social firm more credibility and professionalism.

In this section, we discuss the institutionalization of the social enterprise.

Innovation

The economy is dynamic. New opportunities are always arising due to different factors. The needs of individuals and society change over time. New technologies are always being developed. New information come to light (Santos, 2012). These changes impel improvement and innovation in the organization. Amendments and new developments can inspire the supply and use of resources, and the products and service delivery. In consequence, innovation is imperative for commercial entrepreneurship. Innovation also influences the social enterprise financial mission as it influences the commercial enterprise activities and process (von der Weppen & Cochrane, 2012). In addition, innovation is a significant factor in a successful social entrepreneurship. It is also a vital factor in its social impact, influencing its capacity to realize its social mission (Munro & Belanger, 2017; Weerawardena & Mort, 2012).

Innovation in entrepreneurship pursues new opportunities either by entering a new market, or improving a service or a product or adapting a new operating process aiming to reduce the costs of operation. Entrepreneurship innovation leads changes in the economy. It drives the evolution of entrepreneurship in terms of trend and time (Terjesen & Wang, 2013). Competitors are left without the choice of whether to adapt their business or risking losing their capacity to compete, losing therefore their market shares. Coase and Wang in 2013 mentioned their interest as economists neither for the entrepreneur's personality, nor to their firm's efficiency, but to the lifelong impact on the economy such as new products, new production processes, new startups and new markets, and so forth (Terjesen & Wang, 2013).

Creativity in innovation is a vital capacity for an organization. In fact, entrepreneurial innovation influences organizational performance. It is studied as one of the six most important contributors to the firm's high performance. Continuous entrepreneurial innovation increases the performance of the firm (Lozano et al., 2006). As for the study mentioned above, entrepreneurial innovation is characterized by two dimensions: entrepreneurial spirit and value creation. The entrepreneurial spirit defines the ability of the entrepreneur to start up an innovative idea and continue developing the business by trying new methods and better ways to achieve its goals.

Beyond commercial entrepreneurship, social entrepreneruship aims to create value. On the one hand, commercial enterprises search for achieving the greatest benefits for their stockholders. In the other hand, the social entrepreneur searches primarily to positively impact as many people as possible.

Scalability

Scalability is a word defined by the *Oxford Dictionary* as the ability "to be changed in size and scale." In the business world, scalability is the business potential of a firm. It can concern the number of products it sells and/or the number of markets it serves. It is important to different stakeholders. The creation of job opportunities and tax payments are a business potential from a social and community perspective. From the investors point of view, the business scalability is the foundation of valuation practices (Nielsen & Lund, 2015).

In fact, social enterprise targets a well-defined problem in a certain local geographic area with "global relevance" (Santos, 2012). A scalable social enterprise has an idea, a product and/or a process that has an advantage through being implemented in different geographical areas (Santos, 2012). In other words, scalability means it can be replicable, expanding the geographical area that is benefiting from the social impact. A larger segment of the population would benefit from its social mission and provide new financial resources for the firm.

Scalability gives the company an attractive image for different kind of investors.

It can facilitate and speed up the exit phase, the dream of nearly every entrepreneur. With such a positive image combined with other positive indicators, founders will find buyers such as individuals, international companies, NGOs even governments willing to buy the pattern and implement it on their own for billions of dollars.

By scaling, the company will need to decentralize its activity to ensure effectiveness and efficiently. Doing so, it will create new job opportunities for different type of employees such as white-collar and blue-collar employees.

Institutionalization

Social enterprises no longer depend on the leader. In this case, the social enterprise doesn't rely solely on the person of the social entrepreneur; instead, it becomes efficient and effective through its structure, organization, procedures and policies, etc. (Lozano et al., 2006). The enterprise gains more confidence from society when it moves from being a single entrepreneur working as a one-man-show to a team fully devoted to the social cause of combined skills and backgrounds benefiting the social enterprise. It is the way entrepreneurial decisions are made, it shows the ability to delegate (Lozano et al., 2006), it can be through inviting individuals from different backgrounds to join the board of directors, sharing their shares in return for their experience and education and thus benefiting the company; recruiting, volunteering or increasing the pool of experts around the firm. To be able to share credits or not, the social entrepreneur's decision is influenced by educational level, previous experience, personality, etc. Likewise, the firm gains in professionalism.

A company with a board of directors performs better than a single person taking care of everything. It is true that the decision-making process in a team would consume more time than an individual decision, but the diversity also adds options and creativity to the problem-solving dilemma. Different personalities present different points of view and most probably new perspectives. The company will gain better performance and productivity. New knowledge, expertise and experience are added to the strategic management of the company. Also, responsibilities are divided.

In a study carried out by Davies et al. (2019) entitled *Barriers to Social Enterprise Growth*, nine of the social enterprises studied had multiple founders related by a network of friends and acquaintances.

Low costs and combined skills are the benefits of networking in creating social enterprises. In the case of the Alpha company, named by the company in order to ensure privacy for the participator, it is a social enterprise formed by one business developer specialist who collaborated with his marketer and brand specialist wife, an ex-solicitor and a PR specialist (Davies et al., 2019).

Firm Size and Job Creation

The ability of a firm to create job opportunities is the translation into the increase of firm size. A company that increases in size and recruits more talent is the result of different firm-level modules. When a company grows at the micro level it recruits more talent, in other words, at the macro level it creates job opportunities for the market. This recruiting process can vary from one company to another depending on the culture, vision and business type. Nevertheless, the need to engage new talent into social companies is in general prompted by a certain number of dynamics. To be able to create long-term jobs, the social enterprise needs to be competitive and sustainable in the business.

Social Firm Size: Creation, Growing and Legal Identity

The entrepreneur is an individual who sees a gap in the market and has the courage to try a new venture, resulting in success for solving the problem via a new process or the creation of new services or products. Social entrepreneurs search for gaps in the social life of the society, they aim to have a positive impact on society and to make the world a better place. Social impacts include civic rights, education, environment, safety, health, etc. Social entrepreneurs achieve their financial missions by serving society.

Moving from an idea to a real functional business or creating a social enterprise is the main step to employment potential. The idea takes a legal form in which people join the mission.

In talking about legal identity, the law does not specify any criteria for social enterprises. It is necessary to be recognized as a partner with the government, as this will benefit it from exemption from special treatment in terms of taxation, rules and regulations, financial facilities, etc. This is still a topic in the literature as well as in the business world.

The entrepreneur needs different types of employees, cohorts and/or partners with different or no expertise, to fulfill various positions to achieve the mission.

Recruiting is different for social enterprises than for regular enterprises. Social enterprises search not only for talented and skilled people, but also for potential employees driven by the same social interests.

Social Competitive Advantage and Sustainability

Strategic decision-making is the process that secure advantages for the enterprise and social enterprise over its competitors. Competitive advantage concerns customer loyalty, for example: believing in the social mission of the company, customers would do their part for the social impact by supporting the social enterprise mission and buying its products and/or using its services. In addition, employees or volunteers give the social enterprise company a competitive advantage thanks to their motivations and beliefs in their capability to create social change through their activity in the social enterprise. Also, competitive advantage comes from good relations with stakeholders, especially suppliers, NGOs, governments of the state and country of operation, politicians and so on (Lozano et al., 2006). In consequence, social enterprise resources are increased and their capacity to create value is enhanced. Its legitimacy, internal and external support are greater.

Over and above competitive advantage, sustainability is achieved when the mission and values, the planning and discontinuities and the competitive advantage are all aligned and consistent in order to focus the scope and adjust to environment change. We recall the importance of continuous innovation in any enterprise, especially for the social enterprises studied in this chapter, to maintain social competitive advantage and sustainability. As highlighted in the study conducted by Lozano et al. (2006), creating a sustainable competitive advantage is strategically important in order to apprehend social initiatives and reinforce the firm's operational competencies. Social enterprises can achieve superior competitive advantage. This can be done through two channels: diversified funding sources and innovative community service.

Beyond the positive effects of competition in the business field such as engaging in better decision-making to better serve stakeholders' interests, achieving higher performance and increasing productivity, social enterprises don't consider competition alarming, in fact it is perceived differently. Thus, more entities serving society means more people benefiting from the social mission and correspondingly more positive social impact for society (Santos, 2012). As mentioned earlier, social enterprises have a significant influence on the development of the economy. A larger and more professional ecosystem means higher and more significant results on economy development, and change toward better governance processes and procedures, social impact and environmental culture, resource management and preservation, beyond financial returns, decision-making sustainability, human resource dignity, etc.

Job Creation: Third Mission for Social Enterprise

After elaborating on social entrepreneurship, entrepreneurs and enterprises, it is time for our study to focus on employment and job creation components.

Over the past few decades, the market for ideas has become of particular importance to the market, from being just a concept in law or political science to becoming a fundamental concept in economies. No economy can function without a labor force or human capital, because these factors are a vital input for production. The economy of today is more and more "knowledge-intense," and no input is more important than the idea itself, giving importance to the human resources of the firm (Terjesen & Wang, 2013).

Social enterprises, like any other enterprises, search for and hire talented people in order to achieve their goals. Additionally, social enterprises, more than any other types of firm, search for potential candidates whose values are aligned with its mission and who are driven by their motivation to make social change and have a positive impact on their society (Davies et al., 2019).

Hiring is not a regular activity for social enterprises as in any other enterprise. It is much more than that; job creation is an additional contribution to the society, added to the social mission. In fact, it is considered the third mission of the social enterprise.

According to the GEM (Global Entrepreneurship Monitor) in a special topic report on social entrepreneurship in 2015, when comparing the three factors of "current size of more than five employees," "volunteers' share" and "has growth expectations in the next five years," in Australia, the US and in the Western European economies, the factor of more than five employees is the most dominant, at 55% and 46% respectively (Bosma et al., 2016).

Job creation and hiring is also a factor in high and effectively performing social enterprises. In other words, it includes creating and retaining talented people and talented teams. Effective and efficient social enterprises enhance a culture of innovation. Leaders are oriented to build on people, more than on fulfilling objectives (Lozano et al., 2006).

In addition, the human resources pool, considered as an intangible capital, includes in total the values of skills, capabilities, and talents of employees put at the service of the company to achieve its objective. This capital is a vital and dynamic resource for the company that needs to be managed. It needs to be nurtured and developed, in terms of knowledge and experience in the market, aiming to improve the productivity, performance, effectiveness and efficiency of the company. As for the study conducted by Lozano et al. (2006), it is more protective for an organization to obtain sustainable advantage if it develops this broad approach to the creation of value. In fact, to achieve coherence among the three organizational objectives of the social enterprise, namely, social impact, financial gain and job creation, it is imperative for the organization to act in good faith toward its employees, from the moment of hiring till the moment they leave the company. Overall, a high performance in human resource management in social enterprises is translated into a good labor environment in which employees identify closely with the social enterprise mission.

In a study conducted and published by the OECD, job creation and the ending of paid employee positions are linked to factors such as finance, funding, public contracts, sales of goods, market opportunities and skills availability (Buckingham & Teasdale, 2013).

It is clear that in the Middle East and North Africa region, entrepreneurial initiatives find their way, and they are an attractive occupation for the Arab worlds. Despite the existence of formal job options, entrepreneurial behavior finds a way to emerge through innovative start-ups, entrepreneurship, etc. (Ismail et al., 2017).

Lebanon, with a GDP growth of 0.6% in 2017, and a GDP per capita of $8997 in 2012, is considered to be one of the most entrepreneurial countries in the world (Hill, 2018). In detail, approximately one in four adults starts or runs a new business. It is ranked fourth out of 48 countries participating in the GEM 2018 survey report on adult populations (APS).

Entrepreneurship and social entrepreneurship initiatives' capacities, potentials and expectations are subject to different studies. According to the global entrepreneurship monitor national report on Lebanon in 2018, 3.7% of entrepreneurship initiatives were expected to create six or more jobs over the next five years. New businesses stimulate economic development, and it is an important source of job creation, innovation and income. In Lebanon, a culture dominated by small businesses, especially family-owned and managed, the entrepreneurial spirit and mindset are firmly rooted in Lebanese culture from its antecedents the Phoenicians. Entrepreneurial activities are well supported, both financially and socially; financial support schemes include those developed by the Banque du Liban (BDL) and socially by incubators and accelerators. Moreover, culturally they are viewed with considerable esteem. Young entrepreneurs are well educated and qualified (Faghih & Zali, 2018).

Conclusion

In conclusion, entrepreneurship and social entrepreneurship are making an increased impact on the world, especially in the MENA region and the Arab world. The social entrepreneur makes a social-impact change while making financial income through an institution, the social enterprise. To do so, the social enterprise creates job opportunities not only to make its mission conceivable but also to serve the market. The ability of the social enterprise to create jobs can be influenced by the social entrepreneur's education, experience, family history and financial resources.

To sum up, the identity and history of the social entrepreneur influences its third mission, job creation. A well-educated social entrepreneur, with previous experience and/or belonging to a family with a history in entrepreneurship, and with accurate financing resources, would present a management and governance plan leading the company to higher performance and productivity, and so also to higher job opportunities.

References

Anthony, O., Rey, M.-E., & Mendez, J. G. (2011). *Opportunities and Challenges in the MENA Region.* Arab World Competitiveness Report 2012.

Bae, T. J., Qian, S., Miao, C., & Fiet, J. O. (2014). The Relationship Between Entrepreneurship Education and Entrepreneurial Intentions: A Meta-Analytic Review. *Entrepreneurial Theory and Practice, 38*(2), 217–254.

Bosma, N., Schott, T., Terjesen, S., & Kew, P. (2016). *Special Topic Report: Social Entrepreneurship.* Global Entrepreneurship Monitor Website. http://www.gemconsortium.org/report/49542

Buckingham, H., & Teasdale, S. (2013). *Job Creation Through the Social Economy and Social Entrepreneurship.* OECD.

Davies, I. A., Haugh, H., & Chambers, L. (2019). Barriers to Social Enterprise Growth. *Journal of Small Business Management, 57*(4), 1616–1636.

Gregory, D. J., & Peter Haas, M. (1998). The meaning of social Entrepreneurship. Original Draft: October, 31.

Faghih, N., & Zali, M. R. (2018). *Entrepreneurship Education and Research in the Middle East and North Africa (MENA): Perspectives on Trends, Policy and Educational Environment.* Springer.

Haugh, H. (2007). New Strategies for a Sustainable Society: The Growing Contribution of Social Entrepreneurship. *Business Ethics Quarterly, 17*(4), 743–749.

Hill, P. S. (2018). *Global Entrepreneurship Monitor Lebanon National Report 2018.* UK Lebanon Tech Hub.

Ismail, A., Schott, T., Bazargon, A., Dudokh, D., Al Kubaisi, H., Hassen, M., … Kew, P. (2017). *GEM Middle East and North Africa Regional Report.* Global Entrepreneurship Research Association.

Kruse, P. (2019). Can There Only Be One? An Emperical Comparison of Four Models on Social Entrepreneurial Intention Formation. *International Entrepreneurship and Management Journal,* 1–25.

Lozano, G., Serrano, L., Arenas, D., Vernis, A., Austin, J., Reficco, E., … Teixiera, J. (2006). *Effective Management of Social Enterprises: Lessons from*

Business and Civil Society Organizations in Iberoamerica. (J. Austin, R. Gutierrez, E. Ogliastri, & E. Reficco, Eds.). Harvard University, David Rockefeller Center for Latin American Studies and Inter-American Development Bank.

Mair, J., & Marti, I. (2006). Social Entrepreneurship Research: A Source of Explanation, Prediction, and Delight. *Journal of World Business, 41*(1), 36–44.

Mair, J., Mayer, J., & Lutz, E. (2015). Navigating Institutional Plurality: Organizational Governance in Hybrid Organizations. *Organization Studies, 36*(6), 713–739.

Munro, M. M., & Belanger, C. (2017). Analyzing External Environment Factors Affecting Social Enterprise Development. *Social Enterprise Journal, 13*(1).

Nicholls, A., Paton, R., & Emerson, J. (2015). *Social Finance*. Oxford University Press.

Nick, T., & Wayne, V. (2017). *The World Guide to CSR: A Country-by-Country Analysis of Corporate Sustainability and Responsibility*. Routledge.

Nielsen, C., & Lund, M. (2015). The Concept of Business Model Scalability. *SSRN 2575962*.

Rey-Marti, A., Ribeiro-Soriano, D., & Sanchez-Garcia, J. L. (2016). Giving Back to Society: Job Creation Through Social Entrepreneurship. *Journal of Business Research, 69*(6), 2067–2072.

Santos, F. M. (2012). A Positive Theory of Social Entrepreneurship. *Journal of Business Ethics, 111*(3), 335–351.

Soriano, D. R., & Castrogiovanni, G. J. (2012). The Impact of Education, Experience and Inner Circle Advisors on SME Performance: Insights from a Study of Public Development Centers. *Small Business Economics, 38*(3), 333–349.

Teasdale, S. (2012). Negotiating Tensions: How Do Social Enterprises in the Homelessness Field Balance Social and Commercial Considerations? *Housing Studies, 27*(4), 514–532.

Terjesen, S., & Wang, N. (2013, February). Coase on Entrepreneurship. *Small Business Economics, 40*(2), 173–184.

von der Weppen, J., & Cochrane, J. (2012). Social Enterprises in Tourism: An Exploratory Study of Operational Models and Success Factors. *Journal of Sustainable Tourism, 20*(3), 497–511.

Weerawardena, J., & Mort, G. S. (2012). Competitive Strategy in Socially Entrepreneurial Nonprofit Organizations: Innovation and Differentiation. *Journal of Public Policy and Marketing, 31*(1), 91101.

World Economic Forum. (2018). *The Arab World Competitiveness Report 2018*.
Zahra, S., Gedajlovic, E., Neubaum, D. O., & Shulman, J. M. (2009). A Typology of Social Entrepreneurs: Motives, Search Processes and Ethical Challenges. *Journal of Business Venture, 24*(5), 519–532.
Zawya, Y. S. (2018). *Special Report: Entrepreneurship in the Arab World: The Opportunities, Challenges, the Stakeholders and the Funding Environment*.

Part III

Case Studies of Entrepreneurship

10

The Influence of Entrepreneurship on the Arab Cultures and Economies: Reflections from Egypt's Entrepreneurial Journey

Sherif Kamel

Overview

Emerging economies need an effective entrepreneurial ecosystem that is government-enabled, private sector-led, youth-empowered, innovation-driven, and future-oriented (Kamel, 2016). Startups, especially those based on tech and tech-enabled innovations, have over the last three decades, dominated various societies, communities, and markets in both developed and emerging economies given the growing tech-savvy and interconnected young populations around the world and the potential opportunities offered by emerging information and communication technologies (Schroeder, 2017). However, innovation in general and mainly information and communication technologies (ICTs) cannot solve all the problems or answer all the economic and societal challenges that have developed over many decades, especially in emerging

S. Kamel (✉)
The American University in Cairo, Cairo, Egypt
e-mail: skamel@aucegypt.edu

N. Azoury, T. Hafsi (eds.), *Entrepreneurship and Social Entrepreneurship in the MENA Region*, https://doi.org/10.1007/978-3-030-88447-5_10

economies (Kamel, 2020). While ICTs indeed represent an enabling environment that can make a difference, such technologies should be coupled with the proper legal, regulatory, effective, and comprehensive environment. Building an entrepreneurial ecosystem requires engaging diverse economic stakeholders across the different stages, including the private sector, the government, NGOs, and other institutions, and individuals who can enrich and effectively support an entrepreneurial culture (Ismail et al., 2019).

The culture of entrepreneurship should be built in-sync, bottom-up and top-down, seamlessly and simultaneously. It is a mindset that transforms society into thinking entrepreneurially rather than just focusing on starting-up enterprises (Schroeder, 2013). Noise should be created all along the process to provide the required momentum, passion, drive, and energy. The role of youth, practitioners, academics, industry experts, business leaders, mentors, investors, innovators, educators, trainers, and others can never be discounted within the entrepreneurial space (Kamel, 2012). It must be a collective effort where everyone is effectively engaged, empowered, and positively contributing. There is never a perfect time to start promoting entrepreneurship but, whenever the ball starts rolling, it must be disseminated across the community, and it must be open to risk-taking, problems, challenges, venturing into the unknown, and indeed be ready for failure as a stepping stone to learn from and build on. Success is only one element of the journey. Thinking big from the outset helps the dissemination of an entrepreneurial culture. For emerging economies across the Arab world, such as in Egypt, and from that perspective, it could be the ideal socioeconomic transformational platform (Kamel & Schroeder, 2016). Since the mid-1980s, Egypt has been gradually experiencing a technological makeover with implications for the economy's different sectors (Kamel, 2014). This has been coupled with several socioeconomic opportunities that, moving forward, could hold the keys to a much better and prosperous future. The crucial building blocks in the equation include key primary elements, the human and innovation capital, and the universal and useful information and communication technology diffusion within the society (Kamel & Rizk, 2019).

Youth is a unique opportunity that could and should be captured across the entire Arab world. In Egypt, for example, the population is growing at a rate of 1.9%, or over 2 million people every year, and technology access has been rapidly increasing across the country with over 59% and 99% internet and mobile penetration rates, respectively (Kamel, 2020). Besides, no less than 58% of the population is under the age of 30, reflecting a young society in a nation that is home to around 100 million citizens; where over 22 million students are enrolled in school education and about 2.4 million are enrolled in university programs; in fact, it is a baby population (Kamel & Rizk, 2019). Both elements, schools, and universities in Egypt combined represent the largest educational system in the Arab world; they provide a unique opportunity for change and improvement. The intersection of technology, innovation, youth, and entrepreneurship could be the enabling platform (Kamel & Schroeder, 2016).

Such demographics apply to most emerging economies and across the Arab World. Universal access to ICTs means unlimited access to knowledge, people, opportunities, ideas, and the world at large, regardless of time and distance barriers and should never be confined to specific segments of the society (Kamel & Rizk, 2019; Rizk & Kamel, 2013). This can provide the infrastructure required to create a global competitive edge rather than a liability and a limitation. Investing in creating a pool of energetic, passionate, technology-savvy entrepreneurs and change agents who can make a difference is exactly what emerging economies need, Egypt and the entire Arab world included (Schroeder, 2013). Creating an entrepreneurial culture is never a one-person show nor the playground or the creation of one organization. It is the collective effort towards realizing several common goals for the society, including creating jobs, establishing enterprises, and boosting economic productivity (Kamel, 2011; Kane, 2010). The opportunity enabled through the youth population positions a large segment of the population ready for a more robust, competitive, and mostly service-oriented private sector and a diversified economy. Needless to say, the conditions differ from one country to the other in the Arab world and are based on several elements including but not limited to demographics, size, resources, and, more importantly, the enabling and supportive environment. It is worth noting that an opportunity can be created for every challenge, and that is precisely the entrepreneurial spirit that needs to be embedded in the people's mindset. The more diversified and varying challenges, some more opportunities and breakthroughs could be created given the deployment of an innovative approach customized to local markets (Nazeer, 2017).

In many ways, startups and small- and medium-sized enterprises (SMEs) in general represent the primary avenue by which entrepreneurs provide the economy with a continuous supply of ideas, skills, and innovative products and services. In the context of Egypt and in many ways across the countries in the Arab World, most SMEs are family-owned businesses across different governorates and in various sectors of the economy including agriculture, industry, tourism as well as in a wide variety of services besides, micro-sized enterprises in remote locations especially in villages and underprivileged communities. On this note, in countries with a "*youth opportunity*" such as Egypt, micro-sized enterprises become a viable, effective platform for employment and job creation in different cities and villages and remote locations across the country, which should be significantly emphasized, smartly supported, and rationally encouraged.

Today, Egypt has more than 2.5 SMEs employing around 75% of the workforce with many who are involved in the manufacturing sector; others offer innovative solutions in a variety of industries including biotech, renewable energy, and ICTs coupled with the innovation-driven entrepreneurial ecosystem with around 10% or more led by women, and 90% of the total volume of establishments being family businesses (Kamel, 2015). However, the majority of SMEs are not registered, so most probably more than double these figures are active in the gray "*underground or informal*" economy; all requiring the proper mechanisms and platforms for financial inclusion and integration into the economy which is now being presented through digital transformation, especially in the wake of the repercussions of Covid-19. It is worth noting that when combining the formal and information business transactions and operations, SMEs more or less represent 80% of the total employment in Egypt (Kamel, 2014). Combining these demographics and statistics builds positive momentum and inspires the youth to think in brand new directions.

Over the last decade and across the Arab world, there was a growing number of support institutions represented by associations, non-governmental organizations, and the private sector, all promoting a growing, collaborative, and effective entrepreneurial ecosystem that is diversified, technology-driven, responsible, and committed to societal development and growth. Less than a decade ago, such action was nascent and limited, demonstrating the magnitude of the potential and the untapped opportunities in the market. Today, it is seamlessly growing and impacting different economies. However, there is still a long way to go.

In Egypt, some of the leading players that have been established or joined the entrepreneurial ecosystem over the last decade addressing and supporting the private sector through a variety of critical elements such as growth potential, connectivity and collaboration, talent development, funding and financial support include but are not limited to AUC Venture-Lab, Flat6Lab Egypt, Injaz Egypt, the Egyptian American Enterprise Fund, the Information Technology Industry Development Agency, Cairo Angels, Alex Angels, Innoventures, the American Chamber of Commerce in Egypt, Endeavor Egypt, Techne Drifts, Rise-up Summit, Sawari Ventures, A15, Kamelizer, Enactus, RISE Egypt, Nahdet El-Mahroussa, the Technology Innovation and Entrepreneurship Center, Ashoka, AUC Angels, and many more organizations that are either in the process of being formed or are progressively contributing to a collaborative and increasingly effective ecosystem that can have sustainable and scalable implications on Egypt's economy. They collectively support the ecosystem through a portfolio of services such as education, lifelong learning, crowdfunding, research and development, co-working spaces, acceleration, incubation, mentorship, and media access and visibility, and more.

Egypt is not known for being rich in oil, but it is blessed with one precious resource, its human capital. This is an incredible force that could take the country forward by creating a startup culture that could be scaled-up across the nation's different governorates, and that could also proliferate across other emerging economies given that most countries have similar demographics like Egypt (Kamel, 2015). The name of the game is startups and SMEs and the key to realizing both are investing in human capital and building a robust and state-of-the-art infrastructure with its associated financial and non-financial aspects. They could make a huge difference in society if the proper legal, investment, regulatory, educational, and other support mechanisms are in place. Also, no scaling-up can happen unless the right infrastructure and "*infostructure*" is timely, efficiently disseminated, and well-institutionalized (Rizk & Kamel, 2013).

Startups and SMEs have the potential to create millions of jobs and thousands of enterprises in the years to come, mostly when capitalizing on emerging technologies and the opportunities created by various platforms of the fourth industrial revolution, including artificial intelligence, robotics, cloud computing, big data analytics, mobility, 3D printing, machine language, and many other emerging technologies and innovations (Schwab, 2016, 2018). Investing in these innovations is precisely what emerging economies like Egypt and the entire Arab world should focus on. The world is witnessing a gradual and steady transformation to digitization. However, to be able to promote a scalable and sustainable impact, it is much more rewarding and effective for Egypt and emerging economies, in general, to create an entrepreneurial culture than to promote the concept of promoting an agile and competitive private sector and an innovative entrepreneurship mindset only in the forms of establishing startups and SMEs. What is needed is a paradigm shift that realizes a transformational change (El-Dahshan et al., 2010, 2011).

In the twenty-first century, young graduates are more than ever eager to start their own business, be self-employed, make a difference, and contribute to society. Unlike previous generations, they are not primarily looking for civil servants; they look for self-employment opportunities. They want to take risks and venture into the challenging and exciting business world, even if they do not have all that it takes to succeed in a competitive, global, and dynamic marketplace. With the need to create over 800,000 jobs every year in Egypt, the path for development and growth can only be made through a scaled-up agile, competitive, growing, and inclusive private-sector-led community driven by startups SMEs. The bigger the base of potential entrepreneurs, the more likely an increasing number of startups will prevail. It is all about scalability and the continuous flow of ideas that can go all the way to the next level (Ismail et al., 2019).

With 4000 villages in Egypt, the potential is enormous. With challenging conditions, innovation becomes a model by which underprivileged communities have the passion, determination, and will to make a difference and improve their living standards. The best ideas come in desperate times, and real motivation happens when people are more challenged economically and socially, so what counts is human capital and people's significant role in society as agents of change and, more importantly, the transformational impact they can help realize. During the last few months, the world has seen so many dramatic changes caused by the Coronavirus pandemic. Many legacies were put to the test, and even people who are usually the least receptive to change, have changed and adapted (Kamel, 2020). This offers an opportune moment for innovative entrepreneurs across the Arab world to venture into a space that provides endless openings for business, economic, and social development and growth. Creating a thriving entrepreneurial culture and a startup ecosystem requires talented individuals and a receptive and enthusiastic society (Ismail et al., 2019; El-Dahshan et al., 2010, 2011).

Therefore, while spreading the notion of entrepreneurship to a broader audience across the community, there is a need to identify, mentor, incubate, finance, connect, and support those who possess natural and gifted talents as well as those who are ready to learn and excel in this endeavor and facilitate accordingly their success moving forward. The future will be determined by the millions of youths in Egypt and across the Arab world who are increasingly ambitious, have a lot more technology in their hands, and are tempted by what innovation and creativity have to offer (Kamel & Schroeder, 2016). They can help build a new Egypt and a new region that is hopefully more responsible, sustainable, and prosperous.

It is worth noting that a healthy and agile private sector and a growing, influential, and well-disseminated entrepreneurial culture across the community will change the lives and livelihoods of different countries across the Arab world. This requires a more ambitious, progressive, and action-driven attitude, coupled with a significant shift in the mindset. A lot is happening across the Arab world in terms of promoting and supporting entrepreneurial ecosystems. However, there is still a long way to go, and most countries in the region, if not all, are still scratching the surface. One of the critical challenges is to create an enabling environment that can support in preparing innovative and entrepreneurial leaders who can help transform their respective economies. The first order of business would be to continuously educate and train as many students and learners as possible on change, entrepreneurship, innovation, creativity, discovery, competition, and more critical elements in the entrepreneurial mindset. The essence is not just to focus on starting-up enterprises and creating jobs, but instead helping introduce change to the economy and consequently to the society by addressing priority issues across different economic sectors (Kane, 2010). From a societal perspective, it does not matter where people get employed, whether in the private sector, government, or civil society. The key is to have them contribute effectively to socioeconomic development irrespective of where they are and what they do. There is a need to create leaders, who become game changers, movers, shakers, and agents of change (Kamel, 2016).

For some time, there has been a growing sentiment across Egypt, especially among the new generations, that entrepreneurship is the ideal venue for a better future, and many across the country and for that matter, the entire Arab region got excited and provided all the support needed to help it grow. Ironically, despite all such interest and potential, there is no proper word in Arabic for entrepreneurship. I think that "*reyadet al-aamal*" is being used to mean *entrepreneurship* is anything but encouraging the cause; the term does not bring any of the excitement or passion associated with entrepreneurship. Nevertheless, there has been and remains to be a considerable shift in mindset. In contrast, Egyptians are traditionally risk-averse, preferring to "*wait and see*" overtaking initiatives and actions, a characteristic of the entire region. However, more recently, people started to change, especially as indicated earlier that an overwhelming majority of the population are young; many of them are technology savvy, connected to the Internet, more inclined to work in the private sector. They want to take more risks, explore new venues, venture into startups, learn more, get more exposed but, more importantly, contribute, and make a difference to society.

AUC School of Business: The Journey

The School of Business of The American University in Cairo (AUC) is just an example of many business schools across the Arab world that are continuously trying to impact their constituents. Since 2009, the school has been driven by the notion that *entrepreneurial education* is invaluable for Egypt's development and growth, especially with the population growth rate, the socioeconomic and political developments taking place in the Arab world, and the dynamics and opportunities created through digital transformation and the fourth industrial revolution (Schwab, 2016).

Therefore, the school believes that investing in human capital should always be a priority for individuals, organizations, and societies to move forward, compete, and improve continually. People make a difference; they have been and will always be the differentiating factor in a world increasingly driven by change coupled with the fierce and timely competition. Business and management education must offer a greater level of support and flexibility to existing business owners and entrepreneurs, and that is what the school has been trying to do since it started the journey of promoting entrepreneurship and innovation as a priority area across the board in different programs, activities, and services. The ultimate objective was to support business and economic growth in Egypt and educate students and learners to become leaders who understand the complex and changing context of the global economic climate (Kamel, 2015).

Business schools worldwide regularly look for niches to better serve their local community and search for opportunities to place themselves on the broader educational space and maximize their global footprint. Therefore, as a strategic direction, the school community both on and off-campus collectively decided that focusing on entrepreneurship as an integral element in what is offered through different programs and activities is another journey and that it was high time to pursue while integrating into the curriculum the aspects of innovation, critical thinking, leadership, responsible business, civic engagement, and ethics, to mention a few. The objective was to change entrepreneurship's importance as a significant vehicle for Egypt's socioeconomic development (Kamel, 2020). From the theoretical and academic to the practical and applied, the different school constituents were convinced from the outset that a well-established entrepreneurial culture could be the proper setup for the school to help build Egypt's economy in a more inclusive and impactful way and could be the platform for startup *culture*, a startup *society*, and a startup *nation*.

Entrepreneurial Education

Innovation-inspired and -driven entrepreneurial education is an essential element in creating an entrepreneurial culture and changing society's mindset towards new business behaviors and a new set of endeavors. Business schools, by design, are integral to the national entrepreneurial ecosystem. They should be the strategic educational and learning partners linking the two worlds of business and business schools together (Kamel, 2013a). At AUC School of Business, the rationale behind developing the Entrepreneurship and Innovation Program (EIP) was that entrepreneurial education would change how people think, generate ideas, perceive opportunities, promote innovation, develop alternative solutions, and become impact-driven. Some people claim that entrepreneurship cannot be taught; others believe that some are born gifted with entrepreneurial skills while some are not. I would like to argue that people differ and that each one has an advantage that he/she can capitalize on. Still, there is no doubt that all skills and capacities can be shaped and improved through awareness and customized training, and lifelong learning and development programs coupled with proper and regular guidance and mentorship.

The objective of EIP was to spread the culture of entrepreneurship, both on campus and across Egypt, working with different partners in the ecosystem, which includes entrepreneurs, mentors, venture capital firms, as well as students and learners who have the spirit to venture into the world of startups and the stamina to persevere and take the necessary financial and non-financial risks. It was apparent to all those involved that such an objective will not be realized only through entrepreneurship courses. However, through an environment, a culture, and an ecosystem where curricula, courses, and in-class and out of class experiential learning is crucial; moreover, students and learners' extracurricular activities, engagement in different entrepreneurial endeavors, and internships are invaluable elements to add, coupled with a mission to promote and help create the required infrastructure that would eventually grow and become the core of a university-based entrepreneurial ecosystem that could serve Egypt (Kamel, 2017; Kitagawa & Robertson, 2012).

To realize such a mission, the school decided to start the journey by having its educational programs include entrepreneurship, family business, corporate governance, innovation, critical thinking, leadership, and creativity, embedding and integrating them in both degree and non-degree programs. Moreover, because the school realized that great ideas do not come only from the big cities or urban settings, it was decided that all entrepreneurial services, activities, and events are to be open to everyone, including students and learners at the school, AUC, from across all universities in Egypt, and to promising young entrepreneurs from across Egypt's 27 governorates who wanted to understand what needs to be done to know more about entrepreneurship, get trained, or had an idea and tried to take it to the next level. While many learners came to campus from across Egypt to attend workshops and mentorship sessions and interact with students, faculty, and potential future entrepreneurs, others got access to the services offered online. The motto was, "*all citizens are welcome*."

Investing in human capital should regularly and timely reflect local market needs, which applies to the entire Arab world. Such an attitude helps create job opportunities and close the gap between vacant jobs and a growing pool of graduates looking for employment opportunities. Egypt's youth are passionate, talented, and are experiencing exceptional moments with the increasing penetration and role different innovative technologies are having in their lives. Such a young population is the descendant of a country that is more than 5000 years old. However, it is still the land of opportunity, and so much of it remains untapped. It is the right time for the school of business to build on its role in producing and promoting the next generation of innovative and creative entrepreneurs and private-sector leaders in Egypt. I firmly believe that a thought process should be shared by different business schools and universities from across the Arab world. Each country has its characteristics and has a lot to give in a region with many potentials. We are already seeing massive prospects evolving in the entrepreneurial space from Jordan, the United Arab Emirates, Saudi Arabia, Bahrain, and Tunisia (Wamda & Arabnet, 2020). Egypt's opportunities are spread across different economic sectors, including, but not limited to, agribusiness, manufacturing, oil and gas, energy, information, and communication technology, tourism, entertainment, finance, education, healthcare, and transportation. The solution to effectively move forward was to develop the current capacities and skills and capitalize on existing potentials, which would only materialize by investing in human capital and entrepreneurial education. To maximize the learning curve, the process of promoting entrepreneurship had to take an institutional shape, and that included all academic venues, including research, teaching, service, executive education, and other extracurricular activities both on and off-campus.

EIP aimed to educate, train, and inspire students, learners, and young entrepreneurs in the intricacies of entrepreneurship through a variety of seminars, workshops, networking events, a mentorship program, one-to-one meetings, business boot camps both on and off-campus, and during weekdays as well as weekends in addition to the organization of different formats and schemes of business plan competitions (Kamel, 2013b). The mandate was to create a buzz, help entrepreneurs generate ideas for businesses, and then connect the most viable startups to incubators and help them find venture capitalists, angel investors, and other seed funding sources. From the start, as indicated earlier, the intention was to create a *national buzz*. The school wanted to become the home for entrepreneurial education in the Middle East North Africa region. The origins of EIP dated to 2009 when the school was surveying the local and regional markets. During that time, there was a proliferation of new business schools and programs in the Arab world with a growing interest in supporting and promoting entrepreneurship. EIP was established with a dual-prolonged objective; on the one hand, to help spread the idea of entrepreneurship and innovation to a broader audience by educating students, graduates, and interested individuals and on the other hand, to identify, mentor, connect, and help those who possess natural talents, skills, and capacities to be able to support their endeavors in the entrepreneurial space. To achieve these objectives, EIP has been sowing the seeds and nurturing the ground to pave the way for a rich and prosperous entrepreneurial environment that invests in human capital and caters to organizational and societal needs. Since 2010 and to date, EIP, restructured in 2015 and becoming the Center for Entrepreneurship and Innovation (CEI), has stirred an undeniable impact where the flicker of entrepreneurship started glowing with thousands of smart young Egyptians eager to learn more, get mentored, and take their ideas to the next level.

The interaction, diversity, and networking were essential and represented a real learning experience. Some services were also offered online, so it was more of a blended model. The program gradually became the core educational partner of an ecosystem that is still in the making. By design, EIP looked for talented entrepreneurs to stimulate their ideas, establish a web of those ideas, cultivate a society of mentors, transform those ideas into startup ventures, and open doors for many funding sources to make those ideas become finished products and services. Over the last decade, many local and regional conferences, workshops, seminars, and business plan and case competitions were organized more often with partner organizations from across the Arab world. These partners included local and regional players such as Arabnet, Egypreneur, Enactus, Injaz Egypt, and many others and international organizations such as TechWadi, Intel, the Global Entrepreneurship Program (GEP), and the United States Agency for International Development (USAID).

EIP's experience and its reach across society impacted more than 2500 undergraduate students and 1500 graduate students trained. Moreover, there were 120 faculty and educators trained, and more than 10,000 learners from Cairo and several other governorates in Egypt, including Giza, El-Mansoura, El-Ismailia, Assiout, Luxor, Qena, Alexandria, and Aswan, as well as from other countries in the Arab region including Lebanon, Saudi Arabia, Jordan, Tunisia, Yemen, Sudan, Syria, Oman, Morocco, and the United Arab Emirates. In Egypt, more than 100 public, private, and non-governmental organizations helped create the ecosystem, and more than 25,000 applicants competing to a pool of 50 different startup competitions organized over the past decade. This was just the beginning of a long journey, but it was enough to create the initial buzz.

Building the Entrepreneurial Ecosystem

As an integral part of the school's strategy, EIP includes a broad portfolio of activities and services to address the importance of entrepreneurial education as a mechanism that can help improve most Egyptians' socioeconomic conditions (El-Dahshan et al., 2010). In my mind, entrepreneurship was not just about micro-, small- and medium-sized enterprises, and startups. Egypt needs those young, innovative, passionate, determined, and committed Egyptians to become agents of change and create a better future for the next generations. The question was how to create a momentum that could extend way beyond the campus boundaries. That could have the required scalable and sustainable impact to build a practical and workable market-wide entrepreneurial ecosystem (Ducker, 2015).

Programs such as EIP tried to emphasize the importance of entrepreneurial education through its different activities that extended beyond the university boundaries to benefit many Egyptians across other governorates going north to the delta region and south to upper Egypt down to Dandara and engaging with its entrepreneurial community and realizing an impact which could help create a market-wide entrepreneurial ecosystem and where, since its inception, EIP had positioned itself in the entrepreneurship ecosystem as the national educational partner becoming the primary platform for knowledge sharing and dissemination in the space of entrepreneurship in Egypt.

This was an ecosystem that was created seamlessly and organically (Business Sweden, 2015). It was not led by anyone or any organization or belonged to any specific entity. It was a mushrooming space where individuals and organizations were collectively collaborating and supporting each other. Yet, again in many ways, they were competing in resources, financial support, and bettering their services and offerings, a classic case of co-opetition. It was a learning experience for all. These were exciting times, and everyone was engaged; it was like an open-ended co-working space for creativity and innovation. An experience that should be replicated across the Arab world, given the potential that is growing and enriched, given the triangle of youth, innovation, and prospects that is yet to be tapped across the region. With a large and growing population, such as the case in Egypt, scalability is critical. The same would apply to the Arab world's market if addressed, which is home to more than 420 million people and comprises 22 countries.

The school wanted to take a leading position in the market in the space of entrepreneurship in its journey to establish a university-based incubator eventually, so there was a need to partner with different stakeholders in the marketplace. Moreover, the school's EIP established a network of practitioners, business executives, and academics interested in mentoring and coaching entrepreneurs at various stages of their startup journeys. The entrepreneurial ecosystem approach designed and implemented was primarily based on six building blocks: (a) entrepreneurs, (b) ideas, (c) networks, (d) mentors, (e) funding, and (f) startup ventures. However, the main important element was the creation of an environment where everyone contributed. It was another case of building the right team and engaging everyone to reach the targeted objective, except that this time the team was composed of different institutions, all serving one way or another the space of entrepreneurship.

Human capital is always crucial (Kamel, 2013a). Therefore, finding the correct *entrepreneurs* with ideas was the primary building block. It is always about people. The focus was on raising awareness about entrepreneurs who varied in their education level, socioeconomic background, age, and gender. It was essential to get as many candidates through the cycle as part of the EIP awareness-building effort and search for scalability. Next, it identified and generated attractive and promising *ideas* that address local market needs, conceptualize business opportunities, and help the entrepreneurs develop their business plans and transform the ideas into a potentially viable business opportunity. Entrepreneurship is not about good ideas like many people think but rather about ideas that could be turned into opportunities. During that time, there were many boot camps and workshops organized to mentor the participating entrepreneurs. As indicated before, unlike the traditional wisdom that capitals and large cities of emerging and developing economies are the centers of different resources and prospects, EIP was determined to go unconventional and look for ideas from all over Egypt regardless of their proximity to Cairo, their background, gender, or level of education.

Next was *networking* through the collaboration of different stakeholders, including universities, companies, and international institutions, and the involvement of business executives from various sectors; participants were exposed to real-life examples of entrepreneurship and startups. Meetings and discussions carried out between like-minded entrepreneurs, industry experts, and local leaders is a critical element in creating the culture of entrepreneurship and growing its influence across the board.

The *mentorship* level revolved around coaching potential entrepreneurs by developing their business plans and the launch of their startups. Furthermore, mentors provided internships in startups. The mentoring process was done through the university mentors' network and supported by faculty advice, workshops, and training. This was one of the most invaluable building blocks in the process, given the importance of the *people* factor. Such a network was created by the university alumni who wanted to engage and support potential entrepreneurs. Following this phase, entrepreneurs were encouraged to seek funds. Therefore, the program connected entrepreneurs to venture capitalists, angel investors, and potential investment partners. EIP reached out and managed to solicit financial awards for its different startup competitions and schemes.

Furthermore, the program managed to support potential entrepreneurs with seed funds accumulated during a relatively short period to over one million US dollars divided among the supported startups during their incubation period, and lastly, to connect *startups* to different market stakeholders. Accordingly, some entrepreneurs were connected and consequently admitted to other business and startup incubators and accelerators. Others were assisted in promoting their ideas. Some were introduced to different organizations in the ecosystem. Working with young entrepreneurs highlighted the need for providing additional in-depth services to serious early-stage entrepreneurs and startups as they worked through their business modeling and planning, fundraising, and setting up their operations and partnerships.

These services are best provided to a smaller number of startups through an acceleration or incubation program. This motivated me to expand the scope of the entrepreneurship ecosystem at AUC by establishing a campus-wide incubator/accelerator that provides an infrastructure for an interdisciplinary entrepreneurial learning experience in the form of the university's Venture Lab. It is important to note that startups cannot exist in a vacuum, nor are they isolated from cultural, social, and economic elements. The role of values, norms, beliefs, and habits across the society should be factored in. Accordingly, in one way, the economy of Egypt and in many ways the economies of other countries across the Arab world are characterized by a private sector that is dominated by family businesses, which demonstrates in a way the willingness to invest in creativity, innovation which provides an opening for entrepreneurship to grow. However, from a cultural perspective, there is still a lot of awareness and understanding that needs to take place about issues such as accepting and tolerating failure. It has to be perceived as a step towards realizing success and accomplishment. Therefore, the mindset's transformation should be geared towards the fact that the sharing and exchange of knowledge, best practices, and the regular investment in lifelong learning are critical factors for success as an entrepreneur.

The Venture-Lab (V-Lab)

In 2013, AUC School of Business launched the first full-fledged university-based startup accelerator in Egypt, becoming today one of the leading accelerators in the Arab world and Africa; the Venture Lab (V-Lab) aimed to build on the experience of EIP and to translate technologies and innovations developed by different supported startups across Egypt into commercially viable ventures and to promote and support a growing entrepreneurial culture in Egypt. The V-Lab represented another building block in the school's journey to help establish an entrepreneurial culture and pioneer the notion of university-based incubators and demonstrate its role in building bridges between academia, business, and industry (Manimala & Vijay, 2012). The V-Lab has accelerated 210 startups covering multiple sectors and creative industries, including but not limited to healthcare, energy, retailing, sustainability, supply chain, logistics, transportation, education, wearable technologies, sports, and more. During the past seven years, the V-Lab has helped these startups solicit investments north of 102 million US dollars, creating more than 8000 jobs and generating more than 36 million US dollars.

The V-Lab philosophy is based on the fact that evidence-based entrepreneurship with the support of different business partners and associates, can provide the entrepreneurs with the right business knowledge, industry expertise, tools, resources, and networks to reach their full potential (Kamel & Ismail, 2013). The V-Lab business model is based on capitalizing on the resources and reach of the university at large and its state-of-the-art campus facilities in terms of human, knowledge, and technology infrastructure. The V-Lab was established as an interdisciplinary university-based incubator/accelerator to provide in-depth support services for qualifying entrepreneurs and their startups according to a set of publicly announced criteria and processes for application and qualification. The V-Lab mission is twofold; to help startups commercialize their innovative solutions into viable businesses and provide an experiential learning and research platform for the AUC community to connect and engage with entrepreneurs. The strategic objectives of the V-Lab were identified to include, but not limited to, encouraging employment and job creation; investing in people and innovation; focusing on the development of high-growth small- and medium-size enterprises; empowering youth and building their capacity; and, engaging the private sector in community development such as corporate social responsibility and good citizenship. The V-Lab offered young and promising entrepreneurs various services, including assisting their startups, helping secure access to funding from angel investors, venture capital, and other sources.

Based on the analysis of the findings of several background types of research conducted on startups in Egypt and in across the Arab world, many startups needed a variety of services that could be easily offered by a university-based incubator, such as awareness, training, mentorship and coaching, networking and connections, and access to university facilities, faculty and students (Ensley & Hmieleski, 2005). The V-Lab business model was based on research conducted to study other university-based incubators in the world and build on their journeys, experiences, and lessons learned. This provided insights into the various business models of university-based incubators, which helped shape the V-Lab business model while catering and adapting to the local needs, trends in the market, and the local norms, values, and ways of doing business. The V-Lab offers a few high-impact potential entrepreneurs a variety of customized services to assist the startup process, train them, increase business survival rates, and provide avenues for access to funding from angel investors, venture capitalists, and other sources (Ismail et al., 2019).

The V-Lab builds on the university's brand and rich history with over 100 years of serving the higher education market in Egypt and the Arab world, its diversified alumni network and state-of-the-art capabilities including but not limited to knowledge, faculty, staff, facilities, space, and services to help companies with strong growth potential launch successfully. In terms of its acceleration program design, the V-Lab startup accelerator since its inception has been providing two cycles of incubation each year (Kamel & Ismail, 2013). It is a 16-week program supporting early-stage innovative startups to launch and grow their businesses using evidence-based entrepreneurship and lean startup methods. The number of startup teams selected varies from one cycle to another. However, all applicants go through a competitive process to join the program, with about 400 startups applying each cycle, and around 15 being accepted (3.75% acceptance rate). The V-Lab receives entrepreneurs from all over Egypt, even if they are not affiliated to AUC, and welcomes applicants from the Arab world, as it encourages diversity and meritocracy. During the acceleration stage, the V-Lab provides a small seed fund (in the form of a grant), 3000 US dollars, to each of the accepted startups, along with a set of services and support in return for zero equity. The V-Lab funds itself through sponsorships from external sources coupled with a portion from the school budget.

It is worth noting that the V-Lab as a startup accelerator has been named the Middle East and North Africa Top Challenger for the year 2019–2020 by UBI Global, a Sweden-based research company specializing in mapping, highlighting, and connecting the world of business incubation and acceleration. With three previous UBI recognitions, the V-Lab is the only accelerator in Egypt recognized among 1580 programs assessed this year. The regional Top Challenger award is granted to incubators and accelerators that stand out due to impressive overall impact and performance achievements relative to respective regional peers. Furthermore, the V-Lab Fintech accelerator has also been recognized as a highlight in *Innovations That Inspire* 2020 Challenge organized by AACSB International, the world's largest business education network. The recognition is a testament to V-Lab's work as a catalyst for innovation coupled with the growing impact on society.

More recently, the V-Lab introduced its FinTech accelerator, which is a 16-week customized program for financial technology startups providing entrepreneurs with specialized business, finance, and technology support. Fintech entrepreneurs get to understand the ins and outs of working within the evolving government regulations and gain valuable insights from some of the smartest minds in the startup and fintech worlds. To support the mission of the V-Lab as well as the entrepreneurial ecosystem, the school through the V-Lab launched in 2018 the AUC Angels, which is the first university-based angel investor network in the MENA region, with a mission to create an angel investor community at AUC to invest in innovative Egyptian startups. AUC Angels have access to vetted and scalable startups that have proved traction in the market and have a strong potential for positive returns. AUC Angels provide financial and legal training to new angel investors and help startups develop attractive investment cases while matching them with angel investors. The network now includes over 50 angel investors, have invested in 11 innovative startups, and have so far invested north of 650 thousand US dollars.

In general, university-based incubators are established to empower entrepreneurs and foster innovation to contribute to socioeconomic development by creating jobs. If the proposed ideas can be translated into successful products and services, the economy will most probably be in a much better shape (Mian, 1996, 1997). Entrepreneurship and innovation can be a crucial driver for competitiveness and for accelerating inclusive economic growth. In that sense, this is precisely what the V-Lab was established to realize with an additional mission to support in filling the existing gaps in the emerging entrepreneurial ecosystem in Egypt. It goes without saying that to promote the culture of entrepreneurship across the Arab world, a primary building block is to establish an incubator in each university, given the environment and the ecosystem that is naturally built around it (Kamel & Ismail, 2013).

To date, the V-Lab has developed several key performance indicators to measure its performance and impact, including the number of successful startups it helped create, the number of entrepreneurs trained through the learning program, the number of startups incubated and supported, the percentage of startups that had access to funding, including the amount of funding that was generated as a result of being incubated at the V-Lab, and the mentors' ability to link entrepreneurs with business executives and other entrepreneurs.

Furthermore, the number of partnerships created between startups, businesses, government agencies, and educational institutions were additional success indicators. University-based incubators are increasingly becoming the ultimate resource-base and the convenient environment conducive to developing successful startups and promoting the commercialization of innovative entrepreneurial ideas and ventures. However, some issues remain to be of primary importance for continuous research and development. They relate to different entrepreneurial elements in the equation: the individual, the process, the organization, the financing, and the legal and regulatory environment.

As for the national level, the next journey should be to help all universities in Egypt, both private and public, to establish their entrepreneurial platforms, building on the experience of the school's Center for Entrepreneurship and Innovation and the Venture-Lab. Every university in Egypt must offer such an opportunity to its constituents, which applies to the entire Arab world. Having an incubator/accelerator in each university could be the manufacturing platform for startups that can help students and alumni make a difference in their communities and, consequently, impact society. Furthermore, the timing could provide a unique break because it is often advisable to venture into a new business in challenging economic conditions. It minimizes the cost and offers an opportunity to be ready to thrive when circumstances improve. Accordingly, the growing crowd of innovative and talented tech entrepreneurs in Egypt could be influential and participate in its digital transformation. The following is a sample of promising tech-based and tech-enabled startups that address critical issues of primary importance to society, such as transportation, financial technology (fintech), health care, logistics, and distribution.

In transportation, Swvl—established in 2017 and known as the Uber of buses—is a premium alternative to public transport in Egypt. Through a mobile app, customers can book fixed-rate and affordable bus rides on existing routes; this is an effective solution that is much needed, given the traffic and transportation challenges in Egypt's major cities. Swvl is now operating in Egypt, Kenya, and Pakistan. In fintech, Paymob is an electronic payment enabler established in 2013 that offers integrated infrastructure solutions empowering the masses with instruments that increase financial inclusion. In health care, Rology, established in 2017, is an on-demand teleradiology platform solving the problem of radiologist shortages and high latency in medical reports by remotely and instantly matching cases from hospitals all over the world with the optimum radiologist. In health care, Vezeeta, launched in 2012, is a digital booking and practice management platform for physicians, clinics, and hospitals in the Middle East and North Africa region. In logistics, MaxAB, established in 2018, is an e-commerce wholesale food and grocery marketplace using data-driven technologies and innovative supply chains to serve its customers best. Finally, in distribution, Brimore, set up in 2017, is a social commerce and parallel distribution platform that allows local suppliers to have nationwide coverage through a network of individual distributors, mainly housewives, selling products in their circles using omnichannel.

Egypt is not known for being rich in oil, but it is blessed with a precious, invaluable asset: its youthful human capital. This resource can take Egypt forward by creating a tech-enabled entrepreneurial culture that can be scaled up across the country's governorates. A well-established, innovation-driven, government-enabled, and private sector-led digital transformation strategy can be an effective platform to help grow the economy more competitively and inclusively and presents a unique opportunity for Egypt to autocorrect.

Conclusion

The prospects of the impact of a well-structured, integrated, and diffused entrepreneurial culture across the Arab world are yet to reach their true potential, including the role of small- and medium-sized enterprises and startups. They all play an essential role in economic development and prosperity, obviously depending on need and with variations of the degree of impact from one sector to another, one industry to another, and one country to another. The potential of the impact of a solid and well-supported entrepreneurial ecosystem in the Arab world, emphasizing tech and tech-enabled startups, can help generate from an economic added-value perspective more than ten folds the jobs created and four folds the revenues generated than any other type of business. Creating an entrepreneurial culture should be developed using an approach that reaches out to the entire community for a change in mindset and how a startup nation and a startup Arab world should be perceived as a way for better lives and livelihoods.

References

Business Sweden. (2015). Egypt Entrepreneurship Study. *Research Study*. The Swedish Trade and Invest Council.

Ducker, M. (2015). *Egypt Entrepreneurship: Where Are All Egyptian Entrepreneurs*. Final Report. United States Agency for International Development.

El-Dahshan, M., Tolba, A., & Badreldin, T. (2010). *Enabling Entrepreneurship in Egypt: Towards a Sustainable Dynamic Model*. Entrepreneurship Business Forum.

El-Dahshan, M., Tolba, A., & Badreldin, T. (2011). Enabling Entrepreneurship in Egypt: Toward a Sustainable Dynamic Model. *Innovations, 7*(2), 83–106.

Ensley, M. D., & Hmieleski, K. M. (2005). A Comparative Study of New Venture Top Management Team Composition, Dynamics and Performance Between University-Based and Independent Startups. *Research Policy, 34*(7), 1091–1105.

Ismail, A., Kamel, S., & Wahba, K. (2019). The Impact of Technology-Based Incubators in Creating a Sustainable and Scalable Startup Culture in Emerging Economies: A System Thinking Model. *Communications of the IBIMA, 2019*, 1–16.

Kamel, S. (2011). Managing After the Arab Spring. *Global Focus, 5*(3), 56–59.

Kamel, S. (2012, November/December). Entrepreneurial Uprising. *BizEd. The Association to Advance Collegiate Schools of Business International Magazine*, 46–47.

Kamel, S. (2013a). Investing in Human Capital and Creating and Entrepreneurial Culture: The Egyptian Experience. *The Journal of Information Technology Management, Cutter IT Journal, 26*(5), 32–35.

Kamel, S. (2013b). Is Entrepreneurial Education the Solution? *AUC Business Review (ABR), 1*(1), 10.

Kamel, S. (2014). Investing in Entrepreneurial Lifelong Learning Would Lead to More Entrepreneurs, More Jobs and a Better Economy. *Entrepreneur – Egypt Edition, 1*, 89–91.

Kamel, S. (2015, May 8). Time for an Entrepreneurial Uprising in Egypt. *The Arab Weekly*, 18.

Kamel, S. (2016). Startup. *Global Focus. The European Foundation for Management Development Business Magazine, 10*(3), 52–55.

Kamel, S. (2017, November 6–7). Building an Agile, Competitive and Dynamic Entrepreneurial Ecosystem to Create a Startup Culture, Startup Nation, and a Startup region. *Proceedings of the International Applied Research Symposium on the Transforming Power of the Innovation and Entrepreneurship Ecosystem – Lessons Learned*, Kaslik, Lebanon.

Kamel, S. (2020, October). Does Digital Transformation Present an Opportunity for Egypt to Autocorrect? *Policy Paper*. In M. Mabrouk (Ed.), *Rethinking Egypt's Economy*. Middle East Institute.

Kamel, S., & Ismail, A. (2013, March 4–5). EIP@AUC: A Case Study of a University-Centered Entrepreneurship Ecosystem in Egypt. *Proceedings of the International Conference on Innovation and Entrepreneurship (ICIE)*, Amman, Jordan.

Kamel, S., & Rizk. (2019). The Role of Innovative and Digital Technologies in Transforming Egypt into a Knowledge-Based Economy. In M. Habib (Ed.), *Handbook of Research on the Evolution of I.T. and the Rise of E-Society* (pp. 386–400). IGI Global.

Kamel, S., & Schroeder, C. (2016). Economic Recovery and Revitalization. *Research Study*. Working Group Report of the Middle East Strategy Task Force. The Atlantic Council.

Kane, T. (2010). *The Importance of Startups in Job Creation and Job Destruction*. Kauffman Foundation Research Series.

Kitagawa, F., & Robertson, S. (2012). High-Tech Entrepreneurial Firms in a University-Based Business Incubator. *Entrepreneurship and Innovation, 13*(4), 227–237.

Manimala, M. J., & Vijay, D. (2012). *Technology Business Incubators: A Perspective for the Emerging Economies*. Indian Institute of Management.

Mian, S. A. (1996). The University Business Incubator: A Strategy for Developing New Research/Technology-Based Firms. *The Journal of High Technology Management Research, 7*(2), 191–208.

Mian, S. A. (1997). Assessing and Managing the University Technology Business Incubator: An Integrative Framework. *Journal of Business Venturing, 12*(4), 251–285.

Nazeer, T. (2017, August 13). MENA's Entrepreneurial Ecosystem Has the Potential to Flourish. *Forbes Middle East*.

Rizk, N., & Kamel, S. (2013). ICT and Building a Knowledge Society in Egypt. *International Journal of Knowledge Management, 9*(1), 1–20.

Schroeder, C. (2013). *Startup Rising – The Entrepreneurial Revolution Remaking the Middle East*. Palgrave Macmillan.

Schroeder, C. (2017, August 3). A Different Story from the Middle East: Entrepreneurs Building an Arab Tech Economy. *MIT Technology Review*.

Schwab, K. (2016). *The Fourth Industrial Revolution*. Penguin Random House.

Schwab, K. (2018). *Shaping the Future of the Fourth Industrial Revolution*. Penguin Random House.

Wamda and Arabnet. (2020). *The Impact of the Covid-19 Outbreak on the Entrepreneurship Ecosystem*. Report Published by Wamda and Arabnet.

11

Social Entrepreneurship as a New Institutional Field: Institutional Barriers in the Algerian Context

Sofiane Baba, Taïeb Hafsi, and Meriem Benslama

Introduction

In the last twenty years, social entrepreneurship (SE hereinafter) has gained increased legitimacy in many countries (Raufflet et al., 2016). France has even moved to formalize its existence with the Loi sur l'Écconomie Sociale et Solidaire of July 2014. In the USA, the status of Benefit Corporation[1] plays the same role. Defined as an entrepreneurship with a social purpose, it is perceived by both national and international institutions as a vector of sustainable and inclusive social-economic

S. Baba (✉)
Université de Sherbrooke, Sherbrooke, QC, Canada
e-mail: sofiane.baba@usherbrooke.ca

T. Hafsi
HEC Montréal, Montreal, QC, Canada
e-mail: taieb.2.hafsi@hec.ca

M. Benslama
The Algerian Center for Social Entrepreneurship, Algiers, Algeria

N. Azoury, T. Hafsi (eds.), *Entrepreneurship and Social Entrepreneurship in the MENA Region*, https://doi.org/10.1007/978-3-030-88447-5_11

development. While social entrepreneurs do not neglect financial goals, they do not see them as the firm's main purpose. Battilana (2018) views these organizations as hybrids, which maintain a balance between several goals, whether these are social, environmental, or economic.

Even if its existence is perceived as legitimate in many countries, in particular Western industrialized ones, SE remains a new organizational form (Durand & Paolella, 2013), which is still to be understood, recognized, and encouraged in many others. In these countries, SE can be conceptualized as an emerging institutional field, "a recognized field of institutional life" (DiMaggio & Powell, 1983, p. 148). The field emergence process has been documented for several other domains and industries (Shepherd & Patzelt, 2011; Zietsma et al., 2017). The Cannabis industry in Canada and Social investment in Europe could be mentioned as typical examples. According to neo-institutional scholars, institutional fields are important conceptualizations for understanding social and institutional dynamics (Zietsma et al., 2017). Institutional change issues, and related negotiations, take place at this level of analysis. Scott (2001, p. 84) defines an institutional field as a community of organizations who participate in a system of common meaning, and whose actors interact more frequently and more naturally with each other than with others outside the field.

This chapter deals with SE's emergence as an institutional field, focusing more particularly on the challenges it faces in a country such as Algeria, with turbulent and complex institutional dynamics (Baba et al., 2020, 2021). In Algeria, many organizational actors participate in the process of building institutions in what can be seen as institutional entrepreneurship (Tracey et al., 2011). Their purpose is to transform existing institutions at the cognitive, normative, and regulative levels (see Scott, 2014) to pave the way for SE's development as a legitimate and economically useful organizational form to society. In the early 2020s, the situation of SE in Algeria is still fragile, even precarious. The Algerian Center for Social Entrepreneurship, created in 2016, is the only formal structure promoting SE, with almost no help from established authorities. The Center's activities cover three complementary domains: (1) promoting, even evangelizing among students and civil society; (2) incubating and coaching social entrepreneurs; and (3) pleading with public authorities for the official recognition of SE.

Although much research has been conducted on the difficult process of SE institutionalization (Chandra, 2017; Nicholls, 2010b, 2012), Algeria remains an intriguing context. In the situations described in the literature, often based on experiences in the West, it has been suggested that SE is unlikely to gain legitimacy as a new organizational form, especially where classic entrepreneurship dominates. It has been recommended that there is a need to recognize social enterprise as a novel form of entrepreneurial activity to renew the business firm field, which suffers from too much emphasis on financial performance. In Algeria, the situation is even more interesting, as the private sector enterprise is struggling for legitimacy and facing hostile institutions. In particular, SE, in its hybrid forms with social and financial goals, is facing a double struggle. The first is similar to other classic entrepreneurs, while the second struggle is related to SE's social mission, which is frowned upon by suspicious authorities. Therefore, Algeria is an interesting social and institutional laboratory, which can help understand how a field emerges and gains legitimacy.

This chapter starts with a conceptual conversation around institutional theory, particularly the processes by which new institutional fields emerge and gain legitimacy. Then we explain how this research was conducted from a methodological standpoint, insisting on the context, the choice of the case, and the data collection process and analysis. We shall then propose an empirical description of SE in Algeria before discussing our findings on this poorly known phenomenon and their meaning for both research and practice. As a whole, this chapter helps understand better understudied phenomena in contexts that, for historical reasons, are institutionally hazy at best.

Theoretical Background: Social Entrepreneurship as an Emerging Institutional Field

Beyond a shadow of a doubt, SE has received significant attention and recognition from scholars and institutions in the past two decades (Chandra, 2017; Islam, 2020; Mair, 2020). The economic, social, and environmental issues that accelerated at the turn of the twenty-first century have contributed significantly to this enthusiasm. Considered as "the practice of addressing social problems by means of markets," (Mair, 2020, p. 333) SE has long been applauded "for its ability to challenge the status quo and navigate interactions with markets, institutions and governments to make the world a better place" (Bacq & Lumpkin, 2020, p. 286). Increasing interest in SE gave rise to a whole field of research, qualified by Nicholls (2010a, p. 611) "as a field of action in a pre-paradigmatic state that currently lacks an established epistemology." Overall, it is quite a dynamic and fast-growing field of research which has successfully explored several avenues of research despite remaining "challenging to grasp" because of its ongoing debates at the epistemological, definitional, theoretical and even methodological levels (Saebi et al., 2019, p. 71).

While SE is nowadays recognized as a legitimate entrepreneurial form in the Western world (Doherty et al., 2014; Mair, 2020), the literature has scarcely explored the process that allowed this entrepreneurial form to develop its legitimacy over time. Few exceptions (Hervieux et al., 2010; Newth & Woods, 2014; Nicholls, 2010a, 2010b) delved into this intriguing topic and found that the legitimation of SE is not a linear process but rather a tumultuous one marked by many challenges and resistance to change. In this vein, Nicholls (2010a, p. 625) explored SE legitimation's microstructures through the lens of structuration theory. He found that the field of SE "allows resource-rich actors to shape its legitimation discourses in a self-reflexive way" and that this process "is prioritizing two discourses: narratives based on hero entrepreneur success stories and organizational models reflecting ideal types from commercial business. The former supports internal logics that legitimate new venture philanthropic practices while the latter endorses internal logics that legitimate efficiency and the marketization of the state" (p. 625). Focusing on the same issue of SE legitimation, Hervieux et al. (2010) looked at the role of academics, consultants, and foundations in "theorizing" the SE concept and negotiating its legitimacy. Their study showed how actors' discourses vary in terms of SE's conceptualization, leading to varying definitions of this new field.

Despite the richness of these studies, our understanding of the process of emergence and legitimation of SE remains limited. As is now usual in organization and management theories, emerging countries, especially African ones, are often excluded from reflections and analyses (George et al., 2016; Kolk & Rivera-Santos, 2018). This can be explained by several reasons that should be theorized elsewhere, but as far as SE is concerned, this blinds us on subjects that are still relevant, such as the issue of SE legitimation. This was already clearly stated by Sengupta, Sahay, and Croce (2018, p. 772), arguing that "not much of literature is found in other parts of the world as compared to the developed countries on both sides of the Atlantic … [as] entrepreneurship research is far less pursued in emerging economies, as compared to developed countries." This state of affairs is also implicitly epitomized in an article by Defourny and Nyssens (2010, p. 32) looking specifically at the "conceptions of social enterprise and social Entrepreneurship in Europe and the United States." Their article suggests that "the debates on both sides of the Atlantic took place in parallel trajectories, with very few connections between them, until the years 2004–2005" (p. 33) and that SE in these geographic regions has a long tradition, stretching back at least several decades. Considering the great influence of the institutional and social context on SE dynamics (for a review, see Saebi et al., 2019), it is no exaggeration to assert that what the current literature theorizes about the legitimization of SE is insensitive to the socio-cultural and institutional specificities of emerging countries where institutional environments are usually volatile and more conducive to complexity and resistance.

This is quite unfortunate considering that, as Newth and Woods (2014, p. 194) put it, "resistance to social entrepreneurship undoubtedly does limit the creation and impact of ventures that would have positive social outcomes in many cases." SE's very nature makes it more prone to scrutiny and resistance because of its simultaneous market and social logics, which may conflict (Dacin et al., 2011). Because of its hybrid nature, SE must legitimize its commercial component and its social one, making its legitimation efforts even more sensitive (Battilana, 2018). As suggested by Newth and Woods (2014, p. 196), "resistance is a particularly pertinent issue in social entrepreneurship because such enterprises are likely to face resistance across multiple fronts." Taken together, these insights lead us to investigate how SE legitimizes itself as a new institutional field. We build on the work of Zietsma et al. (2017, p. 392) to define fields as "the bounded area within which meanings are shared and specific institutions operate… [as] fields are presumed to be the predominant source of pressures for institutional conformity and the site of institutional embeddedness." The interest here is not to focus on specific social enterprises and their quest for legitimacy but rather on SE as a field struggling to emerge, grow, and eventually become institutionalized in a context where SE is not part of the existing institutional arrangements. In our case, we are thus conceptualizing SE as a nascent or emerging field (Maguire et al., 2004; Patvardhan et al., 2015). This conceptualization is coherent with the social, cultural, and institutional realities of emerging economies, such as those of the MENA region, given that SE has barely emerged (Baba et al., 2020). In some countries, like Algeria, the private sector itself is still searching for legitimation, which makes resistance to SE even more intense.

Paralleling the interesting work of Newth and Woods (2014) on the Schumpeterian view of resistance to entrepreneurship and innovation, this chapter considers three types of resistance: (a) that of the task itself and the uncertainty related to it, (b) that associated with the preference of the *status quo*, and (c) that of the resistance emanating from the environment in which the entrepreneurial activity is embedded. This chapter mainly focuses on the third type of resistance, which we label as institutional-based resistance, emanating from regulative (laws and regulations), normative (norms and social expectations), and cognitive-cultural (how we think and interpret "things") (Scott, 2014). All in all, these ideas lead us to formulate our research question as follows: *what are the challenges that hinder the emergence of SE as an institutional field?*

Methodology

In this section, we intend to describe and justify our methodological choices. We shall focus on the research design, the empirical context, data sources, and data analysis processes. Taken together, these will explain and justify the use of qualitative research (Lincoln & Guba, 1994; Patton, 2002).

Research Design

This research is qualitative, consistent with the exploratory nature of investigations about a new institutional field emergence (Patton, 2002). More specifically, our study is based on a single case study (Yin, 2003). This choice is appropriate for a detailed, rich exploration of a phenomenon, and the search for new theoretical insights. We must also underline that this research follows an interpretative epistemological tradition, which takes reality as subjective, thus subject to actors' multiple interpretations (Reay et al., 2019).

Choice of Case and Empirical Context

This chapter is based on a revelatory case of SE in Algeria. Algeria has only recently become an independent state, after a hard and bloody colonial war with the French army, and settler extremists (McDougall, 2017). After the independence, the departure of about 1 million European settlers, the new and inexperienced government had no choice but to rely on a socially intense ideology. Socialism and social justice dominated thinking and behavior for two decades. In particular, an institutionalized hostility to private enterprise gave rise to a centralized government and limited local or civil society initiative.

In general, this case is valuable for at least three reasons. First, it helps explore a new emerging institutional field dynamic, especially in a volatile and still developing institutional context. Algeria, like many recently independent states, which came out of the decolonization trend, is institutionally turbulent. As a result, institutions are more malleable, more fragile, and shifting. Also, SE is a fairly new entrepreneurial form, informally established around 2013 and still in formation. The case about the Center of Social Entrepreneurship is amenable to the study of "a detailed contemporary study of a phenomenon in its real context, in particular where the boundaries between context and phenomena are unclear" (Yin, 2009, p. 18). Finally, this case is also a source of insights because it provides information about a rare occurrence of SE emergence in a context where even traditional (business) entrepreneurship's legitimacy is challenged (Baba et al., 2020; Hemissi & Hafsi, 2017). This simultaneous occurrence of dual institutional dynamics can reveal how institutional fields emerging in parallel can influence each other.

Data Sources

To study SE's revealing case in Algeria, we rely on a set of rich qualitative information and data. These help triangulate the information and develop a finer understanding of the phenomenon under study. Three complementary sources were used. First, one of the authors conducted five years of participant observations in the field as it was at birth. This implication in the Algerian SE ecosystem allowed her to interact with public authorities, international funding agencies, social entrepreneurs, and other regional and international actors in the broader field of social entrepreneurship and social and solidary economy. These observations are essential because they provide a unique and detailed account of the emergence and development of the SE field in Algeria. Subsequently, 45 conversational interviews (Burgess-limerick & Burgess-limerick, 1998) have been conducted with key actors of the Algerian SE ecosystem. Conversational interviews are discussions, which can be formal and conducted in the organizational and institutional setting. They tend to facilitate spontaneous behavior and richness of information. Because of the politically sensitive nature of the context, interviews have never been recorded. Finally, and in addition to this information, a variety of documents and archives were consulted. These include studies, reports, and analyses about SE in Algeria, as well as 1200 emails with stakeholders, covering five years of relationships around the buildup of SE.

Data Analysis

As is usual in similar qualitative studies, data analysis was mostly abductive, with a constant back and forth exchange between data and theoretical insights (Timmermans & Tavory, 2012). In so doing, the three authors have debated several times to share meanings about the data gathered by one of the authors. The other two were less immersed in the field but share both the culture and national origins. Being removed from the field, these "outsiders" were able to ask hard questions and ensure the credibility of facts and data interpretations (Nemeth et al., 2001).

Three steps were needed to conduct the analyses. First, the data were analyzed, looking for the details of SE emergence in Algeria, during a specific temporal horizon (2013–2020). This step was based on a detailed chronology of events and was focused on how formalized the field was at each temporal bracket. This step showed three distinct temporal development brackets. First, there was informal emergence, then development and attempts to formalize. Finally, institutionalization was the main purpose. In the second step, we tried to identify the challenges of each of the historical times. Our analyses reveal important challenges throughout the period studied. At this stage of the analysis, we inductively identified challenges at the legal, administrative, financial, organizational, and cultural levels. In the third step, we decided to rely on Scott's three pillars (2014) to structure the challenges identified earlier. In his seminal work, Scott (2014) describes three institutional pillars: regulative (rules and regulations), normative (social norms and practices), cultural-cognitive (beliefs about how things are). From the regulative to the cultural-cognitive, the pillars are first formal, then increasingly preconscious, and taken for granted. Hoffman (1997, p. 36) conceptualizes the pillars as in a continuum, "from the conscious to the unconscious, from the legally enforced to the taken for granted." Using Scott's concepts, we have structured the challenges identified inductively, then reinterpreted them again to fit with neo-institutional pillars.

Empirical Analyses: Social Entrepreneurship in Algeria

Our empirical analyses show that the process of emergence and institutionalization of SE as a new institutional field in Algeria has a triple character, which can be described using the three pillars of neo-institutional theory (Scott, 2014). In what follows, we shall focus on challenges that are specific to each pillar.

Normative Pilar: Social Entrepreneurship Is not a Legitimate Endeavor

Our analyses show the importance of norms in the process of SE development in Algeria. It is recognized that institutions are important vehicles for tacit expectations, which directly influence the behavior of people. When conforming to these expectations, individuals' actions become legitimate. In the case of SE, norms and social expectations about careers and professional success have inhibited the process of recruiting social entrepreneurs. Two hurdles are particularly important: the need for professional stability, and entrepreneurship as a marginal process. These two hurdles directly influence actors' perception of SE's attractiveness and thus their desire to venture into it.

The Stability Factor

The analyses of SE in Algeria show that the search for professional stability is an important barrier in recruiting social entrepreneurs. Social and family expectations favor a stable source of revenue. This norm is probably inherited from the French culture, and the unstable social-political situation of Algeria appears to exacerbate the effect. Young professionals feel more vulnerable, and this leads them to make safe professional choices, even if these are less lucrative than a private entrepreneurial venture. Things are changing, but the norm is still holding that a career in the private sector comes second to a public bureaucracy career.

Historically, after the independence in 1962, the public sector has been the main source of good jobs and exciting careers. It has also been the largest employer, with about 2.5 million civil servants, 85% of them in a permanent position. The private sector is barely taking-off. Its performance is unstable, mostly because of a shifting and hardly predictable institutional/legislative context. Several firms, sometimes industries, have suffered or disappeared as a result of unexpected regulatory changes. The automobile industry, for example, has faced multiple and contradictory regulations, which have been disastrous for private firms involved, and traumatic for thousands of their employees. Therefore, when young workers and professionals envisage a career, SE appears as an unreasonable choice: "*It is clear for us that social entrepreneurship is seen as too unstable… and we know that Algerians more generally prefer a stable public sector job to a risky venture in the private sector… For social entrepreneurship, it is even worse. Family, social and peers' pressures are just overwhelming*" (Interview, 2020). It is also interesting to observe that universities and higher education institutions have no SE programs and teach no such related topics like social innovation, sustainable development, or social and solidary economy. This also contributes to making it less legitimate.

Entrepreneurship as a Peripheral Process

Entrepreneurship, whether classic or social, is marginal in Algeria. Established economic and social norms ignore it. Embarking on an entrepreneurial venture is seen as a marginal behavior. It is generally encouraged neither by social norms nor by formal rules and regulations. Three reasons appear to explain the situation. First, there is pressure from the entrepreneur's relatives to question an entrepreneurial career choice: "*an employment which provides a regular salary is seen as safer and more common in our society… To succeed, a salaried job, in the public sector, remains the option preferred by most new graduates entering the job market*" (Interview, 2020). Second, the lack of institutional and political visibility, in this unstable environment, slows down the entrepreneurial process. In a promotion campaign to recruit entrepreneurs, this argument was often cited as devaluing SE: "*To venture in any enterprise, you have to trust your own country… You have to plan ahead several years… You invest time and money… and here, we know culturally and intuitively that everything can change fast… How can you take initiative without some peace of mind? … it is the very essence of taking risks!*" (Interview, 2020). The regulatory void about SE increases the worries about instability. The third reason is the socialist heritage, which has painted entrepreneurship as incompatible with social justice, and has contributed to a poor image for business enterprise in general.

The Rules and Regulations Pillar: SE in the Heart of an Entrepreneurial Void

Neo-institutional economics research (see Acemoglu et al., 2005; North, 1990) has unequivocally shown the importance of the legal and regulatory framework in the growth of entrepreneurship and in general economic activities. Such a framework clarifies the game rules and guides individuals' initiative, thus giving more visibility to entrepreneurs. Rules and regulations define what is permitted in terms of entrepreneurial initiatives, and encourages some behaviors, discouraging others. A clear framework helps focus entrepreneurial resources where needed. For SE in particular, our analyses show that it faces two major formal hurdles: a persistent legal void and an institutionally discouraging system.

Persistent Institutional Void

The Algerian legal system does not provide any legal status to SE or the social economy. Two possibilities are available to social entrepreneurs. They can build a private enterprise, under the legal business status. They can also create a philanthropic association. All social enterprises in Algeria have followed one or the other of these routes. According to Article 2 of the 12-06 Association law, an association is recognized as a "*contract-based grouping of moral or physical persons, for a limited or unlimited time.*" When deciding to collaborate, these persons "*pool together, for profit or not, their knowledge and other means to promote or encourage activities in all domains' professional, social, scientific, religious, or related to education, sports, environment, philanthropy and humanitarian.*" This chapter emphasizes the association's non-profit side, which leaves aside the more economic entrepreneurship side of social entrepreneurs. As argued earlier, SE does not exclude profits, especially if profits are reinvested to promote the organizations' social mission.

In the history of Algeria, this form of private entrepreneurship is new. With the adoption of socialist objectives and state structure, a choice which appeared to be reasonable after the independence, private enterprise, was shunned until the early 1990s. During the violent civil war at the time, private enterprise was finally recognized as legally legitimate, alongside the dominant public enterprise. The private entrepreneur was then seen as a contributor to economic growth. The legislative decree of 1993 (#93-08, art. 544) argues that "*the commercial character of a firm is related to its legal form or object. Are commercial because of their form, regardless of their object, companies held collectively by a group of shareholders, limited partnerships, limited responsibility companies, and open shareholder controlled or widely-held firms.*" The more dynamic social entrepreneurs, who are close to a business logic choose among these forms. Social entrepreneurs who come from an associative tradition tend to pursue the association route. In both cases, the lack of legal clarity reduces the entrepreneurs' ability to enhance the legitimacy of his/her activity among stakeholders, including potential social entrepreneurs, capital risk national or international firms, and local administrative agencies.

A Discouraging Institutional Framework

The persistent legal void forces SE to live on the margin, a situation where "institutional arrangements that support markets are absent, weak, or fail to accomplish the role expected of them" (Mair & Marti, 2009, p. 419). This institutional void discourages even the most motivated traditional entrepreneurs, let alone those on the margin like social entrepreneurs who try to build a new field. This institutional discouragement is visible at three junctures.

First, the legal void is such that there are no incentives for SE. The lack of an accepted legal status blocks all attempts to promote or coach future social entrepreneurs. They are often worried about the value of this entrepreneurial form, which is present only in speeches, but not in actual laws. The main actor of SE in Algeria, the Center of Social Entrepreneurship underlines this devastating effect of a legal void: "*it is easy for us to encourage young people to give attention to SE, but when comes the time to actually launch the venture, things get much more complicated. Many actors are discouraged by the legal void, and some even abandon their projects*" (Interview, 2020).

Second, this discouraging institutional effect is also felt by those social entrepreneurs who choose the private enterprise route. The Algerian law does not distinguish between the traditional firm and social firm: "*Social entrepreneurs, although motivated by their willingness to resolve social ills, must still pay the same duties and taxes. They don't understand why their contributions to society go unrecognized, which makes them feel cheated*" (Interview, 2020). Since subsidies or international prizes fund most SE initiatives in Algeria, the tax administration looks at these as being taxable income, sometimes at exorbitant rates between 12 and 30%. The subsidies are treated as paying for the production of services. The funds actually devoted to social projects are, as a result, drastically reduced, which further fuels the discouragement and frustration of social entrepreneurs. "*This pushes social entrepreneurs to look constantly for new funding opportunities, and funding schemes, to avoid paying too high charges. Some of them are led to abandon their financial public dotation, because after tax it leads to insignificant funding*" (Interview, 2020).

Third, those social entrepreneurs who choose the route of associations, to avoid taxes, still face other discouraging challenges. The Algerian law 12-06 of associations states that all funds coming from a foreign organization, established in Algeria or not, should be authorized by the ministry of the interior. Some of these authorizations may take months, sometimes years, to come. Some projects did not exist anymore when the funds were finally authorized. As a result, regardless of how social entrepreneurs organize their activities, either as a private enterprise or an association, the institutional void is there to penalize both. The Algerian

Center for Social Entrepreneurship had coached some high-impact projects, to see them die when frustrated entrepreneurs finally abandoned them.

Cultural-Cognitive Pillar: Social Entrepreneurship Is Foreign to Established Mental Schemata

Our empirical analyses also suggest that the cultural-cognitive aspects are important. They refer to values and established mental schemata and have an important place in the process by which SE institutionalization takes place in Algeria. Three issues can be highlighted: the SE concept's conceptual ambiguity, the moral tensions, and the pragmatic tensions affecting social entrepreneurs.

Conceptual Ambiguity

The first issue is related to how ambiguous is the concept of SE. The ambiguity is constantly affecting how people behave. Three preconceptions contribute to the ambiguity. First, the word "social" is often associated with charity or general community-based work in Algeria. Mixing "entrepreneurship" and "social" can be seen as an oxymoron. Those unfamiliar with SE often associate it with charity and solidarity-related activities. The Algerian Center for Social Entrepreneurship has to deal with the issue daily, for example, receiving regular call to support the poor. The Center's entrepreneurial nature is often disregarded, a clear indication of how social engagement is perceived in Algeria. Also, the historical socialism heritage and the related statism or centralization of all decisions at the state center lead people to think that SE is the state's business. The "social thing" is often seen as being in the realm of the state authorities and cannot be delegated to "entrepreneurs" or "enterprise" (more generally, to private initiatives). To deal with these challenges, the Algerian Center for Social Entrepreneurship itself had to adapt to the context using different terminologies such as sustainable or impact entrepreneurship, avoiding the "social" word. This allows the Center to frame its mission within the United Nations' sustainable development goals, to delineate the borders of the "social" concept.

Moral Tension

As mentioned earlier, Algerian social entrepreneurs have often followed a professional volunteering path and are mostly related to the charity and association world. This has shaped their values of solidarity, empathy, and their convictions that entrepreneurship must serve a social purpose. However, transiting from social actor to entrepreneur is fraught with problems. The most important is the complicated relationship to money. These entrepreneurs have a hard time monetizing their products or services, building financial plans, balancing economic imperatives and social missions, and so on. Rationally thinking about social issues means taking into account their financial consequences. This leads to real moral tension, which leads to psychological dilemmas. It represents the conflict between social action as a goal and social action as an entrepreneurial opportunity. This conflict is made more intense by the often-held belief that "social" should not be judged in the commercial but the civil sphere, with an essential role for the state and civil society associations.

Pragmatic Tension

Finally, social entrepreneurs motivated by the entrepreneurial venture itself, with its risk-taking component and the need to develop a business, create value through opportunity. They are often resistant to the SE conceived as a value-based cultural endeavor, and in general, to the drive to the social and solidary economy. Such a conception calls for democratic governance, limited salaries, reinvestment of profit back into the cause. These notions do not resonate well with entrepreneurially minded individuals. They are more inclined to build firms with social principles but with a willingness to generate value and profits and dispose of those as traditional entrepreneurs. In this case, social issues are seen as business opportunities and not constraints, a mode of development rather than submission to prescribed behavior. These individuals wish to free themselves from the constraints that come from the social and solidary economic principles. They are faced with a pragmatic or instrumental tension to balance a social mission with a more common entrepreneurial drive. Interestingly, the Algerian Center for Social Entrepreneurship suggests that this second category of entrepreneurs succeeds better than the more moral one, probably because they are more comfortable with the commercial logic.

Discussion and Conclusion

In this chapter, we presented the nascent SE field in Algeria. We adopted an institutional perspective to show how difficult it is for a new institutional field, even when it is socially worthwhile, to gain space and legitimacy. We have shown to what extent SE in Algeria faces hurdles related to all three institutional pillars (Scott, 2014). Rules and regulations are either inexistent or unclear, norms and cognitive formation have developed a hostile outlook on business and anything which is related. We focused on a key but lonely actor in this emerging field, the Algerian Centre for Social Entrepreneurship. This is the first and only organization of its kind in the country. Its purpose is to encourage and hopefully spread social entrepreneurship in Algeria through raising awareness, lobbying for recognition, training, and coaching potential social entrepreneurs. This institutional perspective findings lead to three significant implications.

First, our analysis suggested that the emergence of SE in Algeria was influenced by a triple institutional constraint, which makes the emergence and legitimization of this new institutional field complex. Paralleling Scott's (2014) work on the three pillars of institutions, our empirical investigation emphasized the importance of regulative, normative, and cultural-cognitive barriers to SE in Algeria. More importantly, we have shown how these constraints are intertwined and mutually reinforcing. For instance, the institutional void in which SE operates in Algeria because of the absence of formal rules encourages SE's perception as a perilous path at the normative pillar. Similarly, the cultural-cognitive understanding of social work as being the state's responsibility undermines the possibility of legislating SE's status, which would grant it an essential legal basis for its progressive legitimation over the long run (Baba et al., 2021). The fact that the obstacles to the emergence and development of SE fall under the three institutional pillars highlights how complicated this field's emergence process is.

The field's difficulties can be hard to understand given Algeria's gloomy reality where social problems are innumerable and where SE can be particularly helpful to a state, which is greatly weakened by enduring socio-political instability. This is even more the case considering the historically rooted issues at the cultural-cognitive level, which prevent the private actor, a key economic determinant, from playing its role. In fact, the historical legacy of post-independence, which takes for granted that entrepreneurship is not interesting and that the social sphere is the prerogative of the state, makes it even harder to envision any radical short-term evolution. How to facilitate a real turnaround remains open to studies, and other countries' experiences could be tapped for insights.

Second, our study also elucidates the invisible, yet important, role of competing fields in explaining an institutional field's emergence success (or lack of). Overall, the literature on SE shows how this new organizational form struggled to gain legitimacy in the face of a classic, more established, and already legitimate entrepreneurial form, that is, the private capitalist enterprise in Western industrialized nations. This antagonism seems natural, as economic and social logics can experience tensions between them. While this might be true for Western societies where classic entrepreneurship has thrived over the past decade or so, developing countries' situation is somewhat trickier. In fact, our empirical analysis showed that classic entrepreneurship itself is not yet completely institutionalized and legitimate in Algeria. In doing so, the strategy of "analogy" in argumentation aiming to show the similarity with a more established entrepreneurial form is less convincing in a context where entrepreneurship more generally is not legitimate (Etzion & Ferraro, 2010). In developing countries, SE is stuck between two realities: on the one hand, the stigmatization of private firms and entrepreneurship in the broad sense, and on the other hand, the appropriation of the "social thing" by the state. Engaging in legitimation work in such a context, with limited resources and an institutional void is, therefore, a major challenge.

Third, our empirical analysis has implicitly hinted that SE is not more problematic in Algeria than entrepreneurship itself. In reality, this is most likely true for most emerging countries in the MENA region where the democratic processes are not yet mature enough to encourage individuals' initiative to its full potential, and where the state adopts behaviors of control and centralization precisely for the fear that private initiative would challenge public authority. Ironically, we see in developed countries that individual initiatives tend to reinforce public authority because entrepreneurship is an ally of development and not its enemy. The study of SE's emergence in Algeria leads us to realize to what extent entrepreneurship in general faces considerable barriers because it is synonymous with freedom and initiative in an environment that rejects them in general. In this context, the institutionalization of SE is still difficult to imagine in the very short term. To facilitate SE's institutionalization, broader institutional changes must take place to free initiatives and change social behavior, perceptions, and expectations vis-à-vis the state and entrepreneurs. In a context where the Algerian state is weakened by limited financial resources, decreasing legitimacy, and accelerating social issues (unemployment, hunger, poverty, homelessness, etc.), the context is perhaps conducive to more aggressive, deliberate, and oriented institutional work on the part of social entrepreneurship actors. The objective here is not so much to weaken the state or to question its legitimacy but to shake it up enough, to recognize SE as an ally and not a competitor. In this vein, the pioneers have difficulty progressing in taking the initiative without frightening the established powers.

Even though difficult, institutional change is possible, even under the most challenging circumstances. Energy, positive emotions, and optimism play a vital role in the feasibility of this change. When conducting this research, we were intrigued by the Algerian Center for Social Entrepreneurship's ability to remain motivated. "Where do you get your energy and motivation from?" we regularly asked. The response of the Director of the Centre probably underlines why there is still much hope for emerging countries like Algeria. Despite all the crises and adversity, these remain contexts where actors believe that change is possible. The Director replied: "I draw my energy from the fire I see in the eyes of the social entrepreneurs we coach. Their satisfaction at having succeeded despite all the pitfalls gives us a reason to stick with the country. What despairs me, however, is the desire of many to go abroad as soon as one faces pitfalls related to the difficult environment in Algeria."

Note

1. In the USA, this legal status covers for-profit firms that have a strong social and/or environmental component in their activities. States are the key actors in regulating these firms. Maryland was the first to act in 2010. In 2020, about 30 states recognize the legal existence of social enterprises.

References

Acemoglu, D., Johnson, S., & Robinson, J. (2005). Institutions as a Fundamental Cause of Long-Run Growth. In P. Aghion & S. N. Durlauf (Eds.), *Handbook of Economic Growth (Part A)* (pp. 385–472). Elsevier.

Baba, S., Hafsi, T., & Hemissi, O. (2020). Construire son entreprise et la société: quatre cas algériens. In S. Frimousse (Ed.), *Africa Positive Impact: Agir pour un meilleur impact sociétal* (p. 424). Éditions EMS.

Baba, S., Hemissi, O., & Hafsi, T. (2021). National Identity and Organizational Identity in Algeria: Interactions and Influences. *M@n@gement, 24*(2), 66–85. https://doi.org/10.37725/mgmt.v24.7809

Baba, S., Sasaki, I., & Vaara, E. (2021). Increasing Dispositional Legitimacy: Progressive Legitimation Dynamics in a Trajectory of Settlements. *Academy of Management Journal, 64*(6), 1–46. https://doi.org/10.5465/amj.2017.0330

Bacq, S., & Lumpkin, G. T. (2020). Social Entrepreneurship and COVID-19. *Journal of Management Studies, 58*(1), 283–286.

Battilana, J. (2018). Cracking the Organizational Challenge of Pursuing Joint Social and Financial Goals: Social Enterprise as a Laboratory to Understand Hybrid Organizing. *M@n@gement, 21*(4), 1278–1305.

Burgess-limerick, T., & Burgess-limerick, R. (1998). Conversational Interviews and Multiple-Case Research in Psychology. *Australian Journal of Psychology, 50*(2), 63–70.

Chandra, Y. (2017). Social Entrepreneurship as Institutional-Change Work: A Corpus Linguistics Analysis. *Journal of Social Entrepreneurship, 8*(1), 14–46.

Dacin, M. T., Dacin, P. A., & Tracey, P. (2011). Social Entrepreneurship: A Critique and Future Directions. *Organization Science, 22*(5), 1203–1213.

Defourny, J., & Nyssens, M. (2010). Conceptions of Social Enterprise and Social Entrepreneurship in Europe and the United States: Convergences and Divergences. *Journal of Social Entrepreneurship, 1*(1), 32–53.

DiMaggio, P. J., & Powell, W. W. (1983). The Iron Cage Revisited: Institutional Isomorphism and Collective Rationality in Organizational Fields. *American Sociological Review, 48*(2), 147–160.

Doherty, B., Haugh, H., & Lyon, F. (2014). Social Enterprises as Hybrid Organizations: A Review and Research Agenda. *International Journal of Management Reviews, 16*(4), 417–436.

Durand, R., & Paolella, L. (2013). Category Stretching: Reorienting Research on Categories in Strategy, Entrepreneurship, and Organization Theory. *Journal of Management Studies, 50*(6), 1100–1123.

Etzion, D., & Ferraro, F. (2010). The Role of Analogy in the Institutionalization of Sustainability Reporting. *Organization Science, 21*(5), 1092–1107.

George, G., Corbishley, C., Khayesi, J. N., Haas, M. R., & Tihanyi, L. (2016). Bringing Africa In: Promising Directions for Management Research. *Academy of Management Journal, 59*(2), 377–393.

Hemissi, O., & Hafsi, T. (2017). *Amor Benamor, une réussite algérienne.* Éditions Casbah.

Hervieux, C., Gedajlovic, E., & Turcotte, M.-F. B. (2010). The Legitimization of Social Entrepreneurship. *Journal of Enterprising Communities: People and Places in the Global Economy, 4*(1), 37–67.

Hoffman, A. W. (1997). *From Heresy Dogma: An Institutional History of Corporate Environmentalism*. New Lexington Press.

Islam, S. M. (2020). Unintended Consequences of Scaling Social Impact Through Ecosystem Growth Strategy in Social Enterprise and Social Entrepreneurship. *Journal of Business Venturing Insights, 13*, forthcoming. https://doi.org/10.1016/j.jbvi.2020.e00159

Kolk, A., & Rivera-Santos, M. (2018). The State of Research on Africa in Business and Management: Insights from a Systematic Review of Key International Journals. *Business & Society, 57*(3), 415–436.

Lincoln, Y. S., & Guba, E. G. (1994). Competing Paradigms in Qualitative Research. In N. K. D. Y. S. Lincoln (Ed.), *Handbook of Qualitative Research* (pp. 105–117). Sage.

Maguire, S., Hardy, C., & Lawrence, T. B. (2004). Institutional Entrepreneurship in Emerging Fields: HIV/AIDS Treatment Advocacy in Canada. *Academy of Management Journal, 47*(5), 657–679.

Mair, J. (2020). Social Entrepreneurship: Research as Disciplined Exploration. In P. W. W. & B. P (Eds.), *The Nonprofit Sector: A Research Handbook* (3rd ed., pp. 333–357). Stanford University Press.

Mair, J., & Marti, I. (2009). Entrepreneurship In and Around Institutional Voids: A Case Study from Bangladesh. *Journal of Business Venturing, 24*(5), 419–435.

McDougall, J. (2017). *A History of Algeria*. Cambridge University Press.

Nemeth, C., Brown, K., & Rogers, J. (2001). Devil's Advocate Versus Authentic Dissent: Stimulating Quantity and Quality. *European Journal of Social Psychology, 31*(6), 707–720.

Newth, J., & Woods, C. (2014). Resistance to Social Entrepreneurship: How Context Shapes Innovation. *Journal of Social Entrepreneurship, 5*(2), 192–213.

Nicholls, A. (2010a). The Legitimacy of Social Entrepreneurship: Reflexive Isomorphism in a Pre-Paradigmatic Field. *Entrepreneurship Theory and Practice, 34*(4), 611–633.

Nicholls, A. (2010b). Institutionalizing Social Entrepreneurship in Regulatory Space: Reporting and Disclosure by Community Interest Companies. *Accounting, Organizations and Society, 35*(4), 394–415.

Nicholls, A. (2012). Postscript: The Legitimacy of Social Entrepreneurship: Reflexive Isomorphism in a Pre-paradigmatic Field. In G. B. & H. Y (Eds.), *Social Enterprises* (pp. 222–247). Palgrave Macmillan.

North, D. C. (1990). *Institutions, Institutional Change, and Economic Performance*. Cambridge University Press.

Patton, M. Q. (2002). *Qualitative Research and Evaluation Methods* (3rd ed.). Sage Publications.

Patvardhan, S. D., Gioia, D. A., & Hamilton, A. L. (2015). Weathering a Meta-Level Identity Crisis: Forging a Coherent Collective Identity for an Emerging Field. *Academy of Management Journal, 58*(2), 405–435.

Reay, T., Zafar, A., Monteiro, P., & Glaser, V. (2019). Presenting Findings from Qualitative Research: One Size Does Not Fit All! In T. B. Zilber, J. M. Amis, & J. Mair (Eds.), *The Production of Managerial Knowledge and Organizational Theory: New Approaches to Writing, Producing and Consuming Theory* (Research in the Sociology of Organizations) (Vol. 59, pp. 201–216). Emerald.

Raufflet, E., Brès, L., Baba, S., & Filion, L. J. (2016). Sustainable Development and Entrepreneurship: Mapping Definitions, Determinants, Actors and Processes. In K. Nicolopoulou, M. Karatas-Ozkan, F. Janssen, & J. Jermier (Eds.), *Sustainable Entrepreneurship and Social Innovation* (1st ed., pp. 289–305). New York: Routledge.

Saebi, T., Foss, N. J., & Linder, S. (2019). Social Entrepreneurship Research: Past Achievements and Future Promises. *Journal of Management, 45*(1), 70–95.

Scott, R. W. (2001). *Institutions and Organizations* (2nd ed.). Sage Publications.

Scott, R. W. (2014). *Institutions and Organizations: Ideas, Interests, and Identities*. SAGE Publications.

Sengupta, S., Sahay, A., & Croce, F. (2018). Conceptualizing Social Entrepreneurship in the Context of Emerging Economies: An Integrative Review of Pastresearch from BRIICS. *International Entrepreneurship and Management Journal, 14*, 771–803.

Shepherd, D. A., & Patzelt, H. (2011). The New Field of Sustainable Entrepreneurship: Studying Entrepreneurial Action Linking "What Is to Be Sustained" with "What Is to Be Developed". *Entrepreneurship Theory and Practice, 35*(1), 137–163.

Timmermans, S., & Tavory, I. (2012). Theory Construction in Qualitative Research: From Grounded Theory to Abductive Analysis. *Sociological Theory, 30*(3), 167–186.

Tracey, P., Phillips, N., & Jarvis, O. (2011). Bridging Institutional Entrepreneurship and the Creation of New Organizational Forms: A Multilevel Model. *Organization Science, 22*(1), 60–80.

Yin, R. K. (2003). *Case Study Research: Design and Methods*. Sage Publications.

Yin, R. K. (2009). *Case Study Research: Design and Methods* (4th ed.). Sage.

Zietsma, C., Groenewegen, P., Logue, D. M., & Hinings, C. R. B. (2017). Field or Fields? Building the Scaffolding for Cumulation of Research on Institutional Fields. *Academy of Management Annals, 11*(1), 391–450.

12

Conclusion

Taïeb Hafsi

Entrepreneurship in the Arab World Is an Engine of Society's Well Being

In the last two decades, entrepreneurship studies have gone beyond economic activities. As a result, entrepreneurship has gradually been conceived to be mostly a process, which can be observed in a variety of situations, economic, social, academic, political, and so on. Institutional theorists have documented a variety of entrepreneurial activities which transform institutions (Maguire et al., 2004), and pushed by recent upheaval in a variety of countries, from Ukraine to MENA countries, the practice of social entrepreneurship emerged as a critical ingredient for social transformation. A bubbling line of research and a lot of social practice are exploring social entrepreneurship. In particular, the CIRIEC international network has focused on social innovation and revealed the importance of social entrepreneurs.

T. Hafsi (✉)
HEC Montréal, Montreal, QC, Canada
e-mail: taieb.2.hafsi@hec.ca

N. Azoury, T. Hafsi (eds.), *Entrepreneurship and Social Entrepreneurship in the MENA Region*, https://doi.org/10.1007/978-3-030-88447-5_12

The chapters in this book go beyond the observation that entrepreneurship is an important strategic solution to a general economic problem, to introduce both context and social institutional intent. First, the Middle East-North Africa (MENA) region is the focus of interest of the book's chapters, and some authors have also addressed the rising topic of social entrepreneurship in the region. They provide a broad historical perspective on how all this happens, and on the process through which the entrepreneur emerges, recognizes opportunities, and builds upon them to achieve his/her transformational goal. The focus on the region and on entrepreneurial intent is in itself a significant contribution.

Recently entrepreneurship in emerging economies and developing countries has attracted attention. Only 10 years ago, of more than 10 000 papers in leading journal, less than 50 dealt with entrepreneurship in these marginal settings. 75% of these articles were published in only two journals, ETP and JBV.[1] They represented a mere 3% of all articles published in these two journals (Bruton et al., 2010).

The region's context is peculiar. In the MENA region, we could argue that there is a high degree of institutional uncertainty (i.e. unstable and underdeveloped institutions, frequent and unpredictable institutional transformation, and institutional changes). Such a dynamic setting in emerging economies is considered a major constrain for entrepreneurship (Luthans & Ibrayeva, 2006). Some scholars have argued that uncertainty in emerging markets can provide important opportunities for entrepreneurs. This is especially true for those who have grown up in these institutional contexts (i.e. local entrepreneurs). Yet, in most emerging economies, survival is the essence of entrepreneurship, which means that being able to deal with a high degree of institutional uncertainty is the first and inevitable step of being an entrepreneur in these contexts.

For traditional entrepreneurs, the context is also critical. More interestingly, entrepreneurs in some of the MENA countries appear to pursue social good as much as economic success (Cherchem & Hafsi, 2018). Their concern for the well-being of communities drives their behavior and is arguably the engine of their economic success (Hemissi & Hafsi, 2017).

An Overview of This Book's Contributions

More specifically, this book contributes to a better understanding of traditional entrepreneurship in MENA. The first part deals with trends and concepts and comprises four chapters. On a general and conceptual note, *Yara Harb (USEK—Lebanon)* addresses entrepreneurship through the lens of Entrepreneurship orientation (EO) and shows how important EO is to understand the behavior of SMEs in building the region and their communities, and to explain their ability to succeed despite steep odds. *Georges Yahchouchy (Amercican University of Middle East—Kuwait) and Vladimir Dzenopoljac (American University of Middle East—Kuwait)* discuss whether entrepreneurship is really important for the region or a fad, which will eventually fade. Their discussion of entrepreneurship also covers social entrepreneurship. They wonder whether the practice is sustainable given the existing institutions. *Sung Joo Park (KAIST Business School, Seoul, Korea)* explores further the innovation side of entrepreneurship and discusses its suitability for the region's well-being. Finally, *Ayman Tarabishy (George Washington University—USA)* is more concerned about sustainability. He goes beyond the previous contribution to argue that social entrepreneurship is more suited to Western nations' context and would face difficulties in the Arab world. Traditions and religious influences have a strong bearing on how individuals and society interact. To ensure that social entrepreneurship is not seen as foreign and rejected, he argues for the emergence of "humane entrepreneurship," which would be more inclusive of stakeholders around frugal innovation.

The second part is focused more specifically on Entrepreneurship in the Arab world—*Thami Ghofri and Imad-eddine Hatimi (ESCA École de Management—Morocco)* discuss the importance of entrepreneurship education, especially if Arab countries want to tap the potential of women and population youth. They argue that this would enhance firm competitiveness and national growth. *Thami Ghorfi (ESCA École de Management—Morocco) and Dora Jurd de Girancourt (American University of the Middle East—Kuwait)* explore how Arab women contribute to entrepreneurship and social entrepreneurship. They see them as providing more impetus to innovation, defined as infusing existing activities with meaningful societal values, to build economic and social value. Finally, *Omar Hemissi (École Supérieure de Commerce d'Alger), Sofiane Baba (Université de Sherbrooke, Quebec, Canada) and Taïeb Hafsi (HEC Montreal-Canada)* study how entrepreneurs and SMEs deal with the turbulent and dynamic institutional context of Algeria. Their study describes the strategies of four Algerian entrepreneurs to support the idea that entrepreneurs can also be institution builders.

The third part provides a valuable peek into entrepreneurial realities of the Arab world, with cases describing economic and social entrepreneurship. *Diala Kozaily (USEK Business School—Lebanon)* studies social entrepreneurship in the Lebanese market. She sees social entrepreneurs' personal demographic characteristics, such as experience, education, and social/family support, as drivers of innovative and sustainable social contributions. Contrary to expectations, social enterprise can supplement the market as an important job creation mechanism. *Sherif Kamel (American University of Cairo—Egypt)* builds on the AUC's School of business experience to provide a broad macro perspective on how a thriving nationwide entrepreneurial ecosystem has been built, with significant effect on many Egyptians' lives and livelihoods. Finally, *Sofiane Baba (Universite de Sherbrook) Taïeb Hafsi (HEC Montréal) and Meriem Benslama (Algerian Center of Social Entrepreneurship*) describe an interesting experience in Algeria with the emergence and legitimation of social entrepreneurship. Their study examines how institutional barriers, whether regulative (laws and regulations), normative (what is considered socially appropriate), and cultural-cognitive (what makes sense given mental schemas), have been impediments of what could be an important source of employment for women and the young.

These contributions address some of the issues which we saw as missing in the literature, those related to context and intent. The focus on the Arab world context, even though limited, provides new insights, mostly about the nature of hindrance and barriers to the development of entrepreneurship. The intent is also important, as most of what is done in these thick religious and cultural settings is driven by the willingness of individuals to go beyond barriers that defy social and economic rationality.

Entrepreneurship is the process by which individuals, sometimes groups, take the lead in questioning practices, imagining alternative ways, making them possible, and fighting to impose them. It can also be social, cultural, political, institutional, and can affect literally any aspect of human collective activities. As a change mechanism, it is truly ubiquitous. It is mostly the entrepreneurs' social ability to change things, thus their leadership and willingness to go against the tide to resist existing norms, and practices, their desire to change things, to generate personal benefits which seem more correlated with the outcomes achieved. A lot more research is needed to uncover the richness of local practices and reveal the whole value of human strivings toward a productive and meaningful life. The peek into Arab entrepreneurs shows that many of them are struggling to build a better world.

Note

1. Entrepreneurship Theory and Practice (ETP) and Journal of Business Venturing (JBV).

References

Bruton, G. D., Ahlstrom, D., & Li, H.-L. (2010). Institutional Theory and Entrepreneurship: Where Are We Now and Where Do We Need to Move in the Future? *Entrepreneurship Theory & Practice, 34*(3), 421–440. https://doi.org/10.1111/j.1540-6520.2010.00390.x

Cherchem, N., & Hafsi, T. (2018). *Hasnaoui, une entreprise citoyenne.* Casbah Editions.

Hemissi, O., & Hafsi, T. (2017). *Benamor: un succès algérien*. Casbah Editions.

Luthans, F., & Ibrayeva, E. S. (2006). Entrepreneurial Self-Efficacy in Central Asian Transition Economies: Quantitative and Qualitative Analyses. *Journal of International Business Studies, 37*, 92–110.

Maguire, S., Hardy, C., & Lawrence, T. B. (2004). Institutional Entrepreneurship in Emerging Fields: HIV/AIDS Treatment Advocacy in Canada. *Academy of Management Journal, 47*(5), 657–679.

Index[1]

A

B

[1] Note: Page numbers followed by 'n' refer to notes.

N. Azoury, T. Hafsi (eds.), *Entrepreneurship and Social Entrepreneurship in the MENA Region*, https://doi.org/10.1007/978-3-030-88447-5